SUCCEEDING GENERATIONS

SUCCEEDING GENERATIONS
On the Effects of Investments in Children

Robert Haveman and Barbara Wolfe

RUSSELL SAGE FOUNDATION / NEW YORK

The Russell Sage Foundation

The Russell Sage Foundation, one of the oldest of America's general purpose foundations, was established in 1907 by Mrs. Margaret Olivia Sage for "the improvement of social and living conditions in the United States." The Foundation seeks to fulfill this mandate by fostering the development and dissemination of knowledge about the country's political, social, and economic problems. While the Foundation endeavors to assure the accuracy and objectivity of each book it publishes, the conclusions and interpretations in Russell Sage Foundation publications are those of the authors and not of the Foundation, its Trustees, or its staff. Publication by Russell Sage, therefore, does not imply Foundation endorsement.

Library of Congress Cataloging-in-Publication Data

Haveman, Robert H.
  Succeeding generations : on the effects of investments in children
/ Robert Haveman and Barbara Wolfe.
    p. cm.
  Includes bibliographical references and index.
  ISBN 0-87154-377-X
  1. Children—United States. 2. Youth—United States. 3. Family—United States.
  4. Parental influences—United States. 5. Success—United States. I. Wolfe, Barbara
  Schull. II. Title.
HQ792.U5H29 1994
305.23'0973—dc20   93-41141
                                                                                 CIP

The paper used in this publication meets the minimum requirements of American National Standard for Information Sciences—Permanence of Paper for Printed Library Materials, ANSI Z39.48-1992.

RUSSELL SAGE FOUNDATION
112 East 64th Street, New York, New York 10021

10 9 8 7 6 5 4 3 2 1

To our Preceding Generations
only some of whom are still with us
and to our Succeeding Generations
who are just that and of whom we are proud

Contents

Preface and Acknowledgments

Succeeding Generations is the culmination of several years of research and writing. It represents the most ambitious single project in which either of us has been engaged. At one level, this volume indicates that the project has been completed. However, a reading of the book will indicate that our research on the question of the determinants of children's attainments is only at a way station. The data base on which our research findings rest—the Michigan Panel Study of Income Dynamics (PSID)—is an ongoing longitudinal survey. Although we chose to cut off the annual observations on the 1700 children that we study at 1988 for the research reported here, the PSID continues to collect data on these children. As of this writing there are an additional 4 years of data that can be exploited on every child. Because we are continuing to add additional years of information on each child to our data base, the volume is but a progress report.

The Preface is the place for acknowledgments, so let us start at the beginning. We would not have pursued this project without the financial and staff support of the Institute for Research on Poverty (IRP). We would like to thank the two Directors of the Institute during the course of the research—Charles Manski and Robert Hauser—for their support and encouragement. We also acknowledge financial support from the Economics Program of the National Science Foundation, the Graduate School of the University of Wisconsin-Madison, the Robert M. La Follette Institute of Public Affairs, and the Russell Sage Foundation.

At the same time, we are indebted to the Michigan Survey Research Center for the collection, editing, and distribution of the PSID data. Over the numerous years that the Center has organized and managed the PSID, the skills and dedication of the staff have not flagged, nor has their willingness to help and assist researchers in understanding where the data came from and what they mean. Greg Duncan, Martha Hill, and their colleagues were very helpful over the entire course of the project.

While the financial support from the IRP kept us from being diverted to other interesting issues, it was the help from the staff that was crucial. Luise Cunliffe was there at the birth. Without her dedication and skills, we could never have gotten the data organized and placed in a relatively easy-to-work-with form. And, as the study moved along and additional years of data became available, we would have been hard-pressed if she had not been there to make sure that updates and extensions were made. Perhaps her greatest challenge on the project was merging the census data onto our individual data. Since she has left the Institute, her skills and dedication have been replaced by those of Jay Dixon.

Several graduate students in the Economics Department have worked with us over the years, and their contributions have also been crucial. James Spaulding, Fung Mey Huang, Chong Bum An, Donna Ginther, and Kathy Wilson not only made contributions to model specification and estimation, but their willingness to persevere in organizing, cleaning, and troubleshooting the data carried us when we were drowning in a sea of information. Our assistant, Joan Sample, came to our rescue in many ways as well.

Our bland prose in the writing of the book—and the many papers from which it draws—was vastly improved by the talented hands of Betty Evanson, Liz Uhr, and Paul Dudenhefer, all of whom are at the IRP, and Alice Honeywell at the La Follette Institute of Public Affairs. Hope Steele, who applied her copious copy editing skills to the final manuscript, helped make a rough manuscript into a coherent story. Lisa Nachtigall provided encouragement and helpful suggestions during the entire editing process, and Charlotte Shelby cheerfully managed it all.

Dawn Duren, Teresa Schiffer, and Pauline Jones contributed typing and secretarial support to the enterprise and stuck with us throughout the many drafts and variations that a project of this size generates. We admire their persistence and good cheer and thank them for their help.

Numerous people read parts or all of the book and made helpful comments to us along the way. Others gave us technical advice. They include Sheldon Danziger, Peter Gottschalk, Gary Sandefur, Sara McLanahan, Robert Hauser, Charles Manski, Robert Mare, Arthur Goldberger, Christopher Jencks, Greg Duncan, Mary Corcoran, Larry Aber, and Lindsay Chase-Lansdale. Robert Moffitt both offered helpful advice and provided data on state welfare benefits. The members of the National Advisory Committee of the IRP also gave us helpful feedback at crucial junctures.

Finally, we acknowledge the support of our colleagues in the several parts of the University of Wisconsin-Madison with which we are associated—the Institute for Research on Poverty, the La Follette Institute of Public Affairs, the Department of Economics, and the Department of Preventive Medicine.

A very special acknowledgment goes to Eric Wanner and the staff of the Russell Sage Foundation. By inviting us to be Visiting Fellows for the 1991–92 academic year, the Foundation contributed more than financial help. We enjoyed an environment and a set of colleagues—both academic and nonacademic—that made our year of research and writing productive, stimulating, and thoroughly enjoyable.

Finally, we thank each other and our children for enduring—often with a smile, but sometimes not—the grumpiness and obsessiveness that is the inevitable accompaniment of the stresses associated with a project such as this. We all deserve a good vacation.

ROBERT HAVEMAN
BARBARA WOLFE

1

The Deteriorating Status of America's Children: Facts and Implications

THE STATUS OF AMERICA'S CHILDREN

American children are not doing well. Much has been written about the precarious situation of many of our youngest citizens—and its implications for the nation's future. There have been a large number of prominent commissions: a House of Representatives Select Committee on Children, Youth, and Families; a Committee on Economic Development Task Force; a National Commission on Children created by Congress and the president; and a National Academy of Sciences Committee, which have studied the problem and offered their recommendations.

In addition, a wide variety of other groups and organizations have studied, written about, and published reports documenting the poor conditions in which many of America's children grow up. Most of these reports have also offered policy recommendations designed to improve the status and well-being of America's children—and their chances for success in life.[1]

A few facts are able to convey the essence of this melancholy picture. By any historical or comparative standard, children in the United States today face a high probability of being born to a unwed mother and of living with only a single parent. More than a quarter of today's infants have been born to an unwed mother; and 4 out of every 10 American children are not living with both biological parents. Less than three-quarters of all children live with two parents. Indeed, each year more than 1.5 million children under 18 (or about 1 child out of 40) experi-

1

ence the divorce of their parents, and about half of all children live with but one parent at some point.

These statistics are far worse for African-American (and to a slightly lesser extent Hispanic) infants and children. Indeed, nearly two-thirds of all African-American children are born to a nonmarried mother, and less than 40 percent of them live with two parents. Current estimates are that only about half of children growing up with a single parent will enter or reenter a two-parent family.[2]

With the rapid increase in the labor force participation of married mothers, substantially less time is spent at home—and with children—than in earlier times. More than 60 percent of all children under 18 have a mother who works in the paid labor force, as do more than half of children under 6. Estimates suggest that the number of hours per week that children have contact with their parents has fallen by one-half since 1964. A variety of other indicators of children's well-being and performance—ranging from the incidence of child abuse, to achievement test scores, to poverty rates, to crime rates—have also turned sour.

The troubling picture that these statistics convey for younger children carries over to teenagers. The suicide rate of teens aged 15–19 is high—more than 11 per 100,000—as is the use of cocaine. Indeed, more than 55 percent of young adults 18–25 have used cocaine at some point. Teenagers continue to drop out of high school at a high rate—15 percent overall, with higher rates for Hispanic and African-American children. And, for those who stay in high school and take the SAT tests, the average combined score of slightly less than 900 is lower than it was 20 or 30 years ago, and is viewed as abysmally low by nearly all observers.

While a large number of these overall indicators of the status of America's children are discouragingly low, this does not mean that the status of all American children is poor. In fact, the average American child today has access to substantial economic resources as well as a number of other advantages, far more than did his counterpart of a few decades ago.

A large part of the problem of children's status is rooted in differences among children, rather than in the status of the average child. The gaps among children today reflect the pattern of economic and social disparities among families. Economic inequality among families with children today is far larger today than it has been since World War II, and the disparities among families in a variety of social and behavioral dimensions seem even greater. While the circumstances of children living in middle-class and upper-income families provide little basis for special concern, the same cannot be said for children growing up poor.

Indeed, many of the dismal national indicators of children's status are heavily affected by the conditions prevailing in the nation's poorest families. As of 1991, nearly 22 percent of all children under the age of 18 lived in families with incomes below the nation's official poverty line, and about 12 percent of them lived in families that could not escape poverty even if all of the adults in the family worked full-time, full-year. The statistic is also far worse for African-American and Hispanic children—more than 40 percent live in families with incomes below the poverty line; about 20 percent of them live in families that are unable to work their way out of poverty.[3]

But just growing up in a family with low income conveys only a portion of the full deprivation that this represents. Children growing up poor are also likely to experience a wide range of other events and circumstances that thwart normal development, aspirations, energy, and hope. They are more likely than other children to be exposed to lead and experience poor nutrition, both of which lead to low and deteriorating health status. And they are less likely to be immunized against common preventable diseases. They have a high probability of living in neighborhoods with high rates of crime, drug dependence, and drug trafficking. Relative to the national average, far higher proportions of poor children attend schools with low capacities to educate or inspire learning, and live in a family with no working adult. They are more likely to give birth out of wedlock, and—by their own testimony—find traditional norms involving hard work, creativity, diligence, organization, stability, and loyalty to be unrewarding. And, to make matters worse, all of these correlates of living in a poor family are substantially higher if the children are African-American or Hispanic.

THE CHANGING STATUS OF AMERICA'S CHILDREN

While the snapshot that this discussion offers is a dismal one, it tells only part of the story. Indeed, a quick tour of the changing landscape of the status of American children is found in the section headings for a lead chapter of the report of the National Commission on Children:

- More Children Living in Single-Parent Families
- More Children with Parents in the Workforce
- More Children Living in Poverty

The fact is that in a wide variety of dimensions—economic, educational, health, nurturing, and behavior—the situation of America's children has deteriorated over time, as have their future prospects.

Over the past 25 years, major changes in both economic and social arrangements have occurred that have fundamentally altered the environment in which children grow up and are nurtured. Table 1.1 provides an overview of a number of these changes. Browsing through these numbers is probably the best way to get a picture of the changing status of the nation's children; our discussion will highlight a few of the most salient patterns.[4]

The children who are born and raised in this country today differ on a variety of demographic indicators from those in earlier decades. First, children have become a smaller proportion of the population—in 1960 children under 15 comprised 31 percent of our total population. By 1989, they made up just under 22 percent of our population. The implication of this change for today's children is substantial: when they reach working age there will be relatively few of them available to support the nonworking elderly and tomorrow's children. Children are increasingly nonwhite: in 1960, 86 percent of children under 18 years of age were white; by 1990 this had dropped to 80 percent.

The pattern of family living arrangements has been radically changed by rapid increases in both the proportion of births to nonmarried mothers and the rate of marital dissolution. Both of these factors underlie the increase in the prevalence of children who live in mother-only families—from 8 percent of children under 18 in 1960 to 22 percent in 1990. The near doubling of the percentage of children with mothers who work—to over 60 percent today—has resulted in a steady decrease in the amount of parental time to which children have access. Whereas in 1965 the average child spent about 30 hours per week interacting with a parent, by the late 1980s this figure had dropped to about 17 hours.[5]

The rising rate of marital dissolution—an increase of more than 30 percent from 1970 to 1990—has also increased the extent to which children are exposed to the stress that inevitably accompanies marital breakup and remarriage. While less than 20 percent of American children experienced family breakup in the 1960s, and 10 percent were born to single mothers, these incidence rates increased to 30 percent and 27 percent, respectively, by the late 1980s. These rates are far higher among African-American and Hispanic families. More than 20 percent of African-American children were born to unmarried mothers in 1960; by the late 1980s, the percentage had increased to more than 60.

TABLE 1.1 Trends in Factors Influencing Children's Well-Being

Changing Factors	Total	White	African-American
Demographics			
Percentage of population under 15 [a]			
1960	31.1	30.3	37.7
1970	28.4	27.6	35.4
1989	21.7	20.7	27.2
Percentage of births to unwed mothers [b]			
1960	5.3	2.3	21.6
1970	10.7	5.7	37.6
1987	24.5	16.7	62.2
Percentage of births to mothers with less than 12 years of education			
1970	30.8	27.0	51.0
1987	20.2	17.3	31.3
Average number of children per family with children [a]			
1970	3.58	3.52	4.13
1980	3.29	3.23	3.67
1988	3.16	3.11	3.43
Parental Time			
Percentage of children living with 2 parents [b]			
1960	87.7	90.9	67.0
1970	85.2	89.5	58.5
1988	72.7	78.9	38.6
Percentage of children under 18 living with never-married mothers [c]			
1970	0.8	0.3	5.4
1990	7.6	3.7	28.3
Rate of divorce per 1000 children under age 18 [a]			
1970	12.5		
1987	16.3		

TABLE 1.1 (*continued*)

Changing Factors	Total	White	African-American
Percentage of children under age 18 with mothers in labor force[b]			
1970	39.2		
1987	61.7		
Percentage of children under age 6 with mothers in labor force[d]			
1970	29		
1987	51		
Health Factors			
Mortality rate for children aged 1–4/ 100,000[b]			
1960	109	95	191
1970	85	75	140
1987	52	49	68
Suicide rate 15–19-year-olds/ 100,000[a]			
1970	5.9	9.4†	4.7†
1980	8.5	15.0†	5.6†
1988	11.3	19.6†	9.7†
Percentage of children aged 1–4 vaccinated against polio (measles)[e]			
1965	74 (33)		
1970	77 (57)	81 (60)	63 (42)*
1985	55 (61)	59 (64)	40 (49)*
Percentage of children in MSA central cities vaccinated against polio[f]			
1970	61		
1985	47		
Percentage of children in MSA central cities vaccinated against measles[f]			
1970	55.2		
1985	55.5		
Percentage of children under age 15 without health insurance[f]			
1980	12.8		
1989	15.9		

Changing Factors	Total	White	African-American
Percentage of young adults (18–25) who ever used cocaine[a]			
1974	52.7		
1988	56.4		
Percentage of young adults (18–25) who ever used heroin[a]			
1974	4.5		
1988	0.4		
Percentage of 12–17-year-olds who ever used alcohol[a]			
1974	54.0		
1988	50.2		
Reported child maltreatment/ 10,000 children[a]			
1976	101		
1980	181		
1986	328		
Income and Poverty			
Percentage of children under age 19 below the poverty line[e]			
1959	26.1	18.8	63.3
1969	15.6	10.4	41.1
1979	17.1	11.7	36.1
1990	20.6	15.9	44.8
Average cash family income, families with children, lowest quintile, 1989 $[c]			
1973	$10,529		
1989	7,714		
Welfare Generosity			
Percentage of children under 18 who are AFDC recipients[c]			
1970	8.8		
1990	11.9		
AFDC child recipients as a percentage of children in poverty[c]			
1970	58.5		
1990	59.9		

TABLE 1.1 (*continued*)

Changing Factors	Total	White	African-American
Average AFDC and Food Stamp benefits for mother plus 2 children with no earnings[c] 1990 $			
1972	10,586		
1991	7,777		
Average AFDC and Food Stamp benefits as % of poverty line[d]			
1982	71.1		
1991	67.1		
Geographic Moves			
Percentage of population age 7 who moved during one year[g]			
1966–1983	19.5		
1982–1983	19.3		
Percentage of population aged 5 or older that changed residences (percentage long distance)[g]			
1955–1960	50 (37)		
1975–1980	46 (46)		
1987–1988[a]	17 (7)		
School Performance			
National Assessment of Education Progress Test Scores (NAEPT), reading, 9-yr.-olds[a]			
1979–1980	215	221	189
1987–1988	212	218	189
NAEPT, math, 9-yr.-olds[a]			
1979–1980	219	224	192
1987–1988	222	227	202
Percentage of 18–21-yr.-olds who are high-school dropouts[a]			
1970	16.4	14.3	30.5
1980	15.8	14.7	23.0
1989	15.0	14.6	17.4
Average SAT scores, verbal[h,c]			
1960	477		
1970	466		
1980	424		
1991	422		

Changing Factors	Total	White	African-American
Average SAT scores, math [h,c]			
1960	498		
1970	488		
1980	466		
1991	474		

NOTES: Following are the page numbers in each footnoted source where the information can be found: U.S. Bureau of the Census: population under 15, p. 13; families with children, p. 51; divorce rate, p. 88; suicide rate, p. 126; alcohol/cocaine/heroin use, p. 121; child maltreatment, p. 182; moves, p. 19; NAEPT scores, p. 155; dropouts, p. 156. Bianchi: births to unwed mothers, p. 9; children living with two parents, p. 10; children under 18 with mother in labor force, p. 17; child mortality rate, p. 34. U.S. House of Representatives: children living with never-married mothers, pp. 1080–1083; cash family income, p. 1371; AFDC child recipients, p. 663; AFDC, Food Stamp benefits, p. 1190; SAT scores, p. 1073. Children's Defense Fund: mothers in labor force, p. 39. Wolfe: vaccinations, p. 53; children below poverty line, p. 45. National Center for Health Statistics: vaccinations, p. 107; children without insurance, p. 291. The Annie E. Casey Foundation: benefits as a percentage of poverty line, p. 18. Long: percent move, pp. 299–304; distance, p. 51.

*Nonwhite.
†Males only.

[a] U.S. Bureau of the Census (1991).
[b] Bianchi (1990).
[c] U.S. House of Representatives (1992).
[d] Annie E. Casey Foundation (1992).
[e] Wolfe (1991a).
[f] National Center for Health Statistics (1991).
[g] Long (1988).
[h] Fuchs and Reklis (1992), p. 42.

Not all such demographic factors affecting children have deteriorated, however. On average, today's parents are better educated than those of any previous cohort. Over 30 percent of children born in 1970 had mothers with less than a high-school education; by 1990 this percentage had declined to less than 20. As of 1970, 61 percent of the parents of elementary-school children had completed high school; by 1990, nearly three-quarters of elementary school children had parents who had completed high school.[6] Although there is no assurance that more-educated parents are better parents, there is substantial evidence—and a common presumption—that parents with more education are better equipped to make choices that enhance the quality of their children's lives than are parents with less education.

Similarly, average family sizes have decreased over the past quarter century. The birthrate of women aged 15–44 (number of births per 1000) declined from 123 to 68 from the mid-1950s to mid-1980s, and has held about steady since then. As a result, the average child has fewer siblings today than in earlier decades, and less competition for parental attention and resources. This decline in the average number of children per family with children has been greater among African-American families than white families, although the average number of children per family remains higher for the former group.

While there has been little increase in geographic mobility in the United States, the movement of American families is substantial. Nearly half of the U.S. population changed residence at least once during a 5-year period during the years from 1960 to 1980.[7] However, a larger percentage of moves are now likely to be longer distance moves than in the earlier 5-year period; in 1955–1960, 63 percent of all residential moves were within the same county. As of 1975–1980, only 54 percent of all moves were within the same county.[8] The children growing up in these mobile families experience the stress of adjusting to the new surroundings—peers, schools, and neighborhoods—that accompany changes in geographic location. Some of the moves within a county may not involve changes in friends, school, or neighborhood, but the longer distance moves surely include changes in all of these.

There have also been important changes in both the income available to children, and in the source of that income. Labor markets did not prosper during the 1970s and 1980s, especially for low- and middle-earnings individuals. Indeed, the median real earnings of all males who worked full-time, full-year actually declined by about 5 percent from 1973 (the beginning of the slide) to 1986. For younger workers and those with a high-school education or less, the drop in earnings is even greater. Real average earnings of full-time male workers with only a high-school education declined 16 percent from 1973 to 1986 among men 25–34, and 7 percent among men 35–44.[9] Moreover, the income gap among American families has widened substantially over the past decade or two. While the median income of families with children in the top 20 percent of the population increased by nearly 10 percent from 1979 to 1990, that for the bottom quintile of families *decreased* by more than 13 percent.

For a time during the 1960s and 1970s, public income support programs contributed substantially to the maintenance of family incomes. Benefit levels rose in real terms, from a four-person family average of nearly $8500 in 1960 (in 1990 dollars) to over $11,000 in 1972. More-over, the coverage of these programs was extended, and an increasing proportion of low-income families received some form of income sup-port. These programs moved an increasing share of earnings-poor fami-lies over the poverty line from the mid-1960s until the end of the 1970s. As the earnings of American workers sagged during the mid-1970s, pro-gram benefit levels were also decreased; by 1991, average benefits available to a mother and two children had fallen to $7777, down from about $10,600 in 1972. In addition, eligibility criteria became tighter, and the receipt of cash income support became tied to requirements for work and/or training. The effectiveness of these government pro-grams in moving working-age earnings-poor families out of poverty fell significantly beginning in the late 1970s.[10] This was the era of re-trenchment.[11]

As a result of these labor-market developments and public-policy measures, poverty rates for children—and for families with children—have risen substantially.[12] From 1974 to 1990, the child poverty rate rose from 15.4 percent to about 21 percent.[13] During the Reagan era period, the rate averaged 20.9 percent—4.7 percentage points higher than during the 1970s period.[14] And the average cash income of the lowest 20 percent of families with children dropped significantly—from about $10,000 in 1973 to less than $8000 in 1989 (in 1990 dollars).

Along with the increase in child poverty has come a decline in child health and in the access of children to health-care services. During the first part of the 1980s, the percentage of children without health-care coverage increased from about 13 percent to 16 percent.[15] Similarly, the percentage of children vaccinated against rubella, DPT (diptheria-pertussis-tetanus), polio, or mumps is lower today than it was during the late 1970s or early 1980s. For measles, the rate of immunization has increased, but it is still just 61 percent for children aged 1–4. Within the central cities of major urban areas the rate of immunization is far lower, and even for measles has hardly increased since 1970. For example, less than 50 percent of children aged 1–4 have been vaccinated for polio in central cities.

Because a far smaller proportion of low-wage intermittent jobs pro-vide health insurance as a fringe benefit than do high-wage jobs, the relative shift in employment toward lower-wage, often service-sector, jobs has led to an increasing fraction of low-wage workers without health insurance. The reduction in employer-based health coverage in response to rapidly rising health-care costs has also contributed to the

growth in numbers of families with children who have to provide for
their own health-care coverage or do without.[16]

These, then, represent a few of the important changes over the last
quarter century in a variety of the most important elements that form
the environment in which children grow up. However, they are not the
only ones.

The quality of the schools that children attend (and their racial and
economic diversity),[17] the levels of crime and dependency in their
neighborhoods, the presence of positive and negative role models (e.g.,
siblings or parents who have been jailed, or who have given birth out
of wedlock),[18] and the access by children to community services and
facilities (e.g., nutritional, recreational, family planning, and health services)[19] are additional attributes of the environment that are likely to
affect the attainments of children when they become young adults. Like
most of the other changes we have discussed, these changes in children's environments have generally been negative.

WHY HAS THE STATUS OF AMERICA'S CHILDREN DETERIORATED?

No one really knows just why this unfortunate state of affairs has developed, although a number of contributing factors are generally agreed
upon. There is no way that the changing structure of the U.S. labor
market can escape some blame. As noted above, real wages have stagnated in the United States since the early 1970s, and have fallen for
young workers—those who are most likely to be parents of young children—and those with little or poor education. This erosion at the lower
end of the economic spectrum has combined with rapid growth at the
top to create large gaps between children growing up in America's well-
to-do and poor families.

But saying this only pushes the inquiry back one step. Why has wage
growth stagnated, and why have the earnings gaps between America's
top and bottom workers grown so rapidly? Numerous speculations—
ranging from changing labor-force demographics, to deteriorating skills
and education, to low rates of capital investment, to the loss of international competitive position, to changes in the organization of the American workplace—have been offered, but in fact no one has yet fully
sorted out the matter.[20]

While this male-earnings stagnation and deterioration at the lower
end might have been expected to lead to more work by spouses and

mothers in order to make ends meet, not much of this response seems to have occurred. Spouses of low-earnings males do not appear to have increased their work effort very much as their husbands' earnings have sagged. The limited availability of jobs considered to be "worthy"—meaning jobs with prospects for advancement and paying above the minimum—has probably accounted for this.

These eroded earnings opportunities have, in all likelihood, encouraged a rise in joblessness and income-generating activities that are illegal (or almost so) for low-education males with few skills. Perhaps this stagnation and alienation from normal work have also contributed to the increase in the number of marital dissolutions and the willingness of teenage girls to give birth out of wedlock. These changes appear to have combined with—and contributed to—a quite new set of social norms concerning sexual activity, spousal loyalty, family stability, and independence and community, and have made traditional institutions such as church, school, neighborhood, grandparents, family, and authority less important in setting standards for behavior and attainment.

WHAT DOES THE DECLINE IN CHILDREN'S STATUS IMPLY?

These changes in the structure and performance of American workers, families, neighborhoods, and schools do not bode well for the future success and attainments of today's children—the next generation of adults. This is especially so for those growing up in poor and otherwise dysfunctional families and neighborhoods. Without some alteration in economic, family, or neighborhood arrangements, or some compensating changes in parental choices and values, the performance of the next generation of America's parents—today's teenagers—is unlikely to be better than that of today's parents. Given the rising disparities among today's children in a myriad of dimensions, we are not likely to see reduced gaps in income and well-being among tomorrow's young families.

These changes in the status of today's children also raise a large variety of questions regarding what goes into making successful children. Does the breakup of a family—or the incarceration or unemployment of a parent, or the need for the family to go on welfare, or the reduction in parental child-care time—adversely affect a child's aspirations, motivations, and attainments? Does the absence of a worker in the family—or below-poverty income, or a neighborhood populated by young high-school dropouts—influence the chances that the child will succeed in life? Does the fact that a mother has children out of wedlock make it more likely that the daughter will also give birth out of wedlock? If a parent is poorly educated, and poorly employed, is it more likely that the children in the family will drop out of school, or end up with a poor—or no—job?

As with the causes for the deteriorating status of America's children, no one has very good answers to these questions. Intuition and common sense take one part of the way. Surely family instability, parental joblessness, and poverty—and their correlates—are unlikely to work to the advantage of children. But the important issue is a quantitative one. Just how much damage are these family-based circumstances or events likely to do to children? Which factors are most likely to hold down children's possibilities in life?

Conversely, of the spectrum of parental decisions affecting children—parental investments in children—which ones are likely to have the greatest impact on the ultimate success and quality of children? And, of those factors that appear likely to have a positive effect on children's attainments, which seem most amenable to change through public policies? It is in order to provide some clues to those who want answers to these questions that we have undertaken the research reported in this book.

CAN THE CHANCES FOR CHILDREN'S SUCCESS BE IMPROVED?

In the following chapters, we report our research on the structure and performance of American families and neighborhoods—the nests in which children are nurtured—and the effects of this structure on children's success.

Our primary purpose is to understand how important decisions made by—and circumstances that characterize—parents and families contribute to the attainments of their children. Do parental decisions to complete school, to work, to earn, to move, increase the chance that their children will be economically successful when they grow up? Does the decision of parents to separate and divorce—or to marry or remarry or to give birth out of wedlock—have an effect on the later educational, reproductive, or economic activities of their children? If parents have earned a high-school diploma or a college degree, are their children more likely to complete high school or become a college graduate? Are the children of higher-income or more-educated parents more likely to be economically active when they become young adults than the children of poorer parents or those with less education?

Viewed one way, then, our study attempts to both define and measure the *linkages* between parental decisions and circumstances—decisions and circumstances that can be thought of as "investments" in their children—and the later achievements of their children. The notion here is akin to what economists call a "production function"—families and neighborhoods are viewed as a production facility, and children and their "quality" as the product of the facility. Decisions made affecting the circumstances and activities of families and neighborhood are seen as determining the outcomes—the ultimate success and attainments—of their children.

Alternatively, our study can be viewed as an effort to measure the strength and character of *mobility* in the United States. To what extent do the characteristics of the families in which children grow up—their income, the education and occupation of the parents, their social class—determine their attainments when they grow up? Is a child who grows up in a family whose parents have low education or low income, or who are welfare recipients or residents of ghetto neighborhoods, or not married, destined to be in a lower economic and social class when he or she grows up? Or do these family circumstances have only a small effect on the ability of children to escape to a higher rung on the success ladder?

In attempting to provide a quantitative answer to these questions, we adopt a framework in which investments are made in children by society as a whole (primarily, by government), by parents, and by the children themselves. Society invests in children by providing schools, libraries, safety, and recreation opportunities, subject to other spending options that exist and to the government budget. Parents observe this social investment, and make their own decisions and choices affecting children. These choices, like those of society, are constrained by a variety of factors. The income-generating opportunities of parents are limited, as is their time.

Finally, children themselves, once they reach the age of discretion, make choices regarding education, work, childbearing, and welfare receipt. Like their society and parents, children's choices are influenced by a variety of constraints and incentives. These include the circumstances, decisions, and values of their parents; the characteristics of the neighborhood(s) in which they grow up; and the economic opportunities available to them.

Viewed in this way, ours is an intergenerational approach: we highlight the effects that one generation's economic resources and decisions have on the next generation—their children.

THE STRUCTURE OF THE BOOK

Following this introductory chapter, we discuss in Chapter 2 the factors that are likely to affect the chances that children will be economically successful in the United States. Of the long list of potential determinants of success, we identify a manageable set around which we organize our thinking and our research.

Although our framework is an economic one, we incorporate the insights and perspectives of other social-science disciplines as well. As suggested above, we characterize several of the choices that affect children, whether made by society (government) or families, as investments in children. Given these choices and the circumstances they create, children themselves make decisions that influence their own attainments and success.

We adopt a sequential view of the world in this theoretical discussion, considering social or governmental decisions involving children first, followed by parental choices and the choices made by children. After noting the wide variety of public-policy issues that are raised by our investment-in-children perspective, we identify the research approach that we follow in the book.

In Chapter 3, we nest our own research in the large body of studies by economists, sociologists, and developmental psychologists on the determinants of childrens' success. This is a long chapter, reflecting the enormous body of prior research on which our own work rests. We organize our discussion by first identifying the primary perspectives—often disciplinary ones—that have guided earlier research, and briefly compare these with our own. Then we summarize the primary findings in this literature, moving from studies of the determinants of educational, occupational, and income outcomes to those involving welfare recipiency, childbearing (especially nonmarital births), and marital stability. We conclude with our summary of what it is we have learned from all of this research.

In Chapter 4, we begin the task of exploring our data (described in Appendix A) and of sorting out the relationships that are implicit in them. We first present a series of cross-tabulations that describe the character of the choices that the children from our data set have made as young adults: choices involving education, nonmarital childbearing and welfare receipt (for the young women), and economic inactivity. These decisions or outcomes are then crudely related to some important characteristics of their families and neighborhoods when they were children. Following this, the same relationships are described more completely through both simple and multiple regression estimates. Our purpose here is to show the primary relationships that our data reveal without attempting to account for potential simultaneity and other subtleties with which only more complex models can effectively deal.

Chapters 5, 6, and 7 present the results of our most full-blown modeling efforts. These three chapters explore the relationships between a variety of family and neighborhood characteristics and the choices made by the children when they are young adults in the areas of schooling (Chapter 5), reproduction (Chapter 6), welfare receipt (Chapter 6), and economic inactivity (Chapter 7). In each chapter we first present the results of our simple base-case estimates revealed in Chapter 4. We then expand our modeling efforts to: (1) include a rich set of family background, family behavior, and neighborhood characteristics; (2) account for a variety of choices that may be interdependent or simultaneous; and (3) explore the sequential nature of some of the choices made.

Over the course of our research, we have tested a variety of models and specifications. Here we report those estimates that meet the dual criterion of being robust over a variety of models and fitting the data most consistently. In addition to reporting the parameter estimates from the models, we have also prepared a series of simulations that reveal how the values of the outcome variables (e.g., years of completed schooling) change in response to changes in the values of the family and neighborhood variables.

Finally, Chapter 8 pulls together the results of our review of past research and summarizes our own findings. It also draws out the policy implications of our research.

Appendix A is a detailed description of the data that we use in our empirical estimation. Our data set is a complicated one, involving 21 years of detailed longitudinal information on each of about 1700 children. For each child, the data include information describing both the economic and demographic characteristics of his or her family and neighborhood during childhood years, and a variety of indicators of the choices made during young adulthood. All of these children were from 21- to 26-years-old in 1988, the final year that we observe them for purposes of this study.

We first describe the principal background and independent variables describing the circumstances during childhood for each of the children, and present some basic statistics on each variable. Following this, similar information is presented on the outcome or success variables reflecting the choices that the children have made when young adults. It is these variables whose values we seek to understand, if not explain. Finally, we discuss one of the most troublesome of the problems with any longitudinal data set, including ours—the issue of attrition from the sample.

NOTES

1. The most prominent of these reports is that of the National Commission on Children: National Commission on Children, *Beyond Rhetoric: A New American Agenda for Children and Families* (Washington, D.C.: Government Printing Office, 1991). Its title belies something of the frustration over the paucity of policy response to the recommendations of a number of other committees, commissions, task forces, and study groups. Among the more prominent of these recent reports are:

- National Commission on America's Urban Families, *Families First* (Washington, D.C.: U.S. Government Printing Office, 1993).

- Committee for Economic Development, *The Unfinished Agenda: A New Vision for Child Development and Education* (New York: Committee for Economic Development, 1991).

- C. D. Hayes, ed., *Risking the Future: Adolescent Sexuality, Pregnancy, and Childbearing* (Washington, D.C.: National Academy of Sciences Press, 1987).

- William T. Grant Foundation Commission on Work, Family and Citizenship, *The Forgotten Half: Pathways to Success for America's Youth and Young Families* (Washington, D.C.: William T. Grant Foundation, 1988).

- U.S. Department of Education, *Schools That Work: Educating Disadvantaged Children* (Washington, D.C.: Government Printing Office, 1988).

- William T. Grant Foundation Commission on Work, Family and Citizenship, *The Forgotten Half: Non-College Youth in America* (Washington, D.C.: William T. Grant Foundation, 1988).

- Carnegie Council on Adolescent Development, *Turning Points: Preparing American Youth for the 21st Century* (New York: Carnegie Corporation, 1989).

- U.S. Congress, House of Representatives, Select Committee on Children, Youth, and Families, *U.S. Children and Their Families: Current Conditions and Recent Trends, 1989* (Washington, D.C.: Government Printing Office, 1989).

- Children's Defense Fund, *S.O.S. America! A Children's Defense Budget* (Washington, D.C.: Children's Defense Fund, 1990).

- National Commission To Prevent Infant Mortality, *Troubling Trends: The Health of America's Next Generation* (Washington, D.C.: National Commission to Prevent Infant Mortality, 1990).

- National Commission on Child Welfare and Family Preservation, *A Commitment to Change* (Washington, D.C.: American Public Welfare Association, 1991).

In addition, there have been a number of prominent books dealing with this problem that should be mentioned:

- E. C. Kamarck and W. A. Galston, eds., *Putting Children First: A Progressive Family Policy for the 1990s* (Washington, D.C.: Progressive Policy Institute, 1990).

- A. J. Cherlin, ed., *The Changing American Family and Public Policy* (Washington, D.C.: Urban Institute Press, 1988).

- L. B. Schorr, *Within Our Reach: Breaking the Cycle of Disadvantage* (New York: Doubleday, 1988).

- J. L. Palmer, T. M. Smeeding, and B. B. Torrey, eds., *The Vulnerable* (Washington, D.C.: Urban Institute Press, 1988).

- J. G. Dryfoos, *Youth at Risk: One in Four in Jeopardy* (New York: Carnegie Corporation, 1989).

- D. Blankenhorn, S. Bayme, and J. B. Elshtain, eds., *Rebuilding the Nest: A New Commitment to the American Family* (Milwaukee, WI: Family Service America, 1990).

- *The Aspen Institute Quarterly* (Special Issue on Children and Families), Winter, 1993, Vol. 5, No. 1.

2. See Bumpass and Sweet (1989). According to Levitan, Mangum, and Pines (1989), 90 percent of all African-American children will spend some time in a single-parent household.

3. See Haveman and Buron (1993).

4. Another source of information characterizing the changing status of America's children is the special Appendix G in the 1992 *Green Book* (U.S. House of Representatives, 1992).

5. These data are from a time diary study by John Robinson, a sociologist from the University of Maryland, cited in Mattox (1991) and Galston (1993). Mattox also cites a 1990 *Los Angeles Times* poll that reported that over 55 percent of fathers and mothers feel guilty about spending too little time with their children.

6. Among African-American children, the increase over this period in the

percentage of parents with a high-school education was even more dramatic: from 36 to nearly 70 percent (National Commission on Children, 1991, p. 32).

7. In particular, 47.1 percent of families moved in the 1965–1970 period and 46.4 percent moved in the 1975–1980 period. See Long (1988), p. 51.

8. The 9 percentage point increase in longer distance moves includes moves between counties but within a state (up from 17 to 21 percent of all moves over this period), moves between states (up from 18 to 20 percent), and moves from abroad (up from 2 to 4 percent). See Long (1988), Table 2.6.

9. The drop was even greater if we look at all men with at least one dollar of earnings: for such men, 25–34, with a high-school diploma, the decline was 20 percent over the years 1973–1986. The same age males with a college degree had their income increase—by 3 percent over this same period. See Levy and Michel (1991) pp. 19–22. See also Haveman (1989), Levy and Murnane (1991), Levy and Murnane (1992), Acs and Danziger (1993), and Haveman and Wolfe (1990).

10. The 1991 *Green Book* (U.S. House of Representatives, 1991, Table 3, Appendix L) provides a comparison of federal programs targeted on children in 1978 and 1987. In constant dollars, the value of all programs decreased by 4 percent (from $50.7 to $48.9 billion). This includes a decrease in income support programs of 10 percent (from $20.6 to $18.6 billion), an increase in nutrition programs of 11 percent (from $13.1 to $14.5 billion), an increase in health programs of 10 percent (from $3.4 to $3.75 billion), a decrease in educational programs of 8 percent (from $7.6 to $7 billion), and a 44 percent drop in training and employment programs (from $3.0 to $1.65 billion). This decrease occurred during a period in which pre-tax and pre-transfer incomes of families with children were declining on average—and poverty rates were increasing.

11. The changing impact of public income support programs in removing children from poverty is reviewed in Danziger (1990).

12. The poverty rate is the percentage of families (or children in families) with cash income below the poverty line corresponding to the size of the family. The poverty line is an official U.S. government definition that is based on an absolute measure of poverty. For a 2- (3-), (4-), (5-) person family in 1992, the poverty lines were $9212, ($11,280), ($14,463), ($17,097), respectively.

13. U.S. House of Representatives (1992), p. 1167.

14. Adjusting for food stamps and housing benefits reduces the poverty rate. Duncan and Rodgers (1991) calculate that the poverty rate for African-American children in 1986 would decline from 43.1 to about 37 percent using these two adjustments.

15. The recent changes in mandated Medicaid coverage will, over time, increase the health-insurance coverage of children. The Omnibus Budget Reconciliation Act of 1990 requires that states provide coverage to all chil-

dren under 19 years of age, born after September 30, 1983, who live in families with income below 100 percent of the federal poverty line. The provision went into effect July 1, 1991.

16. See Wolfe (1991a). Among those employers that do pay for insurance, only one-third now pay for full dependent coverage, compared with 40 percent a decade ago (National Commission on Children, 1991, p. 136).

17. See Mayer (1991) for estimates of the impact of school racial and socio-economic mix on rates of high-school noncompletion.

18. See Case and Katz (1991), who report on the effects of role models on the behavior of a sample of inner-city youth in Boston.

19. See Lundberg and Plotnick (1990b).

20. See Levy and Murnane (1992).

2

Toward Understanding
the Determinants
of Children's Success

Young adults are a relatively little-studied group in contemporary American society. Yet, in a very real sense, they are a pivotally important group. The status and attainments that are observed in young adulthood—say, from ages 18–26—are likely to be a good predictor of the remainder of life's trajectory. Clearly the prospects for the jobless high-school dropout are quite different than those for the college graduate with an engineering degree.

While many of today's youths succeed brilliantly in a variety of life's dimensions—economic, social, and personal—others fail miserably. We read most often about the failures: high-school dropouts, the jobless (especially among minorities), those in jail, teenage unmarried mothers, welfare recipients, and those confined to low-wage jobs with few career opportunities. To be sure, we also read about the successes: the yuppies who have made it in the fast lane of the business world, the young happily married couples with children who own their first home in a middle-class neighborhood, and the college graduate who is working for his master's degree in management.

Although no one has documented it, it seems likely that economic and social inequality among youths is greater than that of any other age group. In no other age group does one find the contrasts of joblessness and high earnings, single welfare mothers with multiple children and unmarried professionals, burger flippers, and fast-track careers. Moreover, though again unmeasured, the increases in social and economic inequality would seem to be larger for this age group than for others.

As indicated in Chapter 1, this book is about success and failure among older children and young adults. It is premised on a basic proposition, namely:

The *resources* and *opportunities* that social and parental decisions have made available to children, together with the *choices* that they make given these resources and opportunities, strongly influence the success that these children achieve when they reach young adulthood.

Because most of these resources and opportunities are conveyed by the family circumstances in which children grow up, the family-based events that they have experienced in childhood, and the characteristics of the neighborhoods in which they have gone to school and sought peers, we focus on these family and neighborhood traits. In short, our task is to measure as accurately as we can the effect of investments in children (especially family-based investments), and of children's own choices, on their performance and attainments when they become young adults.

A moment's thought will reveal how difficult a task this is. While few people doubt that family environment and resources have an important effect on children and their ultimate success, sorting out the influences of parental choices and family circumstances from all of the other factors that influence children's success is difficult. Schools, individual teachers, neighborhood environment, the nature of the labor market in one's area, and especially personal characteristics (such as motivation, ability, drive, and physical appearance) also play an important role. Indeed, these factors are often intricately intertwined with the nature of parental choices and family circumstances. To make things even more complicated, we hope to establish some presumption of causality—that, say, growing up in a poor family causes poor performance—in addition to sorting out independent linkages. This is a far more demanding task than simply observing a statistical relationship.

This chapter sets the stage for the research results that are found in the book. We begin with a discussion of the factors that are likely to account for the successes and failures that young people experience. Although some of these factors cannot be changed in the short run by either individuals or governments—for example, the incentives that young people encounter for working or going to school, or their inherent ability and motivation—others can. We distinguish among choices that can be made by governments, by the parents of children, and by the children themselves.

We follow this discussion with a general description of the research approach that we follow in the study. We briefly describe our data (leaving a more detailed description for Appendix A), the success or failure outcomes on which we focus, the key family and neighborhood variables that are related to these outcomes, and the statistical methods that we employ. We conclude by indicating the sort of statements that we hope to make on the basis of our research.

WHAT DETERMINES SUCCESS FOR YOUNG ADULTS?

Without a great deal of thought, any person can suggest several candidates for inclusion in a list of potential determinants of children's "success," irrespective of how success is defined. The list assembled from the suggestions of, say, a dozen people would be a long one, longer than any researcher would know what to do with. We have done this experiment, and here is a selection of the suggestions we received:

- individual ability or "brainpower"
- motivation or "drive"
- personality
- appearance
- education level and quality
- existence of a special teacher or role model
- race
- ethnic background
- the education of the parents
- the number of parents in the family
- the economic resources of parents
- parental "connections"
- nurturing received when a child
- aspirations of and examples set by parents
- attitudes of friends and peers
- the state of the economy
- the availability of schooling subsidies or other public programs
- the region of the country in which one lives
- "luck"

There is nothing particularly subtle about this list, and nearly everyone believes that everything on it belongs there. Indeed, social scientists—economists, sociologists, and developmental psychologists—who have studied children's behavior and their attainments suggest adding a number of items to the list. These include the following:

- the number of siblings
- whether or not the child was the first born in a family
- stresses encountered while the child is growing up
- neighborhood characteristics, such as welfare recipiency or joblessness
- sociopsychological characteristics (e.g., self-esteem) of parents
- whether or not parents are foreign born
- the source of parental income (e.g., earnings or welfare)
- the quantity of books and reading materials in the home
- parental oversight and monitoring
- religiosity of family
- generosity of public welfare benefits and social services

Just as with the first list, all of these factors seem reasonable, and should be included in any full listing.

The problem, of course, is that one easily becomes baffled and confused when confronted by such a laundry list. Many of the items on these lists are interrelated with other items. For example, having parents with little education probably means having parents with few economic resources. Growing up in a one-parent family probably means having more than the typical share of stressful experiences while a child, and having less nurturing and contact with parents. Little progress can be made unless the independent effects of these various factors can be identified and sorted out.

Another problem is that one never knows all of the things about a young adult that might be relevant in determining his or her success. Available data sets are limited in the information that they convey, and collecting information that is rich in all of these dimensions is prohibitively expensive. As a result, researchers have to work with the data that they have available.

A third problem is that laundry lists such as these give one no anchor, no starting point for organizing research. Providing such a base is the role of theory, and in the case of children's success there is no dearth of theories from which we can draw in beginning our investigation.[1]

A Theoretical Framework: Choices and Investments

To assist in thinking about the determinants of children's success, we have adopted an "investment-in-children" framework. While some will argue that the question of children's attainments is demeaned by casting it into this sort of mold, we disagree. Indeed, as we suggest below, in our view the success of a child is determined by three primary factors: the choices made by the society, primarily the government, regarding the opportunities available to children and their parents (the "social investment in children"); the choices made by the parents regarding the resources to which their children will have access (the "parental investment in children"); and the choices that the child makes given the investments in and opportunities available to him or her.

Several things should be emphasized about this view of the determinants of children's success. First, we have adopted a view of the world that emphasizes the effects of choices that are made. Governments, parents, and children all have their interests, and they make choices that best serve these interests given their resources and the limitations (or constraints) that they face. The attainments of children are viewed as the outcome of this set of choices, together with the inherent talents of the child.

In this sense, then, our framework has a deterministic flavor. If we could identify the various choices that have been made as they pertain to any particular child—or better yet the determinants of these choices—and if we knew about the basic abilities and motivations of the child, we could make a pretty good prediction of how successful that child would be. While "luck" would clearly play a role, with good information on these choices and children's innate talents, we believe that predictions of how children would fare as young adults would be reasonably accurate.

Second, the choices made by the first two actors in this process—society (or government) and parents—relate to investments made on behalf of children by some other party. Consider first, government. Given the wide variety of other demands that it faces, to what extent does society make provision for the nurturing and development of children by devoting resources to schooling, preschool child care, family income support, controlling crime and drugs, ensuring employment opportunities for parents, and so on? For parents, choices are at stake as well. How do they allocate their income and other resources among the various things that give them satisfaction, including their children? How do investments in children stack up against all of the other expenditures that families might make?

Third, while the choices made by government and parents contribute to a child's success, the choices made by the child are also relevant. And, as with government and parents, children are viewed as making decisions in order to maximize their well-being (as they see it), given the resources available to them and their opportunities. To the extent that those choices also contribute to the ultimate attainments of the child, they can be viewed as investments by children in themselves.[2]

Fourth, this way of characterizing the problem suggests a sequential view of the world. Society (government) is viewed as acting first, making some direct investments in children, but more importantly setting the economic environment in which the parents of children operate. Given this environment, parents choose how much to work and earn (given their talents), and how much time to spend with their children, and then, given their resources, they decide how much to devote to their children. They also make decisions about family structure and location that serve their own interests, but that also have an impact on their children.

Finally, given their own talents, the resources that have been invested in them, and the incentives that they confront, children make choices about their education, their childbearing and their family structure, and their work effort. It is the outcomes of these choices, along with a good dose of luck, that we observe, and we assess the extent to which children succeed or fail on the basis of these outcomes.

While this economic framework could be a limiting one, we have broadened it to avoid the blinders that a particular discipline's perspective might create. To begin with, we adopt a very inclusive definition of resources to which a child has access. While we treat the financial resources available to children as contributing to their success, we also view the time, nurturing, and stability resources that parents allocate to children to be investments in them. Similarly, any action by government that creates an environment in which children will prosper and succeed is viewed as a public investment in children.

Most importantly, we attend carefully to the contributions that social scientists who are not economists have made to understanding children's success. Our framework is richly leavened by the insights of sociologists and developmental psychologists.

Social (Governmental) Choices and Children's Success

Government Objectives, Options, and Constraints. In our framework, it is society—or government, as its agent—that sets the basic environment within which families and children make their choices. In this view, government is a decision maker with access to a wide variety of policy instruments: taxing, spending, and regulatory policies; judicial pronouncements; moral suasion; and leadership by example. The use of any of these instruments will affect citizens in a wide variety of ways. Any action will benefit some citizens while hurting others. On balance, one would hope that the benefits that are conveyed by governmental decisions outweigh the harm.

It is the job of government to reflect the collective tastes of its citizens in making decisions. Government must weigh each of the options available within each of the categories of instruments, and choose that set which increases to the greatest extent possible the collective well-being of its citizens, somehow defined. Of course, any possible decision that government might make has costs associated with it. Spending more on school construction, although benefiting children (and teachers), requires that either taxes be raised or public debt be issued. In either case, some group of citizens is forced to bear costs to support the additional resources to be devoted to education.

Viewed in this way, then, government as the agent of society has an objective (to maximize the collective well-being, somehow defined) and has instruments available to accomplish this objective, but it is constrained in a variety of ways in making decisions to accomplish its objective. Indeed, the decisions made by society through government face both economic and political constraints.

We have already mentioned the budgetary constraints facing government. Any action taken requires that some of society's resources be diverted from some activity in which they were being used to another activity, that implied by the policy. Such resource diversion entails costs, and these costs are reflected in the structure of goods and services prices that government faces when it takes action. These prices, then, are one of the constraints that government faces.

Another set of constraints faced by government are political constraints, especially in a democratic system. For example, building a highway will satisfy the road user/road builder constituency, and these interests will make political decision makers aware of these gains in the best way they know how. Conversely, environmentalists, taxpayers, and a variety of other people adversely affected by the decision (including numerous other potential claimants on these same resources) will demonstrate their displeasure with this decision.

Government Choices on Children: Direct and Indirect Effects. Given this general framework, we can now better perceive society's role in affecting children's success. Government policies can be viewed as having both a *direct* and an *indirect* effect on children's chances for success.

Consider, first, policies that have direct effects on children and their chances for future success. Let us call these "social investments in children." For example, primary and secondary schooling has traditionally been assigned to government, and public school budgets and school organization fall within this domain. Public decisions affecting school organization and performance have a direct effect on what and how children learn, and on their chances for success later in life. Similarly, youth job-training programs (e.g., Job Corps) and employment programs for youths fall into this category. Without much of a stretch, police and community efforts to reduce crime in neighborhoods or control drug use among youths are other examples of direct social investments in children. Other examples would include direct expenditures for enriched child care and early education (e.g., Head Start); children's food and nutrition programs; maternal and children's health programs; and children's medical care costs (through Medicaid).

Indirect policies with effects on children and their success are less straightforward to define. A good way to understand such measures is to ask whether or not they enable others—parents, private citizens, and nonprofit organizations—to engage in activities that benefit children. A full employment economy, for example, enables parents to work and earn, and thereby provide resources to children. Provision for the deduction of private child-care purchases and charitable contributions from income in calculating tax liability are further examples. The latter, for instance, encourages citizens to support a variety of private programs that benefit children: Girl Scouts and Boy Scouts, shelters for homeless families, and mental health facilities serving children and youths are examples.

In the larger scheme of things, of course, policies that either directly or indirectly benefit children are but a small portion of the total menu of options open to government. While some parts of this remaining menu may not be viewed as directly or indirectly affecting children in any major way (e.g., highway construction), others are seen as being in direct conflict with social investments in children. Indeed, the debate over intergenerational equity in the United States often views the interests of the elderly population as pitted directly against the interests of children.

Implications for Understanding the Determinants of Children's Success. The lesson of this discussion, then, is a straightforward one: the choices made by society through its government both directly and indirectly affect the success chances of children. Hence, researchers seeking to understand the process by which some children fail and others succeed ignore these social and governmental influences on children at their own risk.

While this lesson is clear, implementing it in research studies designed to identify the determinants of children's success is difficult. Many of government's efforts on behalf of children are "public goods," and hence accurate accounting of their impacts on particular children is difficult. Others are indirect, and with all such governmental efforts, tying the outputs of particular governmental interventions to specific children is also problematic. Although some of these public investments in children are direct and amenable to measurement—for example, the spending on public schools attended by specific children—this information is typically not contained in those data sets containing rich family information on individual children.

Parental Choices and Children's Success

Like government, but even more directly, the decisions made by parents influence how children develop and the level of success that they ultimately achieve. The framework for considering these decisions is very similar to that outlined for governments.

Parental Objectives, Options, and Constraints. Parents have objectives, just as governments do. A standard view is that parents seek to maximize either their own well-being, or the well-being of a broader unit consisting of themselves and their families. Parents make choices that reflect their objectives (or "tastes"), and in so doing they establish the environment in which their children are raised. They choose how many children to have, and when; whether or not to work, and how much to earn; where and in what sort of conditions to live; how much time to spend with their children, and the quality of that time; whether or not to seek and accept welfare benefits; what goods and services to buy and how to allocate these across the members of their families; where to send their children to school, and how much time to spend monitoring their success in school; and whether to stay married, even if the relationship is not a rewarding one, or to divorce. All of these choices (and many others, as well) have influences on their children; all set the family-based environment in which their children grow up. Together they define the level of parental investment in children.

The objectives of parents often conflict, requiring that trade-offs be made. For example, although the provision of time and resources to children appears on the list of things that give parents satisfaction, they are not the only things. Having a new car may conflict with hiring a tutor to work with a child who is performing poorly in school. Working two jobs may detract from quality time spent with children, although it will generate additional income in which children may share. Parental time spent watching television may come at the expense of helping children with school work, or at least monitoring their progress. Having another child may reduce the resources available for existing children— or it may not! Ensuring that inoculations are up-to-date and appropriate health care is provided may require time away from work and jeopardize employment or promotion.

In evaluating these trade-offs and making these choices, parents— like government—encounter restrictions and constraints. They may wish to earn income to buy goods and services (some of which will benefit children), but find that they are unable to find work—the state of the economy may constrain their choices. They are constrained by their own background and characteristics—they may have little education, few abilities, poor usage of language, an unattractive appearance, or an unappealing personality—and these factors also restrict choice. The prices that they face in deciding what to purchase or where to live are also constraints, as is the structure of wages in the labor market in their area. The social mores that prevail among their friends or in their community also restrict their choices. If marital separation and divorce meet with social disapproval, or if accepting welfare benefits is frowned on by family and friends, choosing these options will appear more ''costly,'' and parental choices will be accordingly limited.[3]

Hence, operating in a social and economic environment that is influenced by the decisions and choices made by government, parents, with their objectives, resources, and constraints, make decisions on family structure, consumption levels and saving, work and leisure, and the allocation of income and time. Even more basically, parents choose the sort of monitoring, disciplinary, nurturing, and expectational environment that they create for their children.[4]

Implications for Understanding the Determinants of Children's Success. From this perspective it is clear that a large number of the characteristics of the families in which children grow up are relevant for assessing the level of parental resources that are allocated to them. Family income, and perhaps the stability of that income over time, are relevant, though family income needs to be adjusted to reflect the number of people who share in it. The time allocation of parents is also relevant; one would like to have direct measures of the time parents spend with children, but perhaps the extent of parental working time could proxy for this. Other decisions of parents, sometimes reflecting choices that have been made years earlier, are also likely to play important roles in the development of their children. Parental education, psychological stability and resiliency, and "warmth" all fall in this category. The structure of the family, together with the stresses that come from changes in family structure (e.g., parental separations or remarriages), are also likely to affect children and influence their success later in life. Changes in geographic location may have the same effect. Finally, parental decisions regarding where to live, the source of income (e.g., welfare or earnings) holding its amount constant, and other behaviors and attitudes also contribute to the nature of the family-based environment in which children grow up. All of these family choices represent parental investments in children.[5]

Children's Choices and Their Later Success

The framework that we have suggested for understanding the effect of decisions made by society (government) and parents on children's success applies equally well to the decisions made by children themselves. In this framework, children too are viewed as decision makers seeking to make themselves as well off as possible. It is presumed that they have carefully weighed the benefits and costs associated with the options available to them, and have made the choices that we observe, given their resources and the constraints that they face. In this context, for example, a teenage girl observed to have a nonmarital birth (or observed to drop out of school) is interpreted as having made a choice that leaves her at least as well off, given the constraints that she faces, as not giving birth (or staying in school). Similarly (staying with the teenage nonmarital birth example), subsequent to giving birth, the girl may live with her parents or set up an independent living unit; she may get married or not; she may get a job or choose to receive welfare. All of these options are seen as potential choices for the girl, and given those factors that limit her choices, the decisions that she makes are interpreted as leaving her better off than alternative decisions.[6]

Work and Earnings: A Rational Choice Example. Perhaps thinking about the choices involving working and earning confronting a youth who has completed schooling would make this framework clear. In this example, the youth seeks to leave herself as well off as possible, but her efforts are constrained by a variety of outside forces. She has to accept her own skills and ability, for example, although through additional training, existing capabilities can be further enhanced. She also has to live with the markets in which labor services are sold. If wages are high and rising, or if jobs are plentiful, there will be many opportunities, and these factors alone may lead her to work more hours and receive higher earnings and income. Similarly, the opportunities for securing income by not working will also affect her work effort and earnings. If transfer income or welfare benefits are high and easily accessible, she may choose to be a beneficiary of public programs, to work less, and to have lower earnings.

Such a youth is also limited by other factors that influence the choice of whether or not, and how much, to work. If she is the parent of small children, for example, there is a legal responsibility to have them cared for, whether or not she is available to do the caring; this constraint may affect the amount of work or earnings. A similar consideration is the level of income from other sources to which she might have access, apart from her own work and earnings. The earnings of a spouse would be an example.

From this brief discussion of our framework, we can already see a number of factors that should be included in any analysis of the determinants of the amount of the teenager's earnings. These factors are the determinants of individual labor supply. Ability, education, wages in the labor market, the number of job openings, the generosity of transfer income, the presence of a spouse, the number and ages of children, and the level of assets or income from nonearned sources are all important determinants of labor supply and earnings.

The Teenage Nonmarital Birth Decision: Another Example. When this framework is applied to the options of a teenage girl regarding nonmarital childbearing, we are again assisted in identifying a variety of factors relevant for understanding the decision. These factors can be thought of as determinants of the unmarried teenage girl's "demand for children." Consider the following:

- Is the girl doing well in school? If not, school continuation may be unattractive, and having a nonmarital birth may convey the benefit of an excuse for leaving school.
- A lack of success in school also suggests that her prospects in the labor market may be poor. If the probability that the girl could get a job is low, the jobs for which she is qualified are poor, and the wages that she could earn are low, having a nonmarital birth may give access to welfare benefits that would not otherwise be available.
- Are the girl's parents well-to-do? If they are, the pressures to work if a child is born may be reduced, as will be the pressure to seek welfare, or to leave the parental residence and set up an independent household. Moreover, well-to-do parents probably have values that may lead to censure or strong disapproval of a teenage daughter who gives birth out of wedlock, resulting in cost associated with having such a birth.
- Is family planning information readily accessible to the girl? Are contraceptives available, and are they available at a low price? Are abortions available in the community, and is knowledge of availability widespread? If they are, the cost of avoiding the pregnancy and/or birth will be reduced, and the probability of unplanned or unwanted pregnancies will fall as well.
- What is the situation in the labor market, the marriage market, and the income transfer market in the girl's locality? Plentiful employment opportunities are likely to reduce the benefits of an unmarried birth, as are a large supply of marriageable males, and a stingy and inaccessible welfare system.

This listing illustrates the factors relevant for understanding the nonmarital birth decision faced by a teenage girl. A similar list could be compiled for the rational consideration of whether or not to drop out of high school, or how many years of schooling to pursue, or the sort of employment or marital options to choose once schooling is complete.

The Role of Information in the Economic Choice Framework

Information plays an important role in the economic perspective that we have outlined. In our discussion, individuals make their decisions after appraising their resources and constraints, and weighing the advantages and disadvantages associated with each option. They are assumed to know the magnitude of these gains and losses with accuracy. However, in fact, these benefits and costs are often perceived only dimly.

As a result, the choices made may be quite different from those that would be made in the presence of more complete information.

Consider, again, the case of a teenage girl considering whether or not to engage in behavior that might lead to conception, or, having conceived, whether or not to give birth out of wedlock. These would seem to be classic cases of decisions for which the costs are systematically understated while the benefits are exaggerated. The full money and time costs of raising a child as a lone mother are likely to be ill understood—and as a result, underestimated. Similarly, the full opportunity costs associated with the foregone earnings and marriage possibilities attributable to the nonmarital birth are likely to be understated. On the other hand, the potential psychological benefits of having a child of one's own may be glamorized and exaggerated. Because the information available to teenagers is likely to be poor and asymmetrical, their decisions may tend to be biased toward conceiving and bearing children out of wedlock.

Because the accuracy of these benefit and cost estimates is likely to depend on the characteristics of the girl's parents and the nature of the family in which she grows up, these characteristics should be included in any model designed to explain the nonmarital birth outcome of teenage girls. For example, girls with more-educated mothers and fathers are likely to have more access to reliable information on childbearing costs and the foregone earnings and marriage opportunities associated with a nonmarital birth than are girls with less-educated parents. All else being equal, we would expect that teenage girls with better and more reliable information would have a lower probability of giving birth while unmarried.

Similarly, a child whose parents have devoted substantial time to caring for and interacting with their children is likely to have more reliable information on the relevant costs and benefits of childbearing, work, and welfare decisions than children with small allocations of parental time.[7]

The role of information in the economic model, then, provides the basis for including a variety of parental characteristics as determinants of the choices made by young adults.

Stigma Effects in the Economic Choice Framework

Any full-blown version of the economic model will also admit the relevance of stigma costs in the choices made by children or youths. Those youths whose parents dropped out of high school—or who have siblings who are high-school dropouts, or who grow up in a neighborhood where young high-school dropouts are prevalent—are likely to have a different assessment of the stigma costs attached to this decision than are other teenagers. Similarly, the religious affiliation of the family of a youth is also likely to influence the perceived level of stigma associated with a variety of potential choices. Such differential assessments will influence the probability that a youth will choose to drop out of school, have a nonmarital birth as a teenager, or choose a low-attainment occupation or joblessness.

Investments in Children: Some Policy Issues[8]

We have argued that the choices made by society (government) and parents should be viewed as investment-type choices capable of affecting the success of children when they become young adults. This argument, however, raises a variety of questions about investments in children—for example, the appropriate level of such investment, and the composition of these investments. In the following paragraphs, we discuss a few of the policy issues that derive from this investments-in-children perspective.

Are We "Underinvesting" in Children?

Determining the optimal level of investment in children is, in concept at least, an issue that has a clear answer: keep allocating resources to children until the value of social benefits produced by the last unit of investment is just equal to the value of what could be produced by those resources if they were used in some other way.[9] But that simple textbook response raises as many questions as it answers.

For example, how does one define and measure the "social benefits" of investments in children? If a parent decides to enroll her child in an enriched early childhood education program, the parent is surely benefiting, as is the child. Presumably, the added learning, changed values, and altered behavior that enrollment in such a program confers are what is meant by increased "child quality"; and an increase in child quality provides the parent with satisfaction, and the child with all that comes with these changes.

However, the child quality that is created also benefits persons other than the parents and the child. Because of the program, the child is less likely to engage in crime when he or she grows up, and more likely to contribute to general social well-being through citizenship activities.

These changes benefit society in general. However, the parents do not take into account these social benefits when making the decision on whether or not to enroll the child in the enriched program. Because parents neglect these "external" benefits of their own investments in children, they may devote too few resources to this activity as viewed from the broader perspective of society.[10] This factor may suggest that, as a nation, we underinvest in our children.[11]

The pat answer also gives little insight regarding the value of the resources if they are not devoted to children. One confronts assertions every day about the needs of society to which resources could be efficiently allocated—caring for the homeless, improving the nation's infrastructure, curbing crime and drug abuse, finding a cure for AIDS. It makes a difference where the resources would come from if investments in children are to be increased. Some, for example, would feel more comfortable advocating an increased level of investment in children if the resources came from, say, certain types of consumption such as New Year's Eve celebrations at the Plaza Hotel costing $300 per person, than if they were being diverted from antidrug or homeless shelter activities.

To What Should Investments in Children Be Directed?

Even if it is decided that certain kinds of investment in children would have a very large payoff, it does not follow that, overall, we are investing too few resources in children. We may be allocating resources to activities that we think may lead to increased children's attainments, when in fact these activities may have a very low payoff. For example, a common assertion is that in attempting to increase the quality of education, school systems have added administrators and classroom supplements that serve only to bureaucratize the teaching function and stifle teacher creativity and spontaneity. If this assertion were true, children's attainments could be increased by reallocating resources away from that form of investment in children to other, more productive, investments in children.

This issue of the "best" mix of investments in children is an important one, especially in light of the many perspectives regarding the determinants of children's success that we identified in the previous section. Each of the perspectives may have some claim to being correct. However, for answering questions regarding how effectively to invest in children, that is not enough. The important issue concerns just where the largest payoff in terms of children's achievements lies: formal schooling; enriched early education; more, and more effective, parental time; higher family income; better-adjusted and more-educated parents; or improved neighborhood quality.

From the perspective of public policy, then, the trick is to identify those specific investments in children that have the greatest payoff relative to their cost. While individual analysts would reach different conclusions about the effects of altering various environments (or stimuli) that influence children's attainments—and on the economic costs of the resources required per unit change in attainment—all would agree that identifying the optimal level and composition of such investments in children is a crucial policy issue.

Just to make this issue even more complicated, it needs to be recognized that the effect of changes in various aspects of children's investments is neither constant over various levels of investment, nor independent of the level of other forms of investment in children. For example, increases in parental education (or in family income, or neighborhood quality, or parental time, or parental monitoring efforts, or school quality) are not likely to yield constant returns in terms of children's attainments. Moreover, the effectiveness of one form of investment probably depends on the levels of investments of other types. An increase in parental income probably has a quite different effect on children's attainments if the family lives in a poor-quality neighborhood than if it lives in a higher-quality one. Sound policy also requires that the interactions of these various investments in children in their role as producing quality children be clearly recognized.

Related to this point, not all of the aspects of investments in children that have been identified and discussed in the literature have a *direct* effect on children's success. Some forms of investment may only influence children's accomplishments via other factors—these factors can then be said to mediate the impact of the investment.[12] Moreover, the level of some investments in children may be determined by the very process of improving child quality; in these cases the level of a contributing factor requires no deliberate investment decision, as it may be determined indirectly by changes in other factors or investments. Again, sound policy decisions require that these relationships among investments be clearly recognized.[13]

Even these considerations, as complex as they are, form only part of the story. We have used the term "children's attainments" rather glibly, sweeping aside the fact that children succeed—and fail—in many dimensions. Educational attainment, reproductive behavior, occupation and earnings, dependence on welfare, the quality of personal and family relationships, attitudes toward accepted rules and customs, and self-esteem and other attributes of psychological health are all elements of success and attainment. Somehow, and for each child in differing proportions, these elements combine to form the degree of the child's success. Hence, identifying the optimal level and composition of investments in children requires that one specify clearly those aspects of overall achievement in which one seeks improvement.

To Which Children Should Investments Be Directed?

Even though one might conclude that the overall level of investment in children is too small, it does not follow that all children have too few resources devoted to them. Many children in our society appear to be doing well: they come from intact, supportive, and nurturing families with adequate incomes; they go to quality schools; their parents, their teachers, and their peers have high expectations for their future; and they have easy access to health care, recreational, and, if necessary, counseling services. They are not the cases that are trotted out when it is claimed that, as a nation, we are underinvesting in children.

The underinvestment case is clearly the strongest in the case of children growing up in deprived families—those included in the nation's poverty population or living in the nation's inner cities. These children, in which racial minorities and those living in mother-only families are prevalent, tend to have fewer resources available to them in a whole spectrum of dimensions, as compared with children from middle- and upper-class families. Because the allocation of resources to them is constrained by both family budgets and the "bite" from capital market imperfections, it is likely that the social return on the marginal dollar invested in them is high, relative to both investments in nonpoor children and many alternative uses of the funds.[14]

The "to which children" question is also relevant in considering the ages of children in whom investments are to be made.[15] Is the return at the margin greater for investments in prenatal care, in enriched early childhood programs, in elementary- and secondary-school years, or in adolescence and beyond? A great deal of debate is directed to this question; the knowledge necessary to answer it accurately is in far shorter supply.[16]

Who Should Be Doing the Investing?

Presuming that we have determined the efficient level of aggregate investment in children, the efficient mix of various types of investments, and the efficient pattern of allocation among children, we are still left with the question of who should be doing the investing. Should parents be the primary instrument of investment, with public support for them in case they do not have the resources to provide the socially optimal level of investment in their children? Or should the state itself be the instrument, through increased allocations to schools, nutrition programs, children's health programs, enriched day care programs, and recreation programs?

As with earlier issues, this one generates more heat than light. It is a fundamental question, however, as it rests on an assessment of which type of provider—the family or organized programs—is more effective in producing high-quality children per dollar of cost. Perhaps even more importantly, how one answers this question reflects value judgments on the very nature of social organization. Should the nurturing of the nation's children occur primarily in the privacy of families, with parents as the primary decision makers? Or should society, through the state, play a more active role?[17]

Who Should Pay?

Even after the issue of the direct family versus public provision is settled, there is the question of who is to pay for the investments that are undertaken. Should parents be left to pay all of the costs of whatever their children receive, with perhaps some public subsidization of parents who do not have the financial or time resources to provide a minimum level of these goods and services? Should taxpayers generally—both those with children and the childless—be required to support programs of investment in children, such as public schools or a universal child allowance? Should parental housing, food, clothing, and time allocations to their own children be taken as their contribution, with additional investment support being financed by taxpayers generally, or in particular, childless taxpayers?

Resolving this issue is at least as difficult as any of the others. While this question too can be cast into an efficiency framework, it is far more dominated by equity considerations than many of the others. In some ways, it is but a variant of the traditional question of who should pay for public goods, such as national defense and street lights. As we have seen, investments designed to increase children's attainments and their success have a substantial dose of external or public goods effects, including reduced crime, more informed citizens, and a more productive work force.

CHOICES, INVESTMENTS, AND CHILDREN'S SUCCESS: OUR RESEARCH APPROACH

The empirical research that we present in this book follows directly from the choices-investment framework presented above. In what follows, we attempt quantitatively to measure the relationship between choices made by government and parents—and a variety of other family and neighborhood characteristics—on the attainments of a representative sample of young adults. These public and parental choices and characteristics are interpreted as reflecting various levels of investment in children. We study the relationship of these investments on the attainments of children when they become young adults, in a context in which the youths also make choices.

Within this framework, the specifics of our research have been largely determined by the data that we have available. These data include 21 years of information on each of about 1700 children. These children were born in the years 1962 to 1968, and are 20 to 26 years of age in 1988, the last year for which we have information on them. For each child, we know a great deal about the characteristics of and choices made by the parents in each year of childhood. We also know the characteristics of the neighborhood in which the family of the child lives, and a rich assortment of basic background information (for example, gender, ethnic background, and so on), on the child.

Although these data are rich relative to other sources of available information, they are lacking in several important dimensions. For example, we cannot paint a very complete picture of the public investments that have been made in individual children (for example, the quality of the schools attended), or of the level and composition of parental investments. And, although we cast our analysis in a framework in which children also make choices, we are not able to observe many of the considerations weighed by youths as they make their decisions.

In the following paragraphs we provide a brief overview of our study. We begin by describing the general characteristics of the data with which we work. We then describe the aspects of children's success (or failure) that we study, and provide a description of each. The sorts of determinants of success that we emphasize in our studies are described, and they are related to our investment/choice framework. Finally, we give some insight into the statistical methods we employ, and suggest the sorts of questions that we hope to address with the empirical results that we present.

Our Data: A General Overview

Our empirical estimates are based on detailed information that we have obtained on 1705 children that are included in the University of Michigan Panel Study of Income Dynamics (PSID).[18] All of these children were living in 1968, and they ranged in age from 0 to 6 years old in that year. Each of these children was "dropped in on" in each of the subsequent 21 years (through 1988), and in each year the characteristics of their living arrangements were observed and recorded. In 1993, these children ranged in age from 25 to 31; they have become young adults.

For each child, then, we have 21 annual snapshots, and in each snapshot we are able to observe many aspects of the child and his or her family environment. We see the basic unchanging characteristics of the child: race, gender, and year of birth. We see the kind of family in which the child lives: its income, its location, its religion, how many parents are in the family unit, how much education these parents have, whether these parents work, how much they work if they do work, how many other children are in the family, whether the family is on welfare or not, and so on. We see where the family lives, whether in a rented place or in an owned home, on a farm or in a central city, and in what region of the country.

More importantly, because we have a snapshot of the child in each year, we know about a number of important changes and events that have occurred over the child's lifetime. For example, if the child's parents separate, we know it; if the child's father becomes unemployed, we can observe it; if the family goes on welfare, or changes location, or has another child, we record it. Finally, we know some of the things that have happened to the child, such as losing a grade in school.

Unfortunately, we do not know as much about these children and their families as we would like to know. We do not know what kind of school the child goes to, or the quality of education that it provides. We do not know about the child's social life, the number and types of friends, and activities outside of school. We do not know how much television is watched, or how much reading is done. We do not know the quality of the interactions in the child's family, whether the parents fight, nurture their children, monitor their behavior, go to the school's open house, or leave the children unattended. We do not know a number of seemingly important things about the parents themselves. Do they drink heavily, are they abusive, are they stable and reliable, do they have high or low levels of self-esteem, do they expect much or little from their children, or have they been in jail? And, from the basic data, we do not know very much about the characteristics of the neighbor-hood in which the child grows up.

It would be ideal if we could know all of these things; unfortunately, no available data set contains this rich menu of information. Some data sets have detail that is richer than ours on a variety of issues, but in all cases these data sets are limited in the length of time over which the children are observed. The most prominent of these data sets, the National Longitudinal Survey of Youth (NLSY), begins observing the children only when they reach age 14. As a result, we have had to make a trade-off. We have chosen a data set that is very rich—though not as rich as some others—but that contains year-by-year information on children that spans both their childhood and young adult years.

We have attempted to enrich our data in a number of dimensions so as to offset some of the more serious gaps. For example, using information on the time that parents spend in a variety of activities from another data set, together with matched characteristics from these data and our own, we have imputed a predicted annual measure of the hours of child-care time that parents spend with their children.

Similarly, we have added to our data a variety of detailed characteristics of the neighborhoods in which the families live, obtained by matching information available in our data with detailed tract information available in the 1970 and 1980 censuses.

Finally, because we know the state in which the families of the children live, we have been able to add to our data estimates of the annual state unemployment situation and of the year-by-year value of welfare-type benefits that are available in the state.

Aspects of Success in Young Adulthood

By 1988, the last year that we observe the 1705 children in our data, they have become young adults. In that year, they range in age from 20 to 26. Although we would like to know how they fare even later in their lives, we do have good information on a number of outcomes after they have left their teenage years.

The outcomes or attainments of the children that we have chosen to study are among the most important in terms of forecasting ultimate success. Our first outcome is education. Did the youth finish high school, or did he or she drop out? If he or she graduated from high school, were additional years of schooling or training chosen? How many years of schooling were completed?

We also explore the choices that the girls in our data made regarding whether or not to have a child out of wedlock while they were teenagers, and, if they became an unmarried teenage mother, whether or not they then chose to go on welfare.

A third choice that we study relates to the activities of these young adults when they are in their early twenties. If they are not in school, what are they doing? Do they have jobs, and if so, how much time do they spend working? If they are parents, how old are their children, and what is the extent of their child-care responsibilities? Some of them are not in school, or working, or required to engage in child care—we call them "inactive." Can we understand the determinants of this status?

As part of this last outcome measure, we would like to have added the salary of each young adult when they join the work force on a permanent or long-term basis. Unfortunately, we cannot do this with our sample because our measure of earnings includes part-time jobs while a student or during an intervening year before schooling is completed. The age of the sample during the final year of our observation makes the earnings measure only an imperfect proxy for such a longer-term measure of earnings potential.

We also do not include other possible outcome measures that are of interest in looking at broad indicators of the attainments of young adults. These include criminal activities, broader contributions to society such as volunteer activities, and whether the individual lives in a household with income over the poverty line. The only available measure of criminal activities is whether or not the individual is in jail in a particular year, a very limited measure of the extent of criminal activities.[19] We have no measure of volunteer activities, hence we cannot include it. As for poverty, we would like to measure this when the young adult is responsible for at least part of the income of the family unit: for example, when they are living in their own household rather than that of their parents. Since not all of the sample has their own household by 1988, it is difficult to capture the success of an individual's efforts in avoiding poverty.

Determinants of Choices in Young Adulthood

In studying the determinants of the educational, reproductive, welfare recipiency, and activity choices made by young adults, we have been guided by the theoretical framework discussed earlier. In many cases, however, we have had to compromise, largely because of the limitations of our data.

For example, our data tell us very little about the level of social investment in particular children. We have had to rely on information on a variety of neighborhood characteristics as proxies for information on school quality and other aspects of public investment in children.

Similarly, to form a reliable assessment of the choices parents make in determining the level of investment in their children, we would like to have information on a variety of parental activities and choices—for example, the extent to which parents monitor school work or participate in the PTA—and this information is not available.

Also, although we would like to have information on a number of specific aspects of children's lives during their growing-up years in studying the choices that they make when they become young adults— for example, their grades in school, or the presence of behavioral problems—our data do not include this information.

Finally, while our economic framework has emphasized that youths weigh the gains and costs of each of the options open to them in making choices, we do not have reliable information on many of these cost/ benefit categories, and are required to rely on proxies in a number of cases. Indeed, the youths themselves make their choices on the basis of partial or unreliable information, but we have no indication of the completeness or accuracy of their knowledge.

In the following list, we indicate the primary variables that we use in studying the determinants of the attainments and choices of young adults. Observations on these variables are available for each year that the child is observed in the data. The organization of the variables here begins with true background variables—those that cannot be changed by choices made by anyone. The other categories reflect the economic choice model outlined in the first section of this chapter[20]; in reporting our results, we often use other groupings of variables, largely for purposes of exposition.

Background Variables
  Race
  Gender
  Foreign or domestic birthplace of parents
  The birth position of the child in the family
  Whether or not the child's grandparents were poor

Social (Governmental) Choices: Social Investments in Children
  Education of the child's parents
  Unemployment rate in local labor market

The receipt of welfare benefits by the child's parents
Generosity of public welfare benefits in the state
Housing tenure status of the family

Parental Choices: Parental Investments in Children
Education of the child's parents
Work effort of the child's father and mother
Earnings of the child's father and mother
Occupation of the child's father and mother
The receipt of welfare benefits by the child's parents
Urban/suburban/rural location
Region of location
Number of children in the family
Housing tenure status of the family
Parental time devoted to child care
Number of parents present in the home
Number of parental separations or remarriages
Number of times the family changed geographic location
Age of the child's mother when she first gave birth
Whether or not the child's mother gave birth out of wedlock
Characteristics of the neighborhood in which the child's family lived
Religious orientation of the child's family

Young-Adult Choices Made by Children
Grade lost in school
Split off from parent's home
Years of education[21]
Presence of a teenage nonmarital birth[21]
Teenage welfare recipiency[21]

Empirical Approach Used in the Study

The analyses that we present in this book are based upon the detailed year-by-year data that we have described above.

We begin by presenting raw statistics on the choices made by the children in our sample when they were youths or young adults: high-school graduation rates, years of completed schooling, prevalence of teenage out-of-wedlock births, receipt of welfare benefits subsequent to having a nonmarital teenage birth, and economic activity when the youth is in his or her mid-twenties. Second, for each of the choices made by the young adults (outcomes), we present some simple regressions relating the outcome to a limited number of the background and social and parental investment variables listed above.

Third, we present results that reflect our judgment regarding the choice process of the young adult. For some of the outcomes, a multiple-equation strategy is necessary; for others, we seek to capture the essence of the choice in a single equation. In all cases, we make use of a large number of the variables indicated above. The form in which these variables are expressed often differs, however, depending upon the choice or outcome that we are analyzing.

Although we are often constrained in accurately characterizing the components of the costs and benefits associated with the specific choices made, we exploit the information we have available so as to focus on the determinants of the choices. Throughout our study, we attend carefully to those decisions made by parents that are likely to have important effects on their children, in an effort to discern the effects of family-based choices and characteristics on outcomes in young adulthood.

The Policy Questions Addressed

Throughout our research, we have tried to keep one eye on the public policy implications of our findings. Our starting point was the proposition that the extent of children's success in young adulthood is influenced by choices made by government or choices made by parents (at least some of which can be influenced by government). If this is so, we should be able to extract from our findings some implications for the direction of public policy.

The following are a selection of questions of the sort for which we hope to be able to provide partial answers, or at least relevant information:

- To what extent can increases in the education levels of parents enhance the attainments of their children?

- Does the generosity of public welfare benefits affect the probability that young adults will choose to have a birth out of wedlock, or welfare recipiency?

- Does the poverty status (or income level) of families affect the level of their children's performance and attainments? By inference, can public income support policies improve the chances for success of children in poor families?

- Holding parental income levels constant, does the source of income— say, from working or from welfare—have an effect on the success of children?

- Does instability in families, such as parental separations and household moves, have an adverse effect on the choices made during young adulthood of the children?

- Do the number of years spent living in a single-parent family influence the level of attainment?

- Does the time that a mother works while a child is growing up have an effect on the outcome of the child?

These questions are very basic ones, and they go to the heart of public policy debates on our children and their futures. However, they are not questions that concern the likely success of particular public interventions, such as children's nutrition programs or enriched child care. Hence, at best, our estimates can provide insight into fundamental directions for policy, but little by way of direct evaluation of proposed measures.

NOTES

1. In Chapter 3, we describe several theoretical perspectives, drawn from the sociology, economics, and developmental psychology literatures.
2. Note that this perspective recognizes that children may maximize their utility (or well-being) by making decisions that sacrifice future success in order to satisfy more immediate wants. It follows that our implicit emphasis on children's ultimate success and attainments reflects a judgment that may be inconsistent with children's own evaluation of their well-being.
3. To make matters even more complicated, some of the constraints on parental choices are the effect of social (governmental) decisions made either in the past or currently. For example, some parents are constrained in what they earn or whether they work by the poor quality of education made available to them when they were growing up. Similarly, the failure of public macroeconomic policies to ensure full employment—to some extent reflecting governmental choices—affects the ability of parents to work and earn. The government's approach to welfare policy—its generosity and accessibility—also affects the probability that parents will be welfare recipients. As a final example, government plays an important role in setting the social environment in which family decisions are made. Policies and admonitions regarding reproductive decisions, criminal activities, family structure and lifestyles, housing standards, women's work, and the importance of education can all be viewed as constraining the decisions made by parents.
4. Unlike governmental decisions, the decisions made by parents typically have rather direct effects on children; the distinction between direct and indirect seems much less relevant here. We take the sum of these parental decisions as determining the environment in which children are raised and

develop. This environment reflects the level of parental investment in children.

5. Other parental and family characteristics not reflecting choices are also likely to influence children's success. Race, ethnic background, and parental abilities are examples of such "background" factors.

6. As indicated above, such decisions may simultaneously *increase* an individual's well-being in the short run and *decrease* their future attainment or success. See Note 2.

7. In considering the issue of the amount of time that parents spend with children, the number of siblings with whom a child lives becomes relevant. Any amount of child-care and interaction time spent by parents may be spread over the children, leaving less time available per child in large families than in small ones. On the other hand, parental time allocated to children may be like a public good, available to all children simultaneously when it is provided. Little evidence on this process is available, but clearly the number of siblings with whom a child grows up with may be an important factor in influencing his or her later choices. The research findings of developmental psychologists indicate that family size (the number of siblings) is generally negatively related to the success of any given child.

8. The discussion in this section reflects insights from the thoughtful paper of Fuchs (1990).

9. An alternative, and equivalent, answer is that investment in children should continue until the "social rate of return" on that investment is equal to the social return on alternative ways of using the resources.

10. A review of the literature on the external benefits of education, an important form of investment in children, is found in Haveman and Wolfe (1984) and Wolfe (1993). These studies suggest that the external effects of education are likely to be a significant portion of the total social benefits of this form of investment in children.

11. There are other reasons that also suggest that we undertake too little investment in children. For example, it might be efficient for a particular child to attend a special, and costly, school designed to nurture her unique talents in music. Such an investment might have a social payoff that is greater than that of a business desiring a new office word-processing system. Yet, while the business could probably borrow to finance its planned investment, neither the child nor her parents would be likely to secure bank financing for the training in music. Economists describe this constraint on investing in children as a capital market imperfection, and it too could lead to underinvestment in children.

12. For example, parental participation in a counseling program might lead to higher levels of self-esteem and a greater orientation toward the future. These changes may well be manifest in higher parental expectations for children's success, increased monitoring, or improved family life. In turn, the child may well then be better equipped to cope with stressful events related to school, family, or peers.

13. This is one of the lessons from the extensive empirical work on status attainment that is discussed in Chapter 3.

14. This raises the question of the social desirability of unequal investments in children. Some children, for example, may have the potential to benefit by additional education; others may not. An efficient pattern of investment would concentrate education spending on those children with the greatest potential to benefit from it. This result, however, implies unequal treatment of children, even children within the same family. And, if investments in education result in additional income, unequal educational investments will result in future inequalities of income. If equality of *treatment* of children is desired, families (and society) should find other ways of assisting those children who do not receive the schooling investment. If equality of *outcome* is the goal, families (and society) should increase their investments in children with lower potential to benefit from education, and reduce investments in children with higher potential.

15. This is the primary message of the life course or ecological framework that has been adopted by a number of developmental psychologists. (See Chapter 3.)

16. A growing consensus seems to be that the United States overinvests in children who have graduated from high school (and especially those who go on to posthigh-school education), relative to younger children. See Hamburg (1991). Other evidence suggests that marginal investments in postsecondary education have a higher social payoff than most investment in nonhuman capital. See Haveman and Wolfe (1984), Wolfe (1993), and Ashenfelter and Krueger (1993).

17. This debate plays itself out in issues such as the choice controversy in education; the provision of day-care support through refundable tax credits versus publicly operated day-care centers with subsidized fees; and public support for higher education versus, say, individual capital accounts for youths.

18. A more detailed description of our data is presented in Appendix A.

19. We note that not one of the persons in our sample is reported to be in jail or have served a sentence since turning 18, a highly unlikely situation.

20. In some cases, the classification of a particular variable is problematic. For example, we have classified the birth origin of the parents of a child as a background variable, yet in some cases migration to the United States was a decision made by the parents that could be thought of as a parental investment in the child. In other cases, a variable is listed in two categories, as it contains important aspects of both categories. For example, the educational attainment of the parents of the children reflects decisions made by the government in years past, and it also reflects decisions made by the parents themselves.

21. These variables are used in studying the economic activity of persons in their mid-twenties.

3

A Tour of Research Studies

Before delving into our research findings, and to provide a context for them, we make an excursion through the extensive literature on the determinants of success or attainment of children. Contributors to this literature include economists, sociologists, and developmental psychologists. We attempt to integrate the findings from all of these disciplines.

Encompassing fully all of the social science literature that has explored the causes of children's success and failure would require a volume of its own. We therefore draw a number of boundaries around our discussion.

First, we focus on those studies that examine the determinants of children's success when they have become young adults. Hence our discussion of a substantial amount of research in the field of child development and child psychology, much of which is addressed to behaviors and the performance of young children or adolescents, is very cursory.

Even among the studies of young adult attainment, we emphasize those that analyze the correlates of a limited set of success indicators: in particular, education attainment and socioeconomic success (e.g., occupational status, earnings), teenage nonmarital childbearing, the receipt of welfare income, and marital instability.

Finally, we focus our discussion on empirical studies that employ large microdata bases, in particular those relying on nationally representative samples of individuals and those employing longitudinal data.

Organizing the vast amount of research that remains is difficult. Many of the studies focus on a particular outcome (e.g., educational attainment), and examine a variety of background and parental status and behavior correlates of this outcome. Other studies begin with a specific hypothesis regarding the pivotal role of one or a few particular

51

determinants of success (e.g., growing up in a family that is dependent on welfare income), and examine the effect of variables reflecting this determinant on a variety of outcomes, while controlling for a standard set of background characteristics. Still others have several outcomes of concern and test a variety of potential determinants of these outcomes.

The organization of this chapter emphasizes the primary outcomes of interest. In each section, we first identify those determinants of the outcome in question that are emphasized in the literature. We then discuss the statistical methods employed and the results obtained.

We organize our discussion of the determinants in line with the basic investments-in-children perspective that motivates our own work. However, this perspective has not been used to guide most of the prior studies in the literature, at least not in the form in which we have cast it. Instead, these studies have been motivated by a wide variety of alternative theories or perspectives.

In the first section, we describe the most important of these theoretical perspectives. The second section identifies the major empirical studies and indicates their primary findings, and is organized by outcome. In the third section we attempt to draw out from this research the primary linkages that appear to be established in the research literature. Finally, in the last section we suggest some next steps for data collection and research in this area, and implicitly provide a critique of existing empirical research on children's attainments.

ON THE CAUSES OF CHILDREN'S ATTAINMENTS: THE PRIMARY PERSPECTIVES

Much has been written on why some children succeed while others do not. Depending on one's orientation, quite different factors tend to be emphasized: psychologists, sociologists, and economists all have their own views of the underlying determinants of success.

In the first subsection, we identify and briefly describe the primary perspectives found in the literature, and then recall the investments-in-children perspective that guides our own research. As will be seen, our framework is related to, and draws from, the insights of some of these other perspectives.

Perspectives on the Determinants of Children's Success

One approach to understanding the numerous perspectives that have guided studies of the determinants of children's success is by discipline.

However, several of the theories are difficult to assign to any particular discipline, and are, in fact, employed by researchers from a variety of disciplines. Hence, we directly identify the various explanations—irrespective of the primary discipline from which they stem—and describe the primary variables and linkages they emphasize.

The Economic Deprivation Hypothesis

This hypothesis places heavy weight on the economic circumstances (family income, assets, and housing quality) in which a child is nurtured, and suggests that poverty and economic deprivation contribute to a lack of children's attainments, net of those background variables (such as race, parental education, parental psychosocial characteristics) that also influence achievement. Families living in poverty, it is suggested, are unable to provide the resources and the environment essential for their children to develop their own abilities and potential fully. A clear example of the constraint that inadequate family resources impose on development is the requirement that the child work while an adolescent to contribute to family resources, or leave school early to care for younger siblings, or otherwise assume adult roles.[1]

Empirically, it is difficult to separate economic deprivation from a variety of phenomena that are highly correlated with it. These include growing up in a single-parent family (which may carry with it lower parental control, less parental child-care time, and perhaps increased parental psychological problems), or being a welfare recipient (which may carry its own burden of stigma and dependency).[2]

The Socialization Perspective

This explanation stresses the important effect of role models and socialization during childhood and adolescent years on attainment as a young adult.[3] A variant of this approach emphasizes the importance of having two parents present in a family in order to foster normal personality development and heterosexual interaction. The presence of two parents also strengthens parental control and monitoring, and weakens the potential influence of peers.

The socialization/role-model framework also focuses on the behavior of parents and older siblings, as well as their aspirations, self-image, and other sociopsychological characteristics. Children, it is hypothesized, internalize these behavioral and self-perception attributes of both parents and older family members.

Empirically, this perspective focuses attention on the number of parents in the family, their psychological and social characteristics, and their values and expectations. Because some of these attributes are correlated with earnings capacity and economic position, it is difficult to test this hypothesis reliably against, say, the economic deprivation thesis.

Life Span Development Approach

The life span (or "life course" or "ecological systems") approach to studying families and children has been formulated and utilized primarily by developmental psychologists. This perspective emphasizes that development occurs over the life course of an individual, and that events that impinge on a person have differential effects depending on when during the life course they occur, the length of time since the occurrence of the event, the experiences and interactions that occur subsequent to the event, and the historical context in which the event occurs.[4]

Given this perspective, the task of the researcher is to discover how a variety of environments or events affect alternative patterns of adjustment for individuals with various characteristics at different points during their lifetimes. The process is one of adjustment and adaptation to exogenous forces, in which the nature of the adjustment is affected by the transactions and interactions in which a person engages.

The empirical implications of this perspective involve attention to timing effects (when in the life course significant events occur), the nature of interactions subsequent to events that may either reinforce or offset the effect of the event on the person's development (e.g., whether there is parental support and stability subsequent to a divorce, as opposed to parental conflict), and the environment in which an individual functions during and subsequent to an event. Aside from the emphasis on the timing of events, this perspective is sufficiently broad and complex to encompass a variety of narrower frameworks as special cases.

Stress Theory

Related to both the socialization and the life span perspectives is a theory that emphasizes the tendency of various events and circumstances to dislodge an individual from an equilibrium developmental path.[5] The focus on specific stressful events distinguishes this perspective from the socialization/role-model framework.

Empirical research based on this perspective emphasizes events such as family dissolution, parental unemployment or incarceration, or a change in household location, hypothesizing that such disruptions may lead to emotional uncertainties that impede development and attainment later in life.

The Coping Strategies Perspective

Recent attention, especially among psychologists, has been given to the effects of parental expectations and attitudes on the achievement of their children. The coping strategies perspective suggests that the psychological resources of the family (e.g., parental expectations for their children; the ability to plan for the future; and personal characteristics of ambition, trust, and achievement motivation) are positively related to children's performance and attainments. Parents' expectations, for example, may serve as standards that are internalized by children. These standards may also be revealed in the observed willingness of parents to devote resources to their children. In this sense, then, expectations can become self-fulfilling prophecies.[6] While such resources may be important to child development regardless of the incidence of stressful events with which a child must deal, they may have their greatest impact when negative or stressful events occur.

Other Perspectives

These, then, describe the primary social science perspectives for studying the determinants of children's success. In addition, however, there are a variety of other hypotheses: in some cases, these are but variants of the more full-blown perspectives that we have discussed.[7] Here we describe them only briefly, while providing references to more extended discussions.

The "working mother hypothesis" suggests that the mother's absence from the home may be the source of developmental problems in children, due to the associated reduction in control, guidance, and monitoring.[8] The mother's working, however, may also be associated with income increases for the family, which may offset the negative effects of low income (as emphasized by the economic deprivation hypothesis). A mother's working may also serve as a role model of industry and effort.

The "welfare culture perspective" emphasizes the harmful effects that parental dependence on public assistance may have on children's aspirations and on their capacity for independent actions.[9]

The "family size perspective" focuses on the reasons why large family size (reflected in the number of siblings) may adversely affect development and attainment. These reasons range from the effects of overcrowding, to the dilution of parental time, to the erosion of parental discipline and supervision. Alternatively, some have speculated that the presence of siblings may increase the network of support and monitoring.[10]

Finally, we would mention the "neighborhood/peer group perspective." This viewpoint hypothesizes that the characteristics of neighborhoods and the attitudes and behaviors of peer groups may have a strong influence on the aspirations and, hence the attainments, of children. This conjecture is closely related to, and perhaps a subcategory of, the life span and socialization perspectives, in that it is the interactions of an individual with peers, neighbors, and role models that influence his or her attitudes, aspirations, and ultimately behaviors and achievements.[11]

An Attempt at Synthesis— The Investments-in-Children Perspective

Common to all of the perspectives that we have described is the presumption that the many stimuli that come to bear on children affect the paths along which they grow and develop. Many of these stimuli take the form of resources, or the services of resources, to which children have access, or to which they are exposed. These resources and their services can be categorized in many ways. They include family financial resources, such as the income and the things bought with that income; resources in the form of parental time devoted to children; the emotional energy spent by parents in fostering and nurturing their children; the psychosocial resources (e.g., self-esteem, self-efficacy, future-orientation) that fathers and mothers are able to bring to their parenting role; and public sector services to which children are exposed, such as those related to schooling, health care, recreation, police, counseling, and neighborhood quality or composition.

In all cases, the factors that we have labeled "resources or their services" are increased or decreased by decisions made by individuals. For example, the decision of a parent to work (or to work longer hours) will increase the level of family income to which a child has access. That decision may also influence the level of parental time devoted to the child. Similarly, parents can choose whether or not to allocate time to their children, to invest in their own capacity to produce quality parenting services (e.g., by improving their own psychosocial resources), or to contribute their time to improving the environment in the schools that their children attend.

Viewed in this way, many of the factors identified in the previous section as determinants of children's success can be cast into an economic or an investment framework. Whether it is economic deprivation or socialization or neighborhood characteristics that play the pivotal role in the development process, the factors that serve as inputs to these determinants can be altered by individual decisions regarding them. Such decisions may involve increasing or decreasing the resources— money and time—devoted to children.[12]

If this proposition is true, a corollary is that individual, family, and public decisions—resource allocation decisions—can affect children's success patterns. Such decisions or interventions are properly viewed as *investment-type decisions*—they involve the commitment of real labor and capital resources today in order to secure gains in the future.

Central to this perspective is the proposition that all of the decision makers relevant to the attainment of a child—society (government), parents, and children themselves—are seeking to maximize their own objectives or well-being. The decisions that each of them makes reflect this decision process.

Although we discussed this framework in Chapter 2, relating it to the more formal economic model from which it derives may be helpful. This model is the human capital framework of Becker (1981) and Becker and Tomes (1986), as it is applied to children.

In the Becker-Tomes framework, parents both invest in their children and enjoy their own current consumption, constrained by family economic resources. These resources include both human wealth (the parents' education and their time, for example) and nonhuman wealth (income or assets). The greater the value of parental resources, the larger the investment in children and the greater the children's attainment or success.

For example, family decisions on the schooling of any particular child, or adding to the number of children (fertility), can be viewed as a trade-off between the quantity of children and their quality. Both the number of children and the quality of each child contribute to the well-being of the family. Parental economic security when retired, for example, is positively affected by both the number of children that can assist and support them, and by the capacity and accomplishments of these children. A child's success in school, such as an A on a math test, also provides satisfaction to parents in terms of increased feelings of well-being.

Similarly, increases in either the number of children or the quality of each child require resources in the form of both money and parental time, and these resources are scarce. Hence choices must be made, and the process of making these choices requires assessment of the contribution to family well-being of both child quantity and child quality: increments in either dimension have both costs and benefits. Out of this maximizing framework comes the family demand for the number of children and the schooling (as a proxy for quality) of its children.[13]

In much the same way, the choices of children themselves—for example, whether or not to drop out of school or to bear a child out of wedlock as a teenager—are viewed as the outcome of a comparison of the benefits and costs of the relevant options.

As we detailed in an example in Chapter 2, giving birth out of wedlock provides a teenage girl access to welfare benefits, social services, health insurance, and job-specific training and education, and the potential benefits that these convey. Such a decision also offers independence from parental control that may be perceived as oppressive. The costs of nonmarital childbearing include the sustenance cost of the child, childcare costs (if schooling or market work is chosen), and the earnings from employment foregone because of the presence of the child. Other effects with well-being consequences may include reduced pressure to attend traditional schools (with potential discipline, failure, and boredom correlates), or to work in unpleasant, low-skill jobs; increased feelings of worth and "being needed"; and the ability to form a community with other young women in like circumstances. The result of weighing these considerations is the unmarried teenager's demand for children.

The implications of this synthetic framework for empirical estimation are clear. To the extent possible, variables reflecting both investments by society and parents in a child and those reflecting the child's own evaluation of costs and gains need to be included in an empirical model of the decision at issue. This approach argues for a research strategy that seeks a rich specification of the potential correlates of children's attainment. By adopting such an approach, the dangers of assigning effects to some variable, x, only because another variable, y (which is closely related to it), is not included in the model, can be reduced.

RESEARCH ON THE DETERMINANTS
OF CHILDREN'S ATTAINMENTS

Educational, Occupational, and Income Outcomes

The most studied aspect of children's attainment is clearly education or schooling. The perception of schooling as an important contributor to a wide variety of other behaviors and outcomes no doubt accounts for this emphasis. Various aspects of schooling success are emphasized in the literature, including test scores or grades, whether or not the child drops out of high school prior to graduation, years of schooling, and the character of postsecondary schooling (e.g., vocational training, 2-year college, 4-year college or university, professional school).

In much of the research on children's success, the study of the determinants of schooling attainments is but a way station along the road to understanding the determinants of occupation, earnings, or economic status. Many of the larger studies of economic attainment view education as a prior intervening variable for occupational status and earnings, and occupation as a determinant or intervening outcome prior to earnings or income. Hence, while the following discussion will be cast primarily in terms of educational attainment, subsequent occupational and earning attainments lie only slightly below the surface: the primary results that have been found in studying educational attainment carry over directly to other and subsequent dimensions of economic status.[14]

The Effect of Parental Status on Children's Attainments: Research on Social Mobility

Early research on the determinants of educational attainment (and socioeconomic status) was undertaken mainly by sociologists and demographers, and was largely driven by the question of social mobility: is the occupational status (or income) of children determined by the status of their parent's (primarily their father's) occupation, or is it relatively common for children from families with low occupational status to attain high-status occupations (or high income)?

Blau and Duncan (1967) were among the earliest researchers addressing this question. They relied on a national data set with a limited set of background variables—education and occupation of parents, race, and an indicator of growing up in a single-parent family—to explore the determinants of education and occupational status.[15]

Duncan and Hodge (1963) had earlier set out the conceptual model of the socioeconomic process underlying the Blau and Duncan estimates. This framework viewed family background (e.g., father's occupation) and education to be the primary determinants of children's occupational and earnings attainment, with family background having both a direct effect on occupational status and earnings, and an indirect effect through education. Education, although determined in part by family background, also had its own independent effect on the occupational or income status attained.

The results of the Blau-Duncan study indicated that the son's education was an important determinant of his occupational status, and that education was the most important channel by which the father's education and occupation influenced the son's status. They found that the intergenerational transmission process differed rather substantially between farm and nonfarm families, and among racial and ethnic groups.[16]

Duncan, Featherman, and Duncan (1972) also used the 1962 OCG data, but in addition drew upon a variety of other data sources that allowed them to explore a richer set of determinants of children's attainment. These data included information on intelligence (IQ), parental marital stability, migration, and motivation. They also included a somewhat richer set of background variables, such as number of siblings and farm origin, to understand the determinants of the same outcome variables. Again, parental attainments were significantly and strongly associated with children's socioeconomic outcomes, while the number of siblings, nonwhite race, and growing up in a single-parent family had a negative impact on years of schooling. And, as hypothesized, children's schooling was an important determinant of their occupational status, but schooling was strongly influenced by family background.

These two landmark studies were among the first to document the quite different educational, occupational, and income determination processes affecting nonwhites and whites, suggesting the presence of discrimination at various levels in explaining the differential racial outcomes.

The importance of the findings from the 1962 OCGI data prompted a replication of the survey in 1973; these data are known as OCGII. The primary analysis of this data set was by Featherman and Hauser (1978). In addition to replicating many of the findings from studies using the OCGI data, the authors documented changes over the decade of the 1960s in the effects of various determinants of educational, occupational, and earnings attainments. The substantive findings from this study were many, including a reduction in the effect of parental background on children's educational (and socioeconomic) attainment over the 1960s. The authors concluded that the nation experienced an increase in both "equality of opportunity" and "social mobility" over this period.[17]

At about the same time as the OCG studies, a unique panel data set (a sample of about 9000 individuals who graduated from Wisconsin high schools in 1957) was assembled and analyzed in an effort to disentangle the interrelationships between family socioeconomic characteristics, mental ability, and a set of psychological variables and schooling (and, in turn, the effect of schooling and college quality on earnings and occupational status). The effort here was to expand the domain of explanatory variables that are likely to contribute to socioeconomic success, and hence to estimate more reliably the independent effect of any single factor.

The results of these studies were presented in an important set of works, including Sewell and Hauser (1975) and Hauser and Daymont (1977).[18] These studies also employed the basic model of status attainment developed by Blau and Duncan (1967), but extended it by adding variables describing individual aspirations, the character of the schools attended, and richer social and family background (including indicators of parental encouragement and peer and teacher influences).

Again, the basic determinants of socioeconomic attainment were verified (e.g., parental education, occupation, family structure, and race), but in addition the important effects of parental attitudes, school characteristics, community size, and peer and teacher influences on the achievements of children were established.[19]

Schooling, Economic Inequality, and Attainment

Related to the work on social mobility is another line of research that sought to understand the pattern and persistence of inequality in children's educational and economic achievements, and the potential role of family background and schooling in explaining this persistence.

An early and prominent event in this line of analysis was the 1966 publication of *Equality of Educational Opportunity,* also known as the Coleman Report. Perhaps the most important finding of that report— described by Henry Aaron as "sensational and devastating"—was that the volume of resources devoted to education had very little to do with the educational achievements (i.e., test scores) of children. This conclusion, it should be noted, did not differ in substance from that of a comprehensive review of numerous independent studies done during this period conducted by researchers at the RAND Corporation (Averch et al., 1972).

The themes of the Coleman Report regarding the extent of the disparities in educational resources devoted to different schools, and of the effects of these disparities, stimulated both heated debate and a substantial and influential body of additional research.[20]

One of the subsequent analyses of the effects of schools on children's attainments was a major study by Christopher Jencks and his colleagues (1972), which relied upon both estimates based on the socioeconomic life-cycle model and a wide variety of other analyses of the determinants of success. Their objective was to understand the variation among individuals in both educational and economic attainments. A central question concerned the ability of schools and schooling to override the presumed powerful effects of family background in determining the persistently high level of inequality (in education, occupation, and earnings) in the United States.

The findings of the Jencks et al. study had a significant intellectual and policy impact, in part because of the authors' discouraging conclusions. Variation in those factors that seemed most difficult to change—family background, individual intellectual inheritance (e.g., IQ), and luck—appeared to account for the bulk of the variation in educational attainment (e.g., test scores), while other aspects of socioeconomic success that seemed far more amenable to change—such as parental economic position, school resources, and educational segregation—were found to play a rather minor role.[21] Jencks et al. concluded that schooling in the United States fails to reduce inequality in cognitive achievement and educational attainment (and, hence, income).[22]

While the 1972 volume by Jencks et al. was the most prominent of the studies challenging the view that schooling (and, by inference, school resources) could counter the powerful influence of family background in determining individual socioeconomic attainments and success, several other studies in the 1970s reached similar conclusions. Included in these were the follow-up study by Jencks et al. in 1979, and the even stronger results from the research of several radical political economists. The results from these latter studies led their authors to conclude that the American educational system both validates and perpetuates the significant variation among people in cognitive achievement and educational attainment (and, hence, income inequality).[23]

These discouraging conclusions are not consistent with the results of other research, however. This other research suggests that certain school-based resources do matter for particular children, that the influence is not linear (and, hence, was missed in earlier studies), and that an appropriate allocation of school resources can enable schools to play a significant role in determining children's attainments.

For example, Summers and Wolfe (1977) used detailed data on individual children followed over several years and found that small class size mattered for certain disadvantaged children, that teacher's test scores were indicators of their likely success in the classroom, and that more experienced teachers seemed to improve the learning of certain disadvantaged children. The findings of ongoing research by Ferguson (1991) are similar: he finds that teachers' test scores and class size (in the low twenties or smaller) are important factors influencing student educational performance.[24] Ferguson also finds that such differences in school resources account for somewhere between one-quarter and one-third of the variation in student test scores across school districts.[25]

One final strain of research on the determinants of schooling (and labor market) attainments should also be mentioned: that of sibling studies. A problem that plagues all research on individual attainments is the potential bias in the measured effects (of, say, parental education) due to the presence of unobserved and unmeasured aspects of common family background characteristics (e.g., parental control, aspirations, motivation, neighborhood characteristics).[26]

An example of an unobserved factor likely to cause bias is an individual's genetic endowment. Such endowments are likely to influence expected increases in productivity due to an increase in schooling. Genetic endowment is also likely to be associated with parent's education and perhaps income. Hence, excluding this factor is likely to cause omitted variable bias in the coefficients on parent's education and income in studies of the determinants of children's level of schooling.

Some, but not all, of the effects of these common unobserved family factors can be controlled by modeling the similarity of siblings.[27] The primary focus of this research has been to isolate the "true" role of observed factors, such as parents' education and income on their child's education, and the true effect of a child's own education on his or her later achievements. While research using sibling differences accompanied the development of schooling attainment research from the outset,[28] a large number of such analyses appeared in the 1970s.[29]

The approaches used include fixed effects and random effects models. A review of their findings is in Griliches (1979), who emphasizes the lack of a consistent pattern of findings from these analyses. Griliches also critiques the fixed effects approach, arguing that the fixed effects may underestimate the true relationships.[30]

Recent Research on the Determinants of Children's Educational Attainments

Research since 1980 on the determinants of children's educational attainment has extended the major studies of the 1970s in several directions. These studies have also paid special attention to those specific determinants of children's attainments that reflect current social trends (e.g., parental divorce and separation, living in a mother-only family, mother's work time, and early childbearing). The primary methodological advances involve the application of advanced econometric methods to the data, along with efforts to extend the richness of the environmental and peer variables, primarily neighborhood and school composition factors.

A direct extension of the early intergenerational mobility research is that of Hout (1988), which measured the association between men's and women's socioeconomic outcomes in 1985 with comparable measures of their origins, and compared these relationships with those found in 1962 and 1973. He concluded that the degree of association had declined by one-third between 1973 and 1985, indicating a substantial increase in mobility. This result was due primarily to an erosion of the effect of socioeconomic origin on outcome for those with college degrees, in conjunction with an increase in the prevalence of those with higher education.[31]

Mare and Mason (1980), Corcoran (1980), and Hauser (1984) studied the potential biases in the early research due to the problem of measurement error in the family socioeconomic variables (e.g., most of the early studies used reports by children of the education and economic status of their families). In addition, a number of studies by economists have attempted to measure the correlation between parental and children's income and earnings. There is little agreement among these studies, with the reported correlations ranging from less than .2 (see Becker and Tomes [1986]) to well over .58 (Behrman and Taubman [1990]). The larger estimates are obtained when more permanent measures of income and earnings (e.g., averages of multiple years of observations) are substituted for single-year observations, and when controls for demographic structure are incorporated. Most recently, studies by Solon (1992) and Zimmerman (1992) estimated the extent of intergenerational correlation in earnings with models designed to correct for measurement error in father's lifetime income. Both studies find a correlation of about .4, suggesting considerably less intergenerational mobility than indicated by some of the earlier studies.

An additional line of research extended the school-related variables used to explain educational and labor market attainment. Variables describing curriculum, placement, school and institutional factors, and participation in extracurricular activities have been measured and utilized as supplements to the standard family and environmental factors in models of attainment.[32] A variety of such factors—for example, teacher aspirations—were found to have a statistically significant effect on educational attainment. Other studies have used the Wisconsin data to measure the differences between genders in the process of educational (and occupational, but not earnings) attainment.[33] These studies found that important gender differences exist in the effects of post-high-school education on the status of the first job, but that these differences erode during the employment experience. By midlife, the effects of education on occupational status are similar between genders.

Alwin and Thornton (1984) raised the issue of the duration of exposure by children to various parental and environmental factors, and the differential effects on schooling attainment associated with exposure to these factors at different points during childhood—the issue of timing. Although data weaknesses limited their ability to identify strong differential effects of various family socioeconomic factors present in early childhood and late adolescence, their results did indicate that early family experiences have a stronger effect than the same experiences later in childhood.[34]

A number of studies have focused on particular circumstances and events during childhood, and have inquired about the impacts of these on educational and socioeconomic attainment, controlling for standard family background and environmental effects. The primary circumstances and events studied reflect recent social and economic developments often thought to have adverse family consequences, including growing up in a single-parent family or experiencing a change in family structure[35] (with the measured impacts generally negative and significant); the mother's work time[36] (usually with a negative and significant relationship, perhaps reflecting the fact that mothers with low-earnings capacity are more likely to work); early childbearing[37] (again, having a distinctly negative effect); and the low income or poverty of the child's family[38] (also negatively related to children's educational attainment).

Effects of Neighborhood and Peers on Children's Success

The past three decades have witnessed a continuation of economic and social decline in the urban neighborhoods in which so many poor and minority children are concentrated, and in the schools in these communities. Consistent with this change, economists and sociologists have conjectured that the characteristics of neighborhoods and schools in which children spend so much time affect their attainments. While research interest in neighborhood effects is recent, the basic idea has a long history among developmental psychologists, whose ecological models view individual development as the product of the interaction of personal traits and a variety of "ecosystems": family, relatives, peers, community, schools, and the welfare/criminal justice systems.[39]

Current research on the potential influence of neighborhoods on children's attainments stems largely from the writings of William Julius Wilson in the early 1980s. In his 1987 book, Wilson suggested a process by which neighbors' status, performance, or values can lead to a concentration or growth of joblessness and dependence. Growing up in areas with a high prevalence of nonemployment, transfer recipiency, nonlegal activities, and nonmarital households may lead to the internalization of these outcomes as normal, acceptable, or inevitable. As a result, individual motivation and drive are reduced, and the pattern of present gratification, dependence, and weak labor-force participation is intensified.

Substantial research has focused on the role of adverse neighborhood and environmental factors on child outcomes. Although it would be difficult to claim a rigorous theoretical basis for this interest and these studies, social science researchers have offered several speculations as to how neighborhood characteristics might influence children's outcomes.[40]

In the view of some observers, individual children or youths are influenced by the behavior and status of those with whom they socialize, affiliate, or accept as role models. Hence, the behavior and values of children's friends, the parents of friends, the friends of parents, neighbors, and acquaintances alter their perceptions, influence their behavior, and structure their norms, in much the same way as do the behavior and values of parents themselves. In short, a good neighborhood environment confers benefits on the children that grow up in it. This view is described by various writers as conforming to either "contagion theory" or theories of "collective socialization."[41]

An alternative view is that growing up in a "good" neighborhood may have an *adverse* effect on a child, especially if the child is from a poor or minority family. In this view, poor children growing up in more affluent neighborhoods may view themselves as being in competition with those in their social network. Such competition may be viewed as "zero-sum," in the sense that a fixed stock of community resources is to be divided up among competitors. As a result, a poor or minority child in such an environment may become discouraged or hostile. Such a perspective is related to simple envy—those feelings of hostility as the child compares his or her own economic status with that of his or her better-off peers or neighbors. A common example of this phenomenon is the potentially discouraging effect on grades and class rank that may be experienced by a poor child attending an affluent school, as compared with attending a school populated by other poor children. Unlike alternative perspectives, the logic of these theories (known as "competition" or "relative deprivation" theories) suggests that the presence of middle- or upper-class peers or neighbors can lead to negative behaviors or diminished performance by low-income or minority children or youths.

Published empirical research on the role of neighborhood effects has not been extensive, although emphasis on the potentially powerful role of these factors has stimulated a number of recent studies.[42] The primary studies are those by Datcher (1982), Crane (1991), and Corcoran et al. (1992).[43]

Datcher (1982) studied a sample of about 550 urban males aged 13–22 in 1968 and analyzed their educational attainment 10 years later, when they were 23–32.[44] After controlling for parental age, education, income, educational aspirations, the number of children in the family, region, and community size, she found that the characteristics of the youth's neighborhood (zip code) had an important and significant effect on the years of education attained. A 10 percent increase in the neighborhood's mean family income was related to about a tenth of a year of additional schooling for both blacks and whites. The effects of the neighborhood's racial mix were a good deal less robust, but implied that having more whites (African-Americans) in the neighborhood increased the schooling attainment of African-Americans (whites)—suggesting gains to both groups from racial integration.

Corcoran et al. (1992) also used PSID data and chose zip codes as the neighborhood unit. Her sample was aged 10–17 in 1968, included females as well as males, and controlled for a richer set of background and neighborhood variables than did Datcher's sample. The outcome variables studied by Corcoran et al. were educational attainment and earnings in young adulthood. Again, the results indicate that growing up in a good neighborhood contributes to years of schooling, *ceteris paribus*. Moving from an average African-American neighborhood to an average white neighborhood was estimated to add about .4 years of schooling to the typical male, a larger effect than that estimated by Datcher.[45]

Crane (1991) used a unique 1970 Census data set that permitted the characteristics of about 1500 neighborhood residents to be matched to information on children 16–18 years old and their families. Failure to complete high school was the dependent variable in Crane's study. After controlling for a standard set of family characteristics, he found that the neighborhood's social and economic status, proxied by the percentage of workers with professional and managerial occupations, positively and significantly influenced the probability of graduating from high school. Consistent with his epidemic hypothesis, Crane concluded that the very worst neighborhoods had distinctly large adverse effects on the probability of high-school completion.

In addition to these studies of neighborhood effects, two more recent analyses should be mentioned.[46] A unique collaboration involving economists and developmental psychologists has investigated the effect of the socioeconomic characteristics of neighborhoods on the outcomes of both young children (emphasizing cognitive functioning as reflected in intelligence tests and behavior problem indicators, and using the Infant Health and Development Program sample) and adolescents (emphasizing teenage out-of-wedlock births and dropping out of school, and using the PSID).[47] The design of the study allowed the researchers to examine the effects of neighborhood (and family) characteristics on children at two different points in the life cycle—early childhood and adolescence—and to compare these effects.

Focusing on the adolescent portion of the study (as it compares most closely with our own results presented below), the researchers controlled for differences in the ratio of family income to the family's poverty line when the youth was age 14, the mother's schooling, the race of the family head, and whether or not the family was headed by the mother when the youth was age 14, in obtaining estimates of the effects of neighborhood characteristics. An intervening variable reflecting the mother's perception regarding her ability to control her life ("locus of control") was also included. The neighborhood variables were chosen to reflect the effects of social isolation on individual behavior, and included the fraction of families in the child's age-14 neighborhood with incomes of less than $10,000 or more than $30,000.[48]

Simple regressions indicate that having middle-class neighbors significantly decreases the probability of dropping out of school and having a teenage out-of-wedlock birth. This relationship persists in the case of the childbearing variable, even after the family-level effects are controlled for.[49] When a variable measuring the percentage of mother-only families in the neighborhood (taken as an indication of the inability of the neighborhood to monitor teenage behavior, or as reflecting the effect of a welfare culture on teenage behavior) is included, it too has a significant and large positive effect on both the probability of dropping out of school and having a teenage nonmarital birth. Finally, the variable indicating the mother's locus of control had a statistically significant effect on both the school completion and nonmarital teenage birth outcomes. When the interactions among neighborhood characteristics and maternal locus of control are explored, the authors conclude that the data support William Julius Wilson's hypothesis that "isolation from middle-class and two-parent family neighbors reduces maternal sense of control which, in turn, makes more likely teenage behavior problems such as out-of-wedlock births." (p. 24)

The second recent study of the effects of neighborhood and peer characteristics and behavior is based on a 1989 National Bureau of Economic Research survey of 1,200 youths in three high-poverty Boston neighborhoods in the tight labor market period of early 1989.[50] Six outcome variables are analyzed: criminal activity, illegal drug use, nonmarital childbearing, labor market activity, school attendance, and church attendance. The family background variables are the standard indicators of race, sex, age, single-parent home, and parental education. In addition, data on family members in jail or with a drug/alcohol problem, nonmarried parents, and family religiosity were included as variables. The authors find that specific characteristics (such as criminal activity) of parents or families are closely related to similar behaviors for youths. Even with the inclusion of the other background variables, the race and gender variables are often significant and with the expected sign (e.g., females are less likely to be involved in crime and drugs, more likely to be single parents and idle; African-Americans are more likely to be involved in crime and to be single parents, and less likely to drop out of school).

The unique characteristic of the study is the creation of individual-specific variables that indicate the behavior of youths in narrowly defined neighborhoods surrounding each youth. Estimates using these variables suggest that, even with the family background variables included, similar peer (or neighborhood) behaviors have a significant effect on criminal activity, drug/alcohol use, church attendance, and idleness. This result holds even after statistical adjustments for potential simultaneity bias are included in the estimates.

Taken together, the studies lend substantial support to hypotheses regarding the impact of neighborhoods and peers on youth achievement. While the results are not always consistent across studies, they do suggest that efforts to understand how youths succeed must consider the role of those peers and neighbors with whom they interact and identify.[51]

Effects of School Composition on Educational Attainment

Recent research on the determinants of educational attainment has also investigated the effect of student body composition of the schools that students attend on those students' attainment. The most recent example of this research is that of Mayer (1991), which uses microdata on 26,000 students from the High School and Beyond Survey. The students were in the 10th grade in 1982. Mayer's purpose is to examine the effects of the schools' racial and socioeconomic composition on the probability that students will graduate.

Identifying the independent effect of student mix in schools requires that reliable measures of the characteristics of the students, their parents, their upbringing, and the neighborhood in which they have grown up be included in the analysis. Mayer includes in her analysis variables measuring parental education, father's occupation, home ownership, owning two or more cars and a dishwasher (all combined in an index of parental socioeconomic status, or SES), whether the students lived in female-headed households in the 10th grade, the students' 10th grade math scores and educational expectations, and their race and ethnicity.[52]

When these factors are controlled for, school mix—its SES and African-American and Hispanic proportions—were found to have the expected effects. Other things being equal, attending a school with students from high SES families and with fewer minority students is associated with an increase in the probability of staying in school until graduation. Moreover, Mayer found that these mix effects varied substantially across student SES categories. In general, the effect of the SES level of the school on the probability of dropping out was far stronger for students from low SES families than for those from high SES families.[53]

Mayer then uses these estimates to simulate the effect of reducing both school-based SES inequality and racial/ethnic segregation (homogenization) on the *overall* dropout rate. Surprisingly, SES desegregation is likely to have a small effect on overall dropout rates—the gains in school retention experienced by low SES children would be offset by increases in dropouts by high SES children. Conversely, racial/ethnic desegregation would tend to *increase* the overall dropout rate.[54]

Welfare Recipiency

Although most of the research on the determinants of socioeconomic status and earnings has focused on *individual* attainments—level of schooling, occupational status, and individual earnings—family-based outcome indicators have also been studied. One of the most studied of these outcomes is that of welfare dependency: living in a family that is dependent on welfare benefits for income when a young adult. In this section, those studies that have investigated this outcome are described and their results discussed.

The basic question that has motivated this research concerns the extent to which welfare dependency is intergenerationally transmitted: do the daughters of mothers who are dependent on welfare tend to become welfare recipients themselves? Rein and Rainwater (1978) and Hill and Ponza (1984) are the earliest studies of this relationship. Hill and Ponza used PSID data, and after controlling for a variety of family background characteristics, found a statistically significant but quantitatively small impact from growing up in a household receiving welfare on the individual's welfare experience later in life.[55]

More recent studies, however, have found a stronger relationship. Duncan, Hill, and Hoffman (1988), also using PSID data, found evidence that girls aged 13–15 in welfare-dependent families were substantially more likely to receive welfare when they were aged 21–23 than were teenage girls who grew up in families with a weaker attachment to welfare income. The wide diversity of outcomes among girls growing up in all types of family is noted by the authors: indeed, nearly two-thirds of the girls who grew up in highly welfare-dependent families experienced no dependence on welfare.[56]

The research strategy followed by Duncan, Hill, and Hoffman (1988)—observing the receipt of welfare by mothers at the beginning of a panel of longitudinal data and relating this to the daughter's receipt later in the panel—has been pursued in a number of other studies of intergenerational welfare dependency. These studies generally find a statistically significant relationship between mother's welfare receipt and daughter's recipiency.[57]

Solon, Corcoran, Gordon, and Laren (1991) use data on a sample of sisters to test the strength of the effects of common family background on welfare program participation. They find an extremely high degree of resemblance among sisters in the receipt of welfare, and a high degree of intergenerational welfare resemblance. The former effect, which controls for a more comprehensive array of common family characteristics, was stronger than the latter relationship.[58]

Gottschalk (1992a and 1992b) has explored the intergenerational welfare transmission process using a longer observation period for mothers; he also excluded families who were never eligible (or near eligible) for welfare. Both of these procedures represent methodological improvements on prior studies of intergenerational welfare transmission. His results suggest that parental participation in welfare is correlated with daughters' participation, and that even when parental income and eligibility are controlled for, substantial intergenerational transmission of welfare participation remains.

And finally, Duncan and Hoffman (1990a) find that, for African-American teenage mothers, parental welfare receipt around the time of the teenage birth increases the probability of being a welfare recipient at age 26, after controlling for differences in both family background and the attainments of siblings.

While these studies have investigated the determinants of whether or not a young adult becomes a welfare recipient, other research has focused on the duration of (or dependence on) welfare of those who become recipients. Among the studies relying on either microdata from the PSID or the National Longitudinal Survey of Youth, the generosity of state welfare benefits, number of children, early childbearing, labor market opportunities, previous work experience, education, and whether or not the woman had been previously married have been found to be significantly related to welfare duration. Most of these studies found that African-American recipients remained on welfare for significantly longer periods than white recipients, even after controlling for a wide variety of other factors.[59]

Childbearing and Marital Stability

A variety of reproduction and marital stability behaviors are generally accepted as indicators of the success of the transition to adulthood. These include having a teenage out-of-wedlock birth, or early childbearing, more generally; early marriage; and marital dissolution. Most recent empirical research has focused on the teenage out-of-wedlock birth outcome, since this event is viewed as having serious implications for the long-run well-being of both the mother and the child.[60]

Teenage Out-of-Wedlock Births

Demographic studies in the 1960s and 1970s, using data from the 1950s and 1960s, focused on a variety of marital and reproductive behaviors other than teenage nonmarital births, often with the goal of testing the hypothesis that marital instability and out-of-wedlock childbearing is intergenerationally transmitted. One of the earliest studies of the determinants of adolescent nonmarital births is Hogan and Kitagawa (1985), who also review the preceding literature on this issue, much of which is ethnographic in character.[61]

This early research suggests that teenage women who are African-American, who live in lower socioeconomic class families, who reside in neighborhoods characterized by instability in employment among male youths, and who have grown up in large, mother-only families or who have sisters who have given birth out of wedlock are more likely to become teenage mothers than those with other characteristics. Hogan and Kitagawa note that this research has largely ignored "the impact of family factors, social and economic characteristics, and neighborhood influences" (p. 832), in part because the data used tend to be too crude to describe adequately, and hence control for, the family and personal circumstances that affect the decisions of teenagers.

In their own study, Hogan and Kitagawa estimate the determinants of nonmarital births in a sample of 1000 African-American teenage women in Chicago in 1979. Using a variety of statistical methods and numerous control variables, they found that pregnancy rates among these teenagers were positively related to having parents who were not married, the number of their siblings, the low economic status of the family, low parental control of dating, and having a sister who is a teenage mother.[62]

More recent studies of this outcome are Antel (1988) (using data from the National Longitudinal Survey of Youth [NLSY] 1979–1986 in a bivariate probit specification designed to control for possible unobserved family-specific heterogeneity), Plotnick (1990), and Lundberg and Plotnick (1990a) (also using the NLSY, but adding to the survey data information on state welfare policy, state family planning policy, and the socioeconomic environment proxied by characteristics of the girl's school), and Duncan and Hoffman (1990a) (using data on African-American teenagers from the PSID to model teenage nonmarital births as a rational choice made after comparing income opportunities with and without such a birth).[63]

A number of consistent findings concerning the correlates and determinants of teenage out-of-wedlock births emerge from these studies. They include: (1) the importance of racial differences in the prevalence of teenage nonmarital births, even after controlling for a variety of socioeconomic, attitude, family circumstance, neighborhood, and urban-rural factors; (2) the importance of a variety of risk factors (growing up in a disrupted family, having parents with low levels of educational attainment, living in central cities, close parental supervision, and having a sibling who is a single child-bearer), in addition to race and ethnicity; (3) the effect of easily accessible contraception and abortion services in reducing teenage nonmarital childbearing for whites; and (4) the uncertain effects of a number of important and oft-speculated variables on this outcome, including the generosity and lenience of welfare programs, and the welfare participation and work status of the mother of the teenage woman when she was growing up.[64]

Marital Instability

A number of studies have investigated the correlates of marital and cohabitational patterns among young adults, with most of the analyses focusing on the intergenerational transmission of these patterns. The primary question has been: Does the breakup of the family of young adults when they are children (or does growing up in a one-parent family) have an independent effect on the marital experiences of young adults, after controlling for family background characteristics and other relevant factors?

Numerous theoretical linkages suggest an intergenerational pattern of marital experiences. These include linkages through: (1) economic resources or status attainment (single-parent families tend to have fewer economic resources than do intact families); (2) educational attainment (children growing up in single-parent homes tend to have lower levels of schooling, with schooling being an alternative for marriage or cohabitation); (3) parental social control (single parents tend to have less time to monitor and socialize children); (4) earlier maturation (children growing up in single-parent households tend to be assigned responsibilities, rights, and authority earlier than those in intact families); and (5) attitudes regarding nonmarital sex, cohabitation, early marriage, and marital dissolution (children growing up in a disrupted family—or in a family that married early, or that married postpregnancy, or that remarried after divorce—are likely to have distinct attitudes toward marriage, cohabitation, and marital dissolution).[65]

Although a number of union formation outcomes have been studied (cohabitation, marriage, marital disruption, remarriage), we limit our discussion to the marital breakup outcome. Nearly all of this research has been of the intergenerational variety, seeking to measure the extent to which experiencing a parental divorce as a child (or growing up in a single-parent family) has an independent effect on a person's own marital stability. While much of this research has relied on the recollections of adults regarding the circumstances in which they grew up—in particular the structure and status of their families—a few studies have employed longitudinal data to evaluate this relationship.

In most cases, the variable of interest (parents divorced, or growing up in a single-parent family) has been significantly associated with important "union" events of the adult child (as well as with a number of adult psychological well-being outcomes that are typically included in these studies), even after controlling for important family background and economic status factors. A standard result is that found in a recent study based on a detailed survey of about 1200 adults, 152 of whom experienced a parental divorce or permanent separation prior to age 18 (Amato and Booth, 1991). Although the sample size is rather small, the researchers found that growing up in a divorced family (relative to a "very happy intact" family) was associated with higher levels of spousal disagreements, marital problems, marital instability, and divorce, after controlling for parental education, occupation, age, race, and gender.

Two other more recent analyses using large data sets should be mentioned. The study by Glenn and Kramer (1985) used pooled data from 11 national surveys conducted by the National Opinion Research Center from 1973 to 1985, and found that the divorce and/or separation rate for white women (men) who grew up in a divorced family was 60 (35) percent greater than that for their race-gender counterparts who grew up in an intact family. The standard parental background variables were also included in these results, although they were fairly limited in number.

Finally, the study by McLanahan and Bumpass (1988) should be noted. Using data on nearly 8000 women aged 15–44 from the 1982 National Survey of Family Growth, these researchers investigated the effect of family structure while a child on five marital or reproductive outcomes, including divorce and remarriage. Background variables include parental education, religion, region (and in some specifications, the woman's own education), and the major independent variables of interest include living arrangements prior to age 14, family status at age 14, and the reasons for family disruption if such occurred (family income was not available on the data set). Using hazard rate models to adjust for right-side truncation, family disruption during childhood was found to be significantly related to all of the marital or reproductive outcomes, including marital disruptions. Indeed, white (African-American) respondents who grew up in a single-parent family (because of either divorce/separation or nonmarital birth) were 77 (32) percent more likely to experience marital disruptions than were daughters who grew up in two-parent families.[66]

THE DETERMINANTS OF CHILDREN'S SUCCESS: A SUMMARY

An enormous body of social science research has been directed toward understanding the processes by which children pass through adolescence into adulthood. What factors determine why some children filter to the top of the distribution of outcome rankings, while others are rather middling in their achievements, and still others experience very little success?

Attempts to answer this question have identified a wide variety of indicators of achievement or success—from cognitive and behavioral indices and scores, to schooling levels, to employment and earnings, to reproductive behavior, to interpersonal relationships (e.g., marriage), to dependence on public transfers, to social and psychological adjustment. As with the indicators of success, numerous hypotheses (or theories or models) have guided this research: in the previous section, we identified several of these perspectives. Exploration of this attainment process has occupied scholars in sociology, developmental psychology, and economics, almost always using discipline-specific theoretical and methodological approaches.[67]

Our review of this research has concentrated on studies with particular characteristics. We emphasized studies that measured children's attainments when they were young adults, and that focused on education, earnings, welfare recipiency, and marital and reproductive outcomes. Nearly all of this research involved statistical estimates over large samples of individuals, often employing longitudinal data sets. We entertained studies designed to test nearly any economic or sociological hypothesis.

The results reported in our review are numerous and not always consistent. Moreover, they vary widely in their reliability. Here, we sort out the most salient and robust findings and present them in a series of brief propositions that may not always do justice to their subtleties.

The massive literature on social mobility and *status attainment* established firmly the linkages between family background and occupational status, as they are mediated by the education level of the individual.[68] In particular:

1. The background of the family (size, race, occupation and education of the parents, stability, and structure) in which children grow up has a significant independent influence on their ultimate occupational attainment.[69] Parental schooling and occupational status are robust and persistently related to a wide variety of outcomes.

2. These background characteristics heavily influence the schooling and training attained by an individual; individual educational attainment also appears to have an independent effect on labor market attainments.[70]

3. When additional mediating variables such as measures of intelligence, motivation, and parental and teacher encouragement are added to the analysis, they too, like schooling, contribute to explaining the variation in attainment and mediate the influence of family background on the variation in attainment.

4. Differences in labor market attainments between African-Americans and whites cannot be explained by differences in family background, schooling, motivation, or intelligence measures. Educational, occupational, and wage discrimination would appear to play an important role.

5. Differences in the quality of schools appear to have a relatively small effect on the variation in attainment when crude measures of school quality are employed; studies using more specific and detailed school

quality measures find statistically significant and positive effects on attainment.

6. No more than 40–50 percent of the variation in outcomes (of a variety of sorts) can be explained by family background, motivation, intelligence, schooling and training, parental/teacher encouragement, and school quality. Other factors—labelled "luck" by some—play an important role.

More recent research on the determinants of attainment has proceeded in two main directions. First, additional measures of attainment have been introduced, both as surrogates for ultimate success and of interest in their own right. Distinct literatures seeking to explain differences in education, earnings, poverty status (incorporating both individual earnings and family size/structure), dependence on public transfers, and childbearing out of wedlock have grown up and flourished.

Second, by relying on richer data sources and more advanced statistical methods, children's exposures to additional environmental circumstances and events (e.g., parental separations, mother's work time, parental welfare recipiency, and school and neighborhood characteristics) have been introduced as determinants of attainment. This more recent research can be thought of as attempting to reduce the enormous unexplained variation in outcomes referred to as "luck."[71]

The primary findings from these more recent research efforts include the following:

1. Growing up in a single-parent family (or experiencing a parental separation or divorce) appears to have a negative effect on educational attainment, with a larger effect being recorded for African-Americans than for whites. Some of these adverse effects can be avoided by increased parental monitoring and encouragement. Adverse effects of these factors on the probability that a girl will have a nonmarital birth or experience a dissolved marriage are also recorded.

2. Growing up in a family in which the mother works seems to have a slightly adverse effect on educational attainment, suggesting either that the negative effect of the loss of child-care time outweighs the positive effect of the additional family income, or that mothers with low-earnings capacities have been more likely to work. The mother's work status does not appear to have an effect on the probability that a girl will have a teenage out-of-wedlock birth or be a welfare recipient.

3. Early childbearing by the mother is associated with reduced achievements by her children, indicating that very young mothers are less effective in child rearing than older mothers or that early childbearing constrains education or creates family stress.

4. Growing up in a poor or low-income family is negatively associated with educational and labor market attainments, suggesting that limited economic opportunities while a child increase the chances of low economic attainment. Being poor as a child also has an independent and positive effect on the probability of having a teenage nonmarital birth and of being a welfare recipient.

5. Growing up in a family that was dependent on welfare increases the probability that a girl will herself be a welfare recipient, holding constant the income level of the girl's family: the source of income as well as its level appears to affect children's success. Growing up in a welfare family has little effect on the probability that a girl will have a teenage birth out of wedlock.

6. Growing up in a neighborhood with "good" characteristics (more education and income; less poverty, unemployment, and welfare recipiency) tends to increase schooling and earnings and decrease the probability of an out-of-wedlock birth or involvement in crime or substance abuse. There is some evidence of increasing negative marginal effects of poor neighborhood quality.

7. The economic and racial characteristics of those with whom children attend school affect their attainments, with the effects being stronger for African-Americans and those from low SES families: attending a school with students from higher income/status families increases educational attainment; attending a school with a higher proportion of minority students reduces attainment. These effects suggest uncertain results on attainments from increasing economic or racial diversity in schools.

8. When family background, events, and circumstances are controlled for, belonging to a racial minority appears to have a positive effect on educational attainment; but belonging to a racial minority remains positively related to welfare recipiency, welfare duration, and the probability of having a nonmarital birth.

9. Economic incentives and opportunities (e.g., labor market opportunities, available income support if not working, and contraception and abortion availability) appear to influence a variety of behaviors and outcomes, including earnings, welfare recipiency, and the probability of a teenage nonmarital birth. While estimates of the effect of these variables typically have the expected sign, and are often statistically significant, the magnitude of their impacts is often quite limited.

THE DETERMINANTS OF CHILDREN'S SUCCESS: SOME ITEMS ON THE RESEARCH AGENDA

As our tour through the research literature on the determinants of children's success has shown, much has been learned during these 25 years of active investigation. Studies have moved from reliance on group comparisons using published data to cross-section survey analyses with but few explanatory variables and simple models, to analyses of cross-section and longitudinal data bases with information on family background and environments and experiences early in life that are sufficiently rich to allow a wide variety of hypotheses to be explored (if not rigorously tested).

Data describing the characteristics of the neighborhoods and the schools in which children grow up have been merged with basic household data, permitting still richer analyses. Statistical methods have been developed to permit more confidence that the relationships observed reflect causation rather than simply correlation, and to enable researchers to work reliably with longitudinal data afflicted with censoring problems and missing information. More recently, developmental psychologists and, especially, economists have become involved in using large-sample survey data in "macro" studies of the processes that generate high-quality children. With this diversity of disciplines, the range of hypotheses and theories of the determinants of children's success has flowered.

Still, looking back on the status of this literature that we have reviewed, it is clear that there is still much to be learned. The following list of items still on the research agenda is designed more as a road map for future work in this area than as a critique of work done heretofore.

1. Longitudinal data, tracing large and national samples of children and their families over time, have become the cornerstone of research in this area. Yet few data sets contain information covering a sufficiently long sweep of time to enable *both* detailed family/neighborhood/school circumstances during childhood *and* an assessment of attainments and performance during young adulthood to be recorded. As a result, studies have often had to rely on observations of circumstances and events in late adolescence as proxies for the full range of childhood exposures.[72]

2. This time-limited data problem has forced researchers to make statistical adjustments (often of a somewhat arbitrary character) for the truncation (or censoring) of important variables in models of children's attainments.

3. The same duration-constrained data problem has limited the ability of researchers to study effectively the timing effects of a variety of childhood events and circumstances, and to understand whether particular circumstances have a cumulative effect on outcomes (and if cumulative, whether the relationship is linear or nonlinear). As a result, numerous hypotheses regarding the differential impacts of particular (of-

ten stressful) events occurring at various times during children's lives (e.g., early childhood versus adolescence) have not been tested convincingly.[73]

4. While longitudinal data on children and their families have become increasingly rich over time, some important gaps in information remain. Most social scientists now seem to accept the proposition that parental self-perceptions and self-esteem, parental expectations for and monitoring of children, and parental time spent with children are likely to have an important effect on the children's motivation, behavior, and attainments. Information on these parental psychological variables is sparse, at best.

While gains in tying neighborhood information to children's records have been substantial, contemporaneous data rather than those interpolated from decennial census information would be superior.[74]

Little is known about the characteristics and qualities of the schools that children attend in the large national longitudinal data sets most often used for this research.

Finally, the behavior and attainments of the siblings of children (e.g., their marital, crime, substance abuse, reproductive, and labor market experiences) may well have an important and independent effect on their attainments. In addition, such information can be used as proxies for information on parental and family environment effects that are unmeasured or unobserved.

5. An important hypothesis is that individual behavior and performance responds to available opportunities and incentives. The implication of this economic perspective is that choices made by children, youths, and young adults regarding schooling, marriage, childbearing (in and out of marriage), working, and welfare recipiency are influenced by the relative opportunities available (and implicit "prices" reflected) in organized labor markets, informal labor markets, marriage markets, and public program markets. However, characterizing these opportunity sets and prices is exceedingly difficult. Advances in testing these economic hypotheses could be made if improved information on relevant labor markets, gender ratios, and available public transfers were tied to information on families, neighborhoods, and schools.

6. A puzzling statistical problem arises as information describing the environments (family, school, and neighborhood) in which children grow up and the events/circumstances that impinge upon them (e.g., parental incarceration, geographic moves) becomes increasingly rich. While each of these environmental characteristics and event/circumstances are important in their own right, they are by no means independent of each other. For example, a father's incarceration, parental divorce, living with a single parent, a mother's employment, poverty status, and welfare recipiency may all influence the behavior and attainments of a child. Yet, these separate individual variables are quite likely to be correlated with each other. Without data of prohibitive

size and cost, it is very unlikely that these separate influences can be accurately identified. This issue also raises questions regarding the maintenance of commonly accepted conventions for concluding that results are reliable (e.g., .01 and .05 significance levels). It seems to us that the case for reporting—and emphasizing—results that are significant at lower levels of significance (say, .25) are warranted. After all, as individuals we make many important life decisions on information in which we have far less than 75 percent confidence.[75]

One final point should be mentioned. One of the most severe difficulties faced in teasing out robust conclusions from the very large body of research studies that we have reviewed is the lack of consistency in data, variable definitions, model specification, and interpretation. While no technique for combining the findings from many diverse studies gains universal applause, we have found the few meta-analyses that have been done in this research area to be helpful in understanding which measured relationships have sufficient consistency in sign, significance, and magnitude to be labeled robust.[76] We encourage additional work along this line.

NOTES

1. See Collette (1979), Kelly and Wallerstein (1979), and Weiss (1979).

2. Although this perspective is closely related to our investment-in-children framework, our perspective emphasizes the level of resources of all forms that contribute to children's success and not just the lack of family economic resources.

3. See Hetherington (1972). Chase-Lansdale and Hetherington (1991) review the literature in this area.

4. See Bronfenbrenner (1979, 1989); Furstenberg, Nord, Peterson, and Zill (1983); Elder (1985); Hetherington and Camara (1984); and Lerner (1984). This perspective has been defined by Bronfenbrenner (1989) as follows:

   The ecology of human development is the scientific study of the progressive, mutual accommodation, *throughout the life course,* between an active, growing human being, and the changing properties of the immediate settings in which the developing person lives, as this process is affected by the relations between these settings, and by the larger contexts in which the settings are embedded. [p. 188; emphasis in original]

5. See Elder (1974).

6. See Miller and Turnbull (1986), Newman and Newman (1978), Carver and Scheier (1981), Pearlin and Schooler (1978), and McCubbin et al. (1980).

7. In addition to these more specific conjectures and hypotheses, other writings have suggested broader and more inclusive frameworks for studying the determinants of children's success. For example, Bronfenbrenner (1989) lumps together all of those models emphasizing the effects of environmental factors (e.g., socialization, economic deprivation) into a category that he calls "social address" models. He states:

> Among the most common "social addresses" appearing in the research literature are the following: social class, family size and ordinal position, rural vs. urban residence, differences by nationality or ethnic group, and, more recently, what I have referred to as the "new demography"—one vs. two parent families, home care vs. day care, children in private vs. public schools, mother's employment status, how many times remarried, or—perhaps soon, the number of hours the father spends in child care and household tasks, or homes with and without computers." [Bronfenbrenner and Crouter (1983), p. 193]

He contrasts these with a "personal attributes model" that views development as a function of the characteristics of the individual at an earlier age, and a "person-context model" in which characteristics of both the person and the environment are taken into account jointly.

8. See Hetherington, Camara, and Featherman (1983).

9. Macaulay (1977) presents the essence of this theoretical position most explicitly. The welfare culture hypothesis is related closely to the economic deprivation, or culture of poverty, framework, in that both perspectives suggest that poverty or welfare receipt have negative effects on personal adequacy, independence, and self-esteem.

10. See Rutter (1980).

11. This perspective has been recently emphasized in the writings of Wilson (1981, 1987), and explored in the review by Jencks and Mayer (1990). See also the discussion below.

12. Indeed, even the least economic among these determinants—for example, the extent of contact with positive role models or the incidence of stressful events (or the psychological resources to cope effectively with them)—would seem to be amenable to change through altering the level of resources devoted to producing the services to children that they represent.

13. See Becker and Lewis (1973) and Hanushek (1992).

14. As a result, we use the term "socioeconomic attainment" in much of the following discussion and interpret this term as encompassing education, occupational status, and earnings or income.

15. The data set employed in this study was from a special sample survey, Occupational Changes in a Generation (OCG), conducted as an adjunct to

the March 1962 Current Population Survey of the U.S. Census. It was composed of about 21,000 males aged 20–64 and was weighted to represent the 45 million U.S. men in this age range.

16. They concluded that racial discrimination affects occupational allocations between whites and nonwhites, but not between whites of different ethnic backgrounds.

17. In particular, the OCG studies concluded that while the effect of family background on the son's attainments is statistically significant, its quantitative impact is rather small. Only about 10 percent of the variation in the son's occupational attainment is explained by family background characteristics (net of other characteristics), and this effect declined between the two OCG studies. The variation in the son's own education explained about one-third of the variation in his occupational attainment, and this effect appeared to be increasing over time. Variation in the remaining (and unspecified) factors—including a wide variety of unmeasured family factors (e.g., parental separation, family income, family welfare recipiency), school and neighborhood quality variables, and individual ability and motivation factors—accounted for the remaining variation in the achievement variable.

   These conclusions, emphasized in Featherman (1979, 1981), have been challenged from a number of perspectives. For example, Bowles (1972), Bowles and Gintis (1972–1973, 1976), and Bowles and Nelson (1974) argued that education is primarily determined by true family status, and hence that education serves but to validate and perpetuate that status. These critics, and others as well, concluded that statistical problems related to errors in explanatory variables and unmeasured variables make any firm conclusions regarding the relative roles of family background and other variables impossible.

18. A total of over 60 articles and books have used the Wisconsin data, exploring the determinants of educational and occupational attainments from a wide variety of perspectives. These studies have contributed importantly to the development of causal models designed to disentangle accurately the interrelated determinants of children's educational, occupational, and earnings achievements.

19. Featherman (1979, 1981) and Haveman (1987) review these findings and discuss the contributions of these studies to empirical methodology. Critiques of both the findings and the methods of this work are found in Cain (1974) and Haveman (1987). Jencks, Crouse, and Mueser (1983) used Project Talent data to assess the reliability of the results reported in Sewell and Hauser (1975) (and the results of a similar study of the determinants of educational attainment using data from the Explorations in Equality of Education sample reported in Alexander, Eckland, and Griffen [1975]). They conclude that two of the most serious criticisms of this early research—the quality of the measurement of the variables and the restrictiveness of the sample—have not led to systematic biases in their results.

20. The primary critiques of the Coleman Report are Hanushek and Kain (1972), Bowles and Levin (1968), and Cain and Watts (1970).

21. The Jencks et al. volume was critiqued by numerous analysts and social policy commentators. See *Harvard Educational Review* (1973) for a sampling; see also Haveman (1987).

22. A quite different approach to measuring the effects of schools on children's attainments attempts to measure the impact of the quantity and quality of school resources on the attainments of children. These are known as "educational production function" studies, and they seek to relate the inputs to the schooling process to the outputs of that process, measured variously in terms of test scores, school continuation, and postschool labor market performance. These studies have been reviewed and critiqued in Hanushek (1986).

Hanushek concludes from his review that "Teachers and schools differ dramatically in their effectiveness" (a conclusion that is at variance with the implications of the Coleman Report); that "there appears to be no strong or systematic relationship between school expenditures and student performance"; and, hence, that "schools are economically inefficient because they pay for attributes that are not systematically related to achievement."

23. See the studies by Bowles (1972); Bowles and Gintis (1972–1973, 1976); and Bowles and Nelson (1974).

24. Ferguson (1991) finds the crucial resource to be teacher quality as measured on a standardized teacher's recertification exam.

25. Card and Krueger (1992) also find evidence that school quality (as measured by pupil–teacher ratio, length of the school year, and the relative pay of teachers) influences future socioeconomic success. Bishop (1989) and O'Neill (1990) link scores on standardized tests for youth to future earnings and find that the link has grown both over time and with age. O'Neill finds that the score on the AFQT score, a military qualification test, explains nearly one-half of the difference in the mean hourly wage of white and African-American men in the 1980s.

26. If unobserved family background and neighborhood factors that are important in the true model of the determinants of outcome (say, the years of schooling of the child) are not included in the estimation but are associated with variables that are included in the estimation, omitted variable bias may result in biased estimates of the effects of the observed factors on the outcome.

27. If sibling differences in some background factor lead to differences in educational attainment, there is more assurance that the relationship of that factor to schooling is not an artifact of common family circumstances.

28. The early study by Blau and Duncan (1967), for example, made use of sibling correlations.

29. The two major analyses by Jencks and his associates (1972, 1979) make

use of data on siblings to estimate the determinants of schooling achievements. See also Olneck (1976, 1977); Behrman, Taubman, and Wales (1977); Taubman (1977); Brittain (1977); Chamberlain and Griliches (1975, 1977); Corcoran and Datcher (1981); and Bound, Griliches, and Hall (1986). A 1991 study by Solon, Corcoran, Gordon, and Laren used longitudinal data on siblings from the Michigan Panel Study of Income Dynamics (PSID) to adjust for transitory elements in single-year data and life cycle (time) effects, and concluded that with these adjustments family background accounted for substantially more of the variance in the outcome of permanent earnings, income and income/needs than had been reported in prior studies. See also Huang (1993).

30. Griliches (1979) notes that measurement error leads to more downward bias in estimates of fixed and random effects models than in a "naive" regression that ignores unobserved family factors. Behrman (1984) argues that if there is correlation across siblings in the measurement error (similar direction of error in response), measurement error may cause greater downward bias in individual (traditional) estimates compared to fixed-effect estimates. Behrman further concludes that there are many conditions under which fixed-effect estimates are likely to be unbiased.

   Hauser and Sewell (1986) emphasize the small samples that have been available in the sibling studies, suggesting that these limitations have led to the inconclusive results. Using the Wisconsin data, they were able to assemble data on 928 sibling pairs. Using these data to model education and occupational status (and correcting for random response variability), they find that the results of earlier studies (in particular, Olneck [1977]) do not contain a family bias in, for example, estimates of the effect of mental ability on schooling attainment.

   This approach has also been used to obtain estimates of the relative importance of observed and unobserved family background and other observed factors in determining outcomes such as schooling and income. Total variance (in the outcome) is the sum of between-family variance plus intra-family or within-family variance. Estimates of both individual, family average or mean relations, and family difference (fixed effect) effects are used to decompose between- and within-sample variances into observed and unobserved components. For example, Olneck (1977) found that observed characteristics accounted for 43 percent of the variance in male schooling compared to 18 percent for unobserved family characteristics. Behrman et al. (1980), using white male twins, found that observed characteristics accounted for only 19 percent of observed schooling differences, compared to 58 percent for unobserved factors.

31. See also Ganzeboom, Treiman, and Ultee (1991), who review a wide variety of research studies showing that a child's own education is a more important determinant of adult occupational status than is parental occupational status.

32. These studies are cited in Alwin and Thornton (1984).

33. See Sewell, Hauser, and Wolf (1980).

34. See also Krein (1986).

35. See Hogan and Kitagawa (1985); Krein (1986); Krein and Beller (1988); Keith and Finlay (1988); Hill, Augustyniak, and Ponza (1985); Corcoran et al. (1992); Zimiles and Lee (1991); and Wojtkiewicz (1991). See also Entwisle and Alexander (1992), discussed in endnote 38.

   McLanahan (1985), using 10 years of longitudinal data on 3300 children, tests a variety of conjectures regarding the effects of family structure and economic status on the educational outcomes of offspring. Educational outcomes are interpreted as proxies for poverty, welfare recipiency, and "underclass" status. She concludes that, net of other factors, the absence of a parent has a negative and significant effect on schooling attainment, but for whites much of this effect is accounted for by low income relative to needs and the receipt of welfare benefits. The results also indicate different effects of various types of single-parent families, and rather different patterns across race. (See also Wojtkiewicz [1991].)

   Astone and McLanahan (1991) extend this earlier work by including parenting practices along with family status and change in family status on a variety of educational outcomes. They conclude that parental aspirations, monitoring, and supervision are all positively related to schooling outcomes, after controlling for a variety of background characteristics.

   In recent work, Graham, Beller, and Hernandez (1992) have focused on children living in single-parent settings. They have sought to measure the differential effects of various settings (e.g., widowhood and being divorced) and the receipt of child support (for single parents who are eligible for child support) on the educational attainment of children. They find that children growing up in single-parent families eligible for child support (implying that the mother is not a widow) have a significantly lower level of educational attainment (on six measures) compared to children who live in intact families, but that the children in mother-only families who are both eligible for receipt of child support and recipients of child support do significantly better than those growing up in families that are eligible for support but do not receive it. While child support payments appear to have substantial positive effects on children's attainments, the failure to control effectively for the extent of absent parent contact or other unobserved parental characteristics calls into question the robustness of this finding.

   Hetherington, Camara, and Featherman (1983) review numerous studies of the differences between children living in one- and two-parent families in a variety of school performance and school attainment outcomes. In general, the children living in single-parent families have weaker school performance. The authors, however, emphasize the complexity of the relationship and the apparent ability of effective family functioning and extra-family environments to offset the stressful effects of divorce and single-parent living arrangements.

   Manski et al. (1992) develop a number of estimates of the effect of family structure (primarily, living with a single parent at age 14) on the probability of graduating from high school, depending on the assumptions made regarding the processes determining family structure and high-school outcomes. The estimating procedure adopted allows them to establish bounds around the estimates of effects; these bounds strengthen the conclusion reached in other studies that family structure (and parental education) are important in determining the probability that a child will graduate from high school.

A meta-analysis of the effects of parental divorce on educational attainment (plus 14 other outcomes, ranging from psychological well-being to marital stability to income) was undertaken by Amato and Keith (1991). Eighteen studies of the parental divorce-educational attainment relationship were identified, and the effects were strongly negative and significant. Across the 18 studies, the level of educational attainment (material quality of life, emphasizing income and related indicators of economic position) of adults who experienced divorce during childhood was about .25 (.18) standard deviation units (the mean difference in educational attainment between the groups divided by the within group standard deviation) below that of adults who grew up in intact families.

36. See Hill and Duncan (1987), Datcher-Loury (1986), Stafford (1986), and Krein (1986). Alwin and Thornton (1984), analyzing 18 years of longitudinal data on a sample of 700 white Detroit-area families, find no effect of the mother's work on educational attainment.

37. See Mott and Marsiglio (1985).

38. A number of the studies referred to in the above discussion include family economic status as an independent variable, but they often have difficulty disentangling the effects of this variable from those of family structure and mother's work time. Two studies that explicitly address the independent role of family economic position are Shaw (1982) and Hill and Duncan (1987). In a recent study of the experiences of a sample of Baltimore children entering the first grade, Entwisle and Alexander (1992) used mathematics test score changes over summer periods (when schools are not in session) to test for the effects of home influences on children's educational attainments. They found that family economic status (being in poverty) has the largest effects on attainment, with the extent of school segregation also playing an important role. Parental family structure (intact versus father absent) has a negligible role when family poverty status is included in the analysis.

39. See Bronfenbrenner (1989) for an analysis of this perspective.

40. The varying hypotheses regarding the effects of neighborhoods and peers on attainment are explored in Jencks and Mayer (1990). Our short discussion of these models follows theirs.

41. See the discussion of the role-model perspective in Chapter 2. A variant of these models focuses not on the neighbors and their characteristics, but rather on the quality and character of the institutions—the police, the schools, the public offices—that become part of the landscape of poor neighborhoods.

42. Some of the earliest studies of the influence of peers (or neighborhood) on children's achievements are those focusing on schools, in which measures

of the socioeconomic status of the student body are included as explanatory variables. See, for example, Summers and Wolfe (1977).

43. These studies are also discussed in Jencks and Mayer (1990), and our discussion draws from theirs. Jencks and Mayer also explore the differences in the estimates among the three studies and critique their data and methods. Significant differences among the studies were found in the extensiveness of the family background characteristics used as control variables, the extensiveness of the neighborhood indicators employed, and whether or not the youths in the samples were living with their families at the time that they were observed.

44. Datcher also studied the effects of the characteristics of the neighborhoods in which young males grew up on their earnings as young adults. Neighborhood mean income and racial composition were significant explanatory variables, and the quantitative effect of "bad" neighborhood characteristics on earnings was found to be substantial.

45. The estimates in Corcoran et al. suggest that growing up in a "poor black" neighborhood (one that is one standard deviation below the mean of African-Americans in median family income, percentage of males unemployed, percentage of female heads of household, and percentage of families on welfare) relative to growing up in an average white neighborhood lowers male expected earnings at ages 25–33 by about 18 percent. This estimate is substantially below that of Datcher.

46. A third paper, Duncan and Laren (1990) should also be mentioned. In this study, the dependent variable was the birth of a low birthweight child. The estimates were made using a sample of black women from the PSID. Along with the standard family background characteristics, a variety of neighborhood characteristics were included. A strong relationship between the incidence of welfare recipiency in the neighborhood and the probability of having a low birthweight baby was found and proved robust to alternative specifications. However, the neighborhood's poverty rate or its racial composition did not have a significant relationship with the probability of having a low birthweight child. (The significance of the neighborhood welfare incidence percentage, and the insignificance of the neighborhood poverty rate, has been found in other studies as well. See Corcoran et al. [1992].) The poverty status of the family of a girl was a significant explanatory variable, as were a variety of behavioral factors reflecting high risks of low birthweight babies.

47. See Brooks-Gunn, Duncan, Kato, and Sealand (1991).

48. The researchers also experimented with a number of other neighborhood characteristics, including a severe poverty measure, the percentage of the neighborhood that is African-American, and the fraction of the families headed by a woman. These variables, when added to the poor/rich neighborhood variable, also had significant and expected effects on several of the outcomes.

49. The family-level variables were generally statistically significant and with the expected sign in most of the estimates. However, being African-Ameri-

can is associated with a lower probability of dropping out of school when all of the other variables are controlled for, a result also found in other studies.

50. See Case and Katz (1991).

51. Jencks and Mayer (1990) emphasize a number of measurement issues that should be attended to in exploring the effect of neighborhood characteristics on individual achievements. These include securing a rich set of family characteristics that are not themselves endogenous to the neighborhood in which the family lives; exploring nonlinear specifications of the effects of neighborhood characteristics (consistent with epidemic and contagion theories); and discerning the extent to which neighborhood characteristics have differential effects on rich versus poor, and minority versus white families. They emphasize the dangers of using composite indicators of neighborhood characteristics rather than specific neighborhood variables. Evans, Oates, and Schwab (1992) explore issues of endogeniety of neighborhood and find neighborhood factors are not significant when endogeniety is taken into account.

52. The effects estimated for the control variables are similar to those found in other studies: the student's SES has a large, significant, and negative relationship to dropping out; living in a female-headed family is significantly and positively related to the probability of dropping out; and the student's math scores and educational expectations are negatively and significantly related to dropping out. When these variables are all controlled for, black students have a lower probability of dropping out of high school than do white students.

53. See Entwisle and Alexander (1992), who also find that family economic status of the students in a school plays an important role, along with school racial characteristics, in explaining the educational attainments of children.

54. Mayer's results are somewhat at variance with those of previous research, much of which focused on the effects of high-school composition on college going (Alexander and Eckland [1975], Jencks and Brown [1975], Crain and Mahard [1978]). These studies indicate that the *net* effect of school SES on college going is very low, except for African-Americans, who appear to be somewhat more influenced by high SES peers than are whites. Related research on the effect of school social mix on dropping out (Bryk and Driscoll [1988]) found that decreasing SES and racial/ethnic diversity tended to decrease the overall dropout rate, but that the impact was small. Mayer's results suggested larger effects of these school social mix variables on students' chances of graduating from high school (see also Mayer [1990]). It should be noted, however, that the effects of school composition estimated in these studies are small in magnitude compared to the effects of the economic and other family-based characteristics of students.

55. Because the PSID does not collect information on the sources of income of adult children who live with their parents, the study could not take

account of the potential bias caused by excluding observations of those individuals receiving welfare while still living with their parents.

56. This substantial diversity of outcomes was also found by Furstenberg, Brooks-Gunn, and Morgan (1987) for a sample of poor teenage mothers in Baltimore.

57. See Rainwater (1987) and Antel (1992). Duncan and Hoffman (1990b) review many of these studies. Duncan, Laren, and Yeung (1991) provide interesting tabulations of the fraction of children (by the race and marital status of their mothers) who ever lived in a family that received AFDC and other welfare benefits. They also trace changes in this fraction over time.

58. McLanahan (1988), using a somewhat different methodology, is able to distinguish clearly parental recipiency from other family background characteristics. She also finds that parental recipiency is significantly related to daughter's recipiency.

59. Bane and Ellwood (1983) and Ellwood (1986) studied the duration of welfare spells, finding a small fraction of families with very long (say, 10-year) spells, but with most families completing their spells after a few years. When multiple welfare spells are considered, fewer than one-half of the families who received welfare benefits were on the roles for more than four years. See also, O'Neill, Bassi, and Wolf (1987); Plotnick (1983); and Plant (1984). A recent study by Kimenyi (1991) analyzes the determinants of welfare duration for a sample of Tennessee recipients, finding that a variable that proxies for the size of the pool of marriageable males has a negative and statistically significant effect on welfare duration.

60. Indeed, as noted in our discussion of the determinants of education, children of single mothers or children experiencing family dissolution as children tend to have lower educational attainments (e.g., a higher probability of not completing high school) and lower earnings capacity and employment. See McLanahan (1985); Krein and Beller (1988); Hill and O'Neill (1993); and Hill, Augustyniak, and Ponza (1985). And, as we will see, growing up in a single-parent family tends to increase the probability of being an unmarried mother by increasing the probabilities of both a non-marital birth and marital dissolution. Amato and Keith (1991) surveyed six studies of the effect of family dissolution while a child on the probability of having one-parent status when an adult, and found a significant negative effect of about one-third standard deviation unit. The effect for whites was about twice that for blacks, and the effect for males about three times that for females. Geronimous and Korenman (1992), however, have suggested that teenage unmarried mothers do not experience an adverse impact later in life by this early event, arguing that their low attainments later in life are due to poor family background characteristics that are not measured. Their findings have been critiqued by Hoffman, Foster, and Furstenberg (1993), who do find persistent adverse effects of teenage unmarried childbearing apart from poor, unmeasured family background.

61. More recent reviews can be found in Hayes (1987).

62. Living in a low-quality neighborhood had a gross positive relationship with teenage childbearing, but its effect was mediated by parental control over early dating patterns.

63. See also Abrahamse, Morrison, and Waite (1987). Ribar (1991) estimates a multinomial logit model of the joint decision of high-school completion and teenage nonmarital births, finding results similar to those in the literature cited. He finds that growing up in a mother/stepfather family has significant negative effects on the probabilities of both high-school completion and nonmarital teenage births.

64. Recent papers by Belsky and his associates have suggested a sociobiological model that traces the nature of a child's upbringing (in particular, the presence of stressful events and circumstances such as family dissolution, discord, or economic uncertainty, which induce adverse parenting behaviors) to the child's self-perception and approach to interpersonal bonds, to behavior problems, and biological changes (such as the timing of puberty or menarche), and finally to patterns of postpuberty sexual behavior (such as earlier procreation and sexual activity with multiple mates) that are consistent with a high probability of teenage nonmarital births. See Belsky, Steinberg, and Draper (1991); and Moffitt, Caspi, Belsky, and Silva (1992). See also Ribar (1991), who finds a significant and positive effect of the age of menarche on the probability of a nonmarital teenage birth.

65. Thornton (1991) and Chase-Lansdale and Hetherington (1991) present rather full-bodied discussions of the theoretical linkages between the marital histories of parents and the sexual and marital experiences of their children. This paragraph draws from these discussions. See also Hayes (1987), Hetherington (1979), and Pearlin and Johnson (1977).

66. Other empirical studies that are consistent with these results are Hogan (1985), Mueller and Pope (1977), Hogan and Kitagawa (1985), Keith and Finlay (1988), McLanahan (1988), and Thornton (1991). Hill, Augustyniak, and Ponza (1985), using the same PSID data as McLanahan, did not find evidence of such generational transmission. Research in developmental psychology and child psychology has also investigated a variety of other outcomes of marital disruption or growing up in a single-parent family. In most cases, this research is based on a limited number of observed subjects who are often studied in clinical situations, or for whom detailed outcome and contextual information is available. However, such studies typically observe the children of divorced families within five years after the divorce and concentrate on cognitive achievement and behavioral problems of the children that may be attributable to the family disruption. See Wallerstein (1991) and Chase-Lansdale and Hetherington (1991) for reviews of this empirical literature and for a discussion of the likely processes at work.

   A meta-analysis of the effects of family disruption on the probability that the child will experience a divorce or separation, or the probability that the child will be a single parent, indicates that this event during childhood has a significant negative effect on these outcomes. See Amato and

Keith (1991). The children experiencing family splits during childhood have a probability of experiencing a divorce or separation (living in a single-parent situation) that is about .2 (.36) standard deviations higher than do children who have grown up in an intact family. The negative effect of family splits during childhood on the probability of being a single parent appears to be stronger for males than for females, which is consistent with the thrust of much of the child development literature. However, the negative effect on the probability of experiencing a divorce or separation is similar across the genders. The experience of a parental split during childhood appears to have a greater negative effect on whites than on African-Americans for both of the outcomes.

67. A rough description of the various approaches might read as follows: developmental psychologists typically focus on the early childhood and seek to explain both cognitive and behavioral attributes of children, often using small group experiments with controlled variation in the phenomena expected to influence outcomes. Data analysis is based on intensive and structured interviews and tests.

    Sociologists have been far more pragmatic in their approach, typically relying on interview surveys of large samples of individuals containing information on attained social and occupational status, and other outcomes reflecting social position or social problems such as welfare dependency, having a nonmarital birth, marital instability, or education. Family background characteristics such as education, race, occupation, location, and living arrangements have been the primary determinants of interest. Statistical models (including path analysis and multiple regression) have been employed in estimating a wide variety of models of the social attainment process.

    Economists are relative latecomers to this field, and have typically focused on economic outcomes related to education, employment, earnings, income levels (e.g., poverty), and income sources. Attention to econometric and causal modeling issues and reliance on longitudinal survey data characterize much of this work, as well as efforts to specify outcomes as behaviors in response to budget constraints and perceived prices (or incentives). Research approaches by economists and sociologists have become increasingly similar over time.

68. Alwin and Thornton (1984) have also attempted to summarize the findings of research on status attainment. They state:

    The major findings of this body of research are: (a) education (years of schooling completed) is a major mediator of the effects of socioeconomic origins on socioeconomic achievements; (b) schooling experiences, most notably high school grade performance, curriculum placement, achievement-test performance, and the encouragement of parents and teachers, are largely responsible for transmitting the effects of socioeconomic background on length of schooling; and (c) while the ascriptive influences of race and gender affect these processes, the broad outlines of this ''social-psychological model'' of achievement account for the observed transmission of socioeconomic position from one generation of the family to another across subcategories of race and gender. (p. 786)

69. As noted above, variations in these background factors (independent of other characteristics) were reported by Featherman (1979) to account for about 10 percent of the variation in occupational achievement.

70. The total effect of education on the variation in earnings and occupational attainment is estimated to be about 30–35 percent, but at least one-third of that effect is the influence of family background characteristics operating through educational attainment. The *net* effect of variation in education is, then, about 15 percent. Through its influence on education, the total contribution of family background to the variation in attainment may be about 20–25 percent. See Featherman (1979).

71. While richer data on the circumstances of families in which children grow up add to the proportion of variation in outcomes that is explained, they also partially reflect factors that were captured by the cruder indicators of family background (e.g., parental occupation or education), hence reducing the net contribution of variation in these variables to the explanation of differences in attainment.

72. The implications of this window problem are explored in An, Haveman, and Wolfe (1993).

73. Alwin and Thornton (1984) state: "We do not know, for example, whether the advantaging and disadvantaging influences of social background occur more or less uniformly across the life cycle of the child and essentially cumulate over time, or whether such effects occur during 'critical periods' across the life span, for example, early in childhood." (p. 785)

74. Jencks and Mayer (1990) have emphasized the potential importance of measuring these influences, and investigating the hypothesis that epidemic levels of bad neighborhood characteristics may have an important influence on children's attainments (implying a nonlinear effect of neighborhood characteristics), and the hypothesis that neighborhood characteristics may interact in important ways with both family and school characteristics.

75. We recognize that statistical procedures for dealing with correlated variables are available. These techniques (for example, principal components analysis) have their own shortcomings, such as the necessity of describing constellations of effects that have no necessary tie to common understanding or to relevant policy alternatives.

76. See Amato and Keith (1991).

4

Investments in Children:
Some Simple Relationships

The relationships between important background characteristics and factors that reflect parental and social investments in children (e.g., stressful events and neighborhood characteristics) and our indicators of the attainments of children are complex and interrelated. In this chapter, we explore a variety of these relationships through simple statistical measures, such as cross-tabulations and regressions, run on our unweighted data. Our purpose is to examine the relationships of the outcome or attainment variables that we have identified—high-school completion, level of education, enrolling in postsecondary education, having a teenage out-of-wedlock birth, receiving welfare benefits, and being economically inactive at age 24—with family and neighborhood variables suggested by our investment-in-children framework or found important in prior research. Appendix A presents summary statistics for the data on which our work is based.

In the first section we present a series of simple cross-tabulations. These provide a rough overview of the relationships between selected factors and our measures of outcome, but do so without controlling for other important variables. Next we turn to simple regressions that explore many of the same relationships. We present three sets of regressions and discuss the results of a fourth. In these, the influence of the full set of these background and parental/social investment variables are explored. Ordinary least squares, probit, and tobit estimates are used, as appropriate, although potential simultaneity problems are not accounted for in these estimates. More complete modeling efforts are presented in later chapters in the volume.

RELATIONSHIPS SEEN AS CROSS-TABULATIONS

Background Factors

Race

A common observation is that African-American youths have attainment levels substantially below those of whites, and that these disparities have implications for future success and upward mobility. In the following cross-tabulations (Tables 4.1a–4.1d), we present these patterns for the youths in our sample.[1] The outcomes for these youths are measured in the last year for which we have data, 1988, when they were aged 21–26 years. We compare African-Americans and whites on three dimensions: educational attainment (graduation from high school and years of completed education); having an out-of-wedlock birth during the teenage years of 15–18 (for females); and a measure of economic inactivity.[2]

In all of these aspects of educational attainment, the whites in our sample have substantially higher levels of achievement than do African-Americans. While 87 percent of the white youths in this age 21–26 cohort graduated from high school, only 81 percent of African-Americans had graduated. The percentage of white youths going on to further formal education (college, university, two-year community college programs) was 42; that for African-American youths was 29.

While these raw differences are large, they pale when compared with the racial differences in the prevalence of teenage out-of-wedlock births and economic inactivity, both indicators of undesirable performance. The African-American girls in our sample were four times more likely to have a child out of wedlock when they were aged 15–18 than were white teenagers. However, among those teenagers who did give birth out of wedlock, the probability that they would receive welfare benefits within two years of giving birth does not vary across the races.[3]

While 34 percent of the African-Americans in our sample were economically inactive at age 24, the comparable percentage for whites is 16.

We can learn a bit more about the racial differences in educational attainment by constructing a cross-tabulation of level of education (years of completed schooling) and race. This is presented in Table 4.2. There we observe that white teenagers appear to be substantially more likely to complete two and four years of postsecondary schooling than are

TABLE 4.1a Percentage Who Graduated from High School, by Race

Graduated	White	African-American
No	13	19
Yes	87	81
Percentage of Sample	54	46

TABLE 4.1b Percentage Who Attended College, by Race

Attended College	White	African-American
No	58	71
Yes	42	29

TABLE 4.1c Percentage Who Had a Teenage Out-of-Wedlock Birth, by Race

Birth	White	African-American
No	94	76
Yes	6	24

TABLE 4.1d Percentage Who Are Economically Inactive at Age 24

Inactive	White	African-American
Yes	16	34
No	84	66

African-Americans; conversely, African-Americans are more likely to terminate their schooling during or at the end of high school than are whites. The zero-order correlation between race and years of school completed is − .17, implying that African-Americans, on average, have about .2 fewer years of schooling than do whites.[4]

TABLE 4.2 Level of Completed Education, by Race

Level of Education (years)	White (percentage)	African-American (percentage)
< 10	1	1
10	7	9
11	5	9
12	45	52
13	6	6
14	20	16
15	4	4
16	11	3
17	1	0

Gender

Another background factor of general concern is gender: How do males and females compare in terms of educational attainment and economic inactivity? Tables 4.3a and 4.3b provide evidence on gender differences in educational attainment among the observations in our sample. The results are easy to summarize: women are slightly more likely to graduate from high school than are men (86 versus 83 percent), but

TABLE 4.3a Percentage Who Graduated from High School, by Gender

Graduated	Male	Female
No	17	14
Yes	83	86
Percentage of Sample	49	51

TABLE 4.3b Percentage Who Attended College, by Gender

Attended College	Male	Female
No	69	59
Yes	31	41

TABLE 4.4 Percentage Who Are Economically Inactive at Age 24, by Gender

Economically Inactive	Male	Female
Yes	19	29
No	81	71

women are 10 percentage points more likely than men to go on to college (41 versus 31 percent).

This raises the question of whether such differences appear at every level of schooling. Here the picture is more mixed[5]: Women are more likely than men to drop out of school during the 10th grade (9 versus 7 percent). Perhaps this reflects the impact of pregnancy. However, women are more likely to complete 14 years of education than men (22 versus 14 percent) and somewhat more likely to complete college (8 versus 6 percent). Men, however, are more likely to attain a maximum of 11 or 12 years of schooling than are women (9 versus 5, and 52 versus 45 percent).

Table 4.4 presents gender differences in economic inactivity. While 19 percent of males are economically inactive at age 25, 29 percent of females are not engaged in sufficient work, schooling, or the care of young children to classify them as active.

Parental Choices/Opportunities

Mother's Education

One of the most important factors that previous research has identified as contributing to children's success is the education level of the child's mother. The level of schooling of a mother may proxy for a wide variety of maternal—and family—activities of an investment character that are likely to contribute to a child's adjustment, motivation, and performance. Perhaps more-educated mothers are able to convey to their children a value of learning, or perhaps these mothers monitor school and other behaviors more carefully or live in higher-income families and better neighborhoods. Perhaps simply they are more effective in parenting and processing information.

Our cross-tabulations in Tables 4.5a and 4.5b show the expected strong relationship between whether a mother graduated from high

**TABLE 4.5a Percentage Who Graduated from High School,
by Whether Mother Graduated from High School**

	Mother Graduated	
Graduated	No	Yes
No	24	8
Yes	76	92
Percentage of Sample	48	52

**TABLE 4.5b Percentage Who Attended College,
by Whether Mother Graduated from High School**

	Mother Graduated	
Attended College	No	Yes
No	76	52
Yes	24	48

school and the education level of her child. Among children with a mother who finished high school, 92 percent also finished high school; among children with a mother who did not complete high school, only about 76 percent completed high school. College attendance is also strongly related to mother's education: the rate of college attendance for children with a mother who graduated from high school is twice that of other children (48 versus 24 percent).[6]

Table 4.6 shows that the pattern of educational levels attained by children relative to their mother's education is quite pronounced over all levels of the children's education. Far lower percentages of our sample with a mother who is a high-school graduate dropout prior to graduating, or stop their education with high-school graduation. Conversely, far larger percentages of children with a mother with a high-school diploma continue on beyond high school, resulting in a higher proportions of children at each level from 13–17 years of schooling for children

**TABLE 4.6 Level of Education,
by Whether Mother Graduated from High School**

	Mother Graduated	
Level of Education (years)	No	Yes
< 10	2	0
10	12	4
11	9	4
12	53	44
13	5	7
14	14	22
15	3	5
16	2	12
17	0	1.2

whose mother completed high school relative to those whose mother dropped out prior to graduation (see Table 4.6).

The pattern of substantial differences in outcome related to the mother's education also holds for the undesirable outcomes: teenage out-of-wedlock births and economic inactivity. As Table 4.7a shows, the probability that a teenager with a mother who did not graduate from high school has had an out-of-wedlock birth is nearly five times larger than the probability of a nonmarital birth for a teenager whose mother completed high school. The zero-order correlation between these two variables is − .27.

Table 4.7b shows that about 17 percent of those children whose mothers are high-school graduates are economically inactive; the proportion is nearly twice as high for children whose mothers do not have high-school diplomas.

Household Moves

A variety of challenges and disruptions often accompany a geographical location move: leaving old friends, making new ones, starting a new school, and adjusting to a new neighborhood are common examples. Developmental psychologists have found that such disruptions are often difficult to deal with and create stress and insecurity for those children

TABLE 4.7a Percentage Who Had a Teenage Out-of-Wedlock Birth, by Whether Mother Graduated from High School

Birth	Mother Graduated	
	No	Yes
No	76	95
Yes	24	5

TABLE 4.7b Percentage Who Are Economically Inactive at Age 24, by Whether Mother Graduated from High School

Economically Inactive	Mother Graduated	
	No	Yes
Yes	32	17
No	68	83

who experience them. The reactions to such stress can be manifested in ways that vary substantially among children. Often school behavior problems are observed, where class progress and curriculum might be quite different from the child's prior experiences. Such problems may also be revealed in higher school dropout probabilities or lower school attainments. For females, this insecurity may lead to premature sexual encounters, resulting in pregnancy and out-of-wedlock births.

In Tables 4.8a–4.8d we present cross-tabulations relating our educational, reproductive, and economic inactivity variables to the number of household moves.

A direct and negative relationship is observed between the number of household moves and the probability of graduating from high school (see Table 4.8a). Less than 10 percent of those who did not move when they were aged 6–15 failed to graduate from high school; conversely, nearly a third of those who moved five or more times during these ages failed to graduate. In general, for those with at least one household move, the probability of graduating decreases as the number of moves

TABLE 4.8a Percentage Who Graduated from High School, by Number of Household Moves During Ages 6–15

	Number of Moves					
Graduated	0	1	2	3	4	5 or more
No	9	14	21	18	22	32
Yes	91	86	79	82	78	68
Percentage of Sample	33	29	14	10	6	8

TABLE 4.8b Percentage Who Attended College, by Number of Household Moves During Ages 6–15

	Number of Moves					
Attended College	0	1	2	3	4	5 or more
No	54	66	73	68	63	75
Yes	46	34	27	32	37	25

TABLE 4.8c Percentage Who Had a Teenage Out-of-Wedlock Birth, by Number of Household Moves During Ages 6–15

	Number of Moves					
Birth	0	1	2	3	4	5 or more
No	92	85	83	74	79	85
Yes	8	15	17	26	21	15

TABLE 4.8d Percentage Economically Inactive at Age 24, by Number of Household Moves During Ages 6–15

	Number of Moves					
Economically Inactive	0	1	2	3	4	5 or more
Yes	18	26	31	34	18	26
No	82	74	69	66	82	74

increases. Going from no moves to one move is associated with an increase in the probability of not graduating of more than 50 percent. Similarly, going from four to five or more moves is associated with an increase of not graduating of 10 percentage points.

Table 4.8b shows the substantial differences in the probability of attending college by the number of geographic moves. Among those children who experienced no household moves, nearly half attended college: among those with five or more moves, only a quarter attended college. For those with one to four moves, no clear pattern exists, except that the probabilities of attending postsecondary schooling for those with one to four moves are intermediate to those at the extremes.[7]

The relationships between the undesirable outcomes—teenage nonmarital childbearing, and economic inactivity—and the number of geographic moves are seen in Tables 4.8c and 4.8d.

A positive relationship between household moves and the probability of a teenage out-of-wedlock birth exists, but again it is not linear (Table 4.8c). Daughters who experience no moves during the ages of 6–15 are not likely to give birth—only 8 percent of them do so. However, daughters who moved once and those who moved five or more times have an equal probability of giving birth out of wedlock—15 percent—while those with from two to four moves were more likely to give birth as a nonmarried teenager. The probability rises to 26 percent for those experiencing three moves. The simple correlation coefficient is a relatively low .11, reflecting this nonlinear pattern.

Table 4.8d shows a similar nonlinear relationship. Those children experiencing an intermediate number of household moves—two to three moves—over ages of 6–15 are substantially more likely to be economically inactive at age 24 than children who either did not move or who moved several times.

Parental Separations

Family breakup during a child's formative years is another stressful parental choice, and one likely to influence development and attainments when a young adult. Tables 4.9a–4.9d explore the relationship between these parental decisions and educational, out-of-wedlock birth, and economic inactivity outcomes. The link between this decision and the undesirable teenage out-of-wedlock birth outcome appears to be stronger than the linkage between parental separations and schooling attainments: the zero-order correlation is .17 with a teenage out-of-wedlock birth, but only −.06 and −.05 with high-school graduation

**TABLE 4.9a Percentage Who Graduated from High School,
by Number of Parental Separations During Ages 6–15**

	Number of Separations		
Graduated	0	1	2 or more
No	15	19	22
Yes	85	81	78
Percentage of Sample	78	20	2

**TABLE 4.9b Percentage Who Attended College,
by Number of Parental Separations During Ages 6–15**

	Number of Separations		
Attended College	0	1	2 or more
No	62	69	69
Yes	38	31	31

**TABLE 4.9c Percentage Who Had a Teenage Out-of-Wedlock Birth,
by Number of Parental Separations During Ages 6–15**

	Number of Separations		
Birth	0	1	2 or more
No	89	77	63
Yes	11	23	37

**TABLE 4.9d Percentage Who Are Economically Inactive at Age 24,
by Number of Parental Separations During Ages 6–15**

	Number of Separations		
Economically Inactive	0	1	2 or more
Yes	23	27	38
No	77	73	63

and postsecondary school attendance, respectively. The simple correlation coefficient between parental separations and economic inactivity is .05.

Children of parents who never separated are somewhat more likely to graduate from high school (85 percent) than those whose parents did separate (about 80 percent). There also appears to be a zero-order relationship between this event and continuing schooling past the high-school level, as well: 38 percent of those whose parents did not separate or divorce when they were aged 6–15 attended college, compared to 31 percent of those who did experience a parental separation or divorce. In this case, the number of separations or divorces beyond the first appear to play no role.

In terms of the probability of a teenage out-of-wedlock birth, there are far larger differences. In this case the number of separations beyond the first also appears important: 11 percent of those who experienced no parental divorce had a teenage nonmarital birth, while 23 percent of those who experienced one divorce or separation had such a birth. More than a third—37 percent—of girls who experienced two or more parental divorces or separations had a birth out of wedlock as a teenager. Much the same pattern is observed with the economic inactivity outcome, except the existence of a single parental separation appears to have a rather small effect: it is multiple separations or divorces that take their toll here.

Parental Economic Resources

Poverty

Children who live in households with few economic resources tend to have fewer opportunities in a number of dimensions, compared with children who grow up in more well-to-do families. We look first at the relationship between number of years that a child lives in a poor family between the ages of 6–15 and our four primary outcomes. Tables 4.10a and 4.10b present these results for the educational outcomes.

Children who experienced no poverty while growing up are far more likely to graduate from high school than those whose parents experienced at least one year of income below the poverty line. Ninety-two percent of children whose parents were never poor graduated from high school. Those children whose families were poor for some of the period were less likely to graduate, although the relationship is not linear. However, those who lived in a persistently poor family are the least

**TABLE 4.10a Percentage Who Graduated from High School,
by Years Poor During Ages 6–15**

	Years						
Graduated	0	1	2–3	4–5	6–7	8–9	10
No	8	21	36	23	30	25	37
Yes	92	79	64	77	70	75	63
Percentage of Sample	52	10	11	10	7	7	5

**TABLE 4.10b Percentage Who Attended College,
by Years Poor During Ages 6–15**

	Years						
Attended College	0	1	2–3	4–5	6–7	8–9	10
No	52	70	71	77	77	82	91
Yes	48	30	29	23	23	18	9

likely to graduate—less than two-thirds do so. The zero-order correlation between years in poverty and high-school completion is −.21.

We would expect a stronger relationship between poverty and continuing education beyond the secondary level. Attending college requires the outlay of economic resources, even with financial aid. The association is, indeed, stronger and, as Table 4.10b shows, it is nearly monotonic. Nearly one-half of those who lived in a family that escaped poverty for the entire childhood period attend college. Conversely, less than 10 percent of those who spent all ten of the years from age 6–15 in poverty do so. The drop between one year and no years in poverty is stark—48 percent continuing education beyond the secondary level, compared to 30 percent. The changes are also large at the other end of the poverty intensity spectrum. While only 9 percent of those who lived in poverty during their entire childhood went on to postsecondary education, for those whose families were able to escape poverty for even one year, the percentage doubles to 18 percent.[8] The zero-order correlation of poverty persistence and postsecondary schooling is −.24.

A clear tie between years in poverty and the probability of giving

TABLE 4.10c Percentage Who Had a Teenage Out-of-Wedlock Birth, by Years Poor During Ages 6–15

	Years						
Birth	0	1	2–3	4–5	6–7	8–9	10
No	93	88	82	75	79	68	67
Yes	7	12	18	25	21	32	33

TABLE 4.10d Percentage Who Are Economically Inactive at Age 24, by Years Poor During Ages 6–15

	Years						
Economically Inactive	0	1	2–3	4–5	6–7	8–9	10
Yes	16	31	31	25	35	32	44
No	84	69	69	75	65	68	56

birth out of wedlock as a teenager also exists, and this is shown in Table 4.10c. While only 7 percent of those who grew up in a family that was never in poverty had such a birth, one-third of those whose families never escaped poverty had a nonmarital teenage birth. Again, the relationship is nearly monotonic, and the zero-order correlation is .22.

As Table 4.10d shows, for the experience of some poverty—from 1 year to 8–9 years—there seems to be little effect on economic inactivity. The percentage of youths inactive through this range varies from 25 to 35 percent, with no consistent pattern. However, for youths who experience zero years in poverty, only 16 percent are inactive; in stark contrast almost one-half of those who lived in poverty for the entire 6–15-year period were inactive.

Years Lived with One Parent

Children who live with only one parent are constrained in the number of potential hours of parental time that can be invested in them. Single-parent families typically also have lower family income (in total and per person) than do intact families and are more likely to receive income from public transfer programs. This nexus of experiences may also affect children's outcomes.

In Tables 4.11a–4.11d, we show the relationships between the number of years spent living with one parent and our four children's attainment variables. Table 4.11a suggests a fairly strong connection between years lived with one parent and high-school graduation. Those who spent their entire childhood in an intact family are very likely to graduate—89 percent do so. On the other hand, only 73 percent of those who spent all 10 years living with one parent graduated from high school. Among those who spent some, but not all, years living with one parent, 76–85 percent graduated from high school. Within this intermediate group there seems to be no real pattern between the number of years living with one parent and the probability of graduating. As we have seen with several of the other relationships, most of the impact appears to be at the extremes of the intensity scale. The zero-order correlation is −.16.

Turning to the choice of postsecondary schooling, the relationship is even stronger. Those children who lived with both parents in all of their childhood years are twice as likely to attend school after graduating from high school as those who spent all (10) years living with just one parent—42 percent versus 21 percent. Those who spent some years—1 to 8–9—in a single-parent family have about a 30 percent chance of continuing education beyond high school, a value intermediate to those at the extremes. The zero-order correlation between these two variables is also −.16.

Tables 4.11c and 4.11d present the zero-order relationships between the time that a child lived with but a single parent and the undesirable reproductive and inactivity outcomes. In both cases the relationship is a strong one: for the teenage out-of-wedlock birth outcome, even stronger than that for the education outcomes. Daughters who lived all (10) years with a single parent are more than four times as likely to have given birth as a nonmarried teen (a 29 percent probability) than daughters who spent their entire childhood living in an intact family. The percent who had such a birth among those who spent only 1 year living with one parent is similar to that of those who spent no years; the experience of those who spent 2–9 years is closer to that of those who spent no time living in an intact family. The zero-order correlation (.25) reflects the stronger relationship of family structure to this aspect of reproductive behavior than to educational attainment.

A similar, though less strong, relationship is observed between the

**TABLE 4.11a Percentage Who Graduated from High School,
by Years Living with One Parent During Ages 6–15**

	Years						
Graduated	0	1	2–3	4–5	6–7	8–9	10
No	11	15	24	17	16	24	27
Yes	89	85	76	83	84	76	73
Percentage of Sample	59	3	6	6	5	5	16

**TABLE 4.11b Percentage Who Attended College,
by Years Living with One Parent During Ages 6–15**

	Years						
Attended College	0	1	2–3	4–5	6–7	8–9	10
No	58	68	67	67	71	71	79
Yes	42	32	33	33	29	29	21

**TABLE 4.11c Percentage Who Had a Teenage Out-of-Wedlock Birth,
by Years Living with One Parent During Ages 6–15**

	Years						
Birth	0	1	2–3	4–5	6–7	8–9	10
No	93	90	75	76	76	76	71
Yes	7	10	25	24	24	24	29

**TABLE 4.11d Percentage Economically Inactive at Age 24,
by Years Living with One Parent During Ages 6–15**

	Years						
Economically Inactive	0	1	2–3	4–5	6–7	8–9	10
Yes	20	21	29	25	36	29	34
No	80	79	71	75	64	71	66

number of years lived with one parent and economic inactivity. The range extends from a 20 percent inactivity rate for those who lived their entire childhood in an intact family to 34 percent for those children who spent 10 years living with a single parent. Those who lived but 1 year with a single parent also have a low (21 percent) probability of being economically inactive. Between the two extremes, the proportion of inactive youths lies between these two values, though the highest proportion inactive occurs among those who experienced 6–7 years living with but one parent. The zero-order correlation coefficient between these two variables is .13.

Receipt of Welfare

Children who grow up in families that choose to receive welfare at some time are more likely to themselves receive welfare when they become young adults. (The linkage here is typically through having an early birth, either in wedlock followed by a divorce, or out of wedlock. Receipt of welfare is, by and large, conditioned on being unmarried and having a child.) Children who grow up in families that receive welfare are likely to have fewer ties to the work force because of the lower probability that a parent is working, and as a result, they have more limited information about the work force. Both of these factors may encourage fewer years of education to be chosen, and increase the likelihood of having a birth out of wedlock and being economically inactive.

Clearly, the underlying reasons for these outcomes may be factors other than welfare receipt—poverty, single-parent living arrangements, and parents with limited education are examples. However, here we look only at the simple relationship between the receipt of welfare by the parent and the child's decisions regarding education, having a teenage nonmarried birth, receiving welfare (dependent on such a birth), and being economically active at age 24. Tables 4.12a–4.12e present these relationships.

Children who live in families that received welfare while they were aged 6–15 are somewhat less likely to graduate from high school than those whose families were not recipients. They are also far less likely to attend college. About 42 percent of children from families who were not welfare recipients chose education beyond high school, but only 22 percent of the children from recipient families so continued their education. The zero-order correlations for these education outcome variables are −.22 and −.19, respectively.

TABLE 4.12a Percentage Who Graduated from High School, by Whether Family Ever Received Welfare During Ages 6–15

	Family Received Welfare	
Graduated	No	Yes
No	11	28
Yes	89	72
Percentage of Sample	71	29

TABLE 4.12b Percentage Who Attended College, by Whether Family Ever Received Welfare During Ages 6–15

	Family Received Welfare	
Attended College	No	Yes
No	58	78
Yes	42	22

TABLE 4.12c Percentage Who Had A Teenage Out-of-Wedlock Birth, by Whether Family Ever Received Welfare During Ages 6–15

	Family Received Welfare	
Birth	No	Yes
No	91	72
Yes	9	28

TABLE 4.12d Percentage Who Had A Teenage Out-of-Wedlock Birth and Received Welfare Within Two Years of that Birth, by Whether Family Ever Received Welfare During Ages 6–15

	Family Received Welfare	
Teenage Receipt of Welfare	No	Yes
No	49	24
Yes	51	76

TABLE 4.12e Percentage Who Are Economically Inactive at Age 24, by Whether Family Ever Received Welfare During Ages 6–15

	Family Received Welfare	
Economically Inactive	No	Yes
Yes	19	38
No	81	62

TABLE 4.12f Percentage Who Are Economically Inactive at Age 24, by Whether They Graduated from High School

	Graduated	
Economically Inactive	No	Yes
Yes	36	22
No	64	78

Larger differences appear in the relationships between parental welfare receipt and the two undesirable outcomes. For girls who lived in families that received welfare, the probability of having a nonmarital birth as a teenager is 28 percent, more than three times greater than the 9 percent of those growing up in a nonrecipient home who experienced a nonmarital birth. The zero-order correlation between these two variables is .24.

The receipt of welfare during childhood also appears to be related to the postbirth experience of those girls who did have a nonmarital birth as a teenager. This pattern is shown in Table 4.12d. Nearly three-quarters of such girls whose mothers were on welfare themselves became recipients within two years of giving a birth. However, about one-half of those girls whose family did not receive welfare became a recipient within two years of having a child out-of-wedlock as a teenager.

The relationship of family welfare recipiency and the child's activity pattern at age 24 is shown in Table 4.12e. For children who grew up in a family that received welfare, the probability of being economically inactive at age 24 is about .38; it is one-half this level—.19—for children whose families were not recipients. The zero-order correlation coefficient between these variables is .15.

One final economic inactivity relationship is shown in Table 4.12f. It shows the relationship between two outcomes: high-school graduation and economic inactivity. For those in our sample who graduated from high school, 22 percent were inactive; more than 35 percent of the dropouts were economically inactive at age 24. The zero-order correlation coefficient between these two variables is $-.13$.

Neighborhood Attributes

In recent years, social scientists have paid increasing attention to the potential effect of neighborhood characteristics, especially those of inner-city or disadvantaged neighborhoods, on the outcomes of children (see Chapter 3). Research on this question has focused on neighborhood characteristics that bring residents into contact with circumstances and people that either serve as models of success or as exemplars of failure.

Here we present the zero-order relationships between two neighborhood characteristics that are likely to influence adversely the ultimate attainment of children who grow up in them and our four indicators of success. The two neighborhood characteristics are: (1) the proportion of households that are headed by single females, and (2) the proportion of the individuals aged 16–19 in the neighborhood who are high-school dropouts.

Proportion of Households Headed by a Female

Tables 4.13a and 4.13b show the relationship between the proportion of households headed by a single woman in the neighborhood in which children grow up and the educational attainment of these children. The association between these variables is clear: those children who grow up in neighborhoods with few female-headed households are far more likely to graduate from high school (89 percent) than those who grow up in neighborhoods where a majority of households are headed by women (71 percent). Between these extreme proportions the relationship between the proportion of households headed by a woman in the neighborhood in which children grow up and the probability that they will graduate from high school is not monotonic, and a clear break point appears when the proportion of female heads reaches about 40 percent. The zero-order correlation is $-.13$.

The relationship between the proportion of female-headed households in the neighborhood and college attendance patterns in our sample is even stronger. (The zero-order correlation is −.15.) Among the children growing up in neighborhoods with few households headed by a female, about one-half attend college. Conversely, of those growing up in neighborhoods in which over 40 percent of the households are headed by a female, only 24 percent attend college. The percentage between these two extremes shows a nonlinear pattern.

Table 4.13c shows the relationship between the probability that a girl will have a teenage out-of-wedlock birth and the extent of female headship in the neighborhood in which she grows up. Because the level of stigma associated with being an unmarried parent is likely to be less in a neighborhood with more women in this circumstance, the expected relationship between these two variables is positive. We find such a zero-order positive relationship.

However, while the relationship is positive, it is distinctly nonlinear. When a girl grows up in a neighborhood in which less than 20 percent of the households are headed by a woman, her probability of having a teenage birth out of wedlock is low—less than 11 percent. However, as we have seen in some of the other patterns reported above, a contagion-type effect seems to be present here. For girls growing up in neighborhoods in which a quarter or more of the households are headed by a woman, the probability that she will have a nonmarital birth exceeds 25 percent, and ranges to over 35 percent when 40 percent of the households are headed by single women. The zero-order correlation stands at .22.

Finally, we present the relationship between the prevalence of female-headed households in the neighborhood in which a child grows up and the probability that he or she will be economically inactive. While the conceptual reasons for expecting such a relationship are not strong in the case of males, we have seen that the concentration of female-headed families is related to the probability that a girl will have an out-of-wedlock birth. Such a choice is typically followed by a spell of welfare recipiency, and hence economic inactivity.

As Table 4.13d shows, the relationship between this neighborhood characteristic and economic inactivity is a rather strong one. While only about 14 percent of the youths in our sample who grew up in a neighborhood dominated by two-parent families (more than 90 percent) are economically inactive, those who grew up in neighborhoods in which female-headed families were common (say, 20 percent or more) had inactivity rates well in excess of 30 percent. Those in communities with a majority (more than 50 percent) of households headed by single moth-

TABLE 4.13a Percentage Who Graduated from High School, by Proportion of Female-Headed Households in Neighborhood

	\multicolumn{6}{c}{Proportion}					
Graduated	<10	10–20	20–30	30–40	40–50	>50
No	11	14	22	17	28	29
Yes	89	86	78	83	72	71
Percentage of Sample	52	37	15	10	5	3

TABLE 4.13b Percentage Who Attended College, by Proportion of Female-Headed Households in Neighborhood

	\multicolumn{6}{c}{Proportion}					
Attend College	<10	10–20	20–30	30–40	40–50	>50
No	50	68	69	70	75	76
Yes	50	32	31	30	25	24

TABLE 4.13c Percentage Who Had a Teenage Out-of-Wedlock Birth, by Proportion of Female-Headed Households in Neighborhood

	\multicolumn{6}{c}{Proportion}					
Birth	<10	10–20	20–30	30–40	40–50	50+
No	95	89	75	79	64	74
Yes	5	11	25	21	36	26

TABLE 4.13d Percentage Who Are Economically Inactive at Age 24, by Proportion of Female-Headed Households in Neighborhood

	\multicolumn{6}{c}{Proportion}					
Economically Inactive	<10	10–20	20–30	30–40	40–50	>50
Yes	14	27	30	36	29	37
No	86	73	70	64	71	63

ers had a 37 percent probability of being economically inactive at age 24. The zero-order correlation coefficient is .16.

High-School Dropouts

Another neighborhood characteristic that is likely to influence the outcomes of the children who grow up in them is the prevalence of high-school dropouts among young adults living in the neighborhood. Here, we focus on the proportion of the neighborhood's residents aged 16–19 who have not finished high school, and relate this variable to each of our four outcomes.[9] Tables 4.14a–4.14d present the relevant cross-tabulations.

As expected, the relationship between the prevalence of dropouts in a neighborhood and the educational attainments of the children who grow up in that neighborhood is a strong one. Among those in our sample who live in areas in which more than 90 percent of the young adults have finished high school, over 90 percent graduate from high school. At the other end of the scale, nearly 60 percent of the children who have grown up in a neighborhood in which more than 40 percent of those aged 18–25 have failed to graduate from high school are themselves dropouts. This is the highest proportion of nongraduates by any of the factors employed in our cross-tabulations. As with some of the other relationships we have explored, there is a clear nonlinearity in this relationship as well: a distinct tipping point seems to exist when about 20–30 percent of the youths in the neighborhood are dropouts. The zero-order correlation coefficient between these two variables is −.18.

A similar, but somewhat less strong, relationship also exists between the proportion of dropouts in a neighborhood and the postsecondary schooling attendance probabilities of the children who grow up in the neighborhood. About one-half of those children who have grown up in areas with very few dropouts attend college, while less than a quarter (23 percent) of those in areas with a high proportion of dropouts continue on beyond high school. The zero-order correlation coefficient is −.17.

The relationship between the neighborhood high-school dropout variable and the proportion of the girls in our sample who have a teenage out-of-wedlock birth is also strong. This is shown in Table 4.14c. Six percent of the girls who grew up in neighborhoods with few youths who were high-school dropouts had such a birth, while 27 percent of those who grew up in neighborhoods in which more than 40 percent of the youths had failed to complete high school gave birth out of wedlock as

**TABLE 4.14a Percentage Who Graduated from High School,
by Proportion of Young Adults in Neighborhood Who Dropped Out**

| | Proportion Dropped Out | | | | |
Graduated	<10	10–20	20–30	30–40	>40
No	8	15	22	22	58
Yes	92	85	78	78	42
Percentage of Sample	28	40	24	6	2

**TABLE 4.14b Percentage Who Attended College,
by Proportion of Young Adults in Neighborhood Who Dropped Out**

| | Proportion Dropped Out | | | | |
Attended College	<10	10–20	20–30	30–40	>40
No	50	67	70	79	77
Yes	50	33	30	21	23

**TABLE 4.14c Percentage Who Had a Teenage Out-of-Wedlock Birth,
by Proportion of Young Adults in Neighborhood Who Dropped Out**

| | Proportion Dropped Out | | | | |
Birth	<10	10–20	20–30	30–40	>40
No	94	87	77	76	73
Yes	6	13	23	24	27

**TABLE 4.14d Percentage Who Are Economically Inactive at Age 24,
by Proportion of Young Adults in Neighborhood Who Dropped Out**

| | Proportion | | | | |
Economically Inactive	<10	10–20	20–30	30–40	>40
Yes	18	26	25	31	43
No	82	74	75	69	57

a teenager—a 4.5-fold difference. The zero-order correlation coefficient for this relationship is .18.

Finally, Table 4.14d shows the relationship between the prevalence of youths who failed to complete high school in the neighborhoods in which the children in our sample grew up, and the economic activity levels of these children when they are 24. The neighborhood differences are very large. For those who grew up in neighborhoods in which virtually no high-school dropouts lived, the rate of economic inactivity is less than 20 percent. However, those in our sample who grew up in neighborhoods in which more than 40 percent of the youths failed to complete high school had economic inactivity rates in excess of 40 percent.

AN ANALYSIS OF RELATIONSHIPS
BASED ON MULTIPLE REGRESSIONS

Cross-tabulations such as those presented in the previous section allow only simple relationships—those without controlling for other important factors—to be observed. In this section, we first present the results of regressions using as dependent variables either those education, childbearing, and economic inactivity outcomes discussed earlier, or variants of them: whether the individual graduated from high school, the years of schooling completed, whether a female had an out-of-wedlock birth when she was between the ages of 15 and 18, and whether the individual was economically inactive at age 24.[10]

We present two estimates for each of the four dependent variables: first, an ordinary least squares estimate in which the coefficient can be readily interpreted as a partial derivative; second, an appropriate maximum likelihood (probit or tobit) estimate appropriate to the dependent variable in question. In the case of high-school graduation and having a teenage out-of-wedlock birth—both limited dependent variables—probit analysis is used.[11] In the case of years of completed schooling,[12] we set the maximum level of education to be 14 years (which provides accurate information on the entire sample) and employ a tobit maximum likelihood model.[13] For the second set of results, those employing maximum likelihood methods, only the t-statistics are presented as the coefficient values have little quantitative meaning.

The Basic Model

In our basic model, we relate our four primary outcome or attainment variables—high-school graduation, years of education, teenage out-of-wedlock birth, and economic inactivity—to a limited set of background, parental activity, and investment choice variables. The independent variables are:

Background
  Female
  African-American

Parental Choices/Opportunities
  Mother a high-school graduate or more
  Father a high-school graduate or more
  Any religion
  Average posttax family income ÷ poverty line, ages 6–15
  Average number of siblings, ages 6–15
  Number of years lived in an SMSA, ages 6–15

Family Circumstances
  Number of years family head disabled, ages 6–15
  Number of years mother worked, ages 6–15
  Number of years lived with one parent, ages 6–15

The results of these estimates are presented in Table 4.15.

We also present a modified version of this base model in Table 4.16. In this model, we replace years lived in an SMSA with years lived in the South, and years lived with one parent with average annual hours of parental time spent with children, ages 6–15. We discuss results from both models in this section, describing the impact of the explanatory variables on our dependent, or outcome, variables.

Background Variables

Gender. For all three of the models estimated using the sample with both genders included—high-school graduation, years of education, and economic inactivity—the gender variable (female = 1) is statistically significant, and the signs are as expected. Holding all other factors constant, being female is associated with a higher probability of graduating from high school and having more years of education when schooling is complete than is being male. Women are also more likely to be economically inactive at age 24 than are men.

Race. Controlling for the other variables included in the model, we find that African-American persons are more likely to graduate from high school, have more years of education, and to be economically inactive at age 24 than are whites. The results on the education out-

TABLE 4.15 Multiple Regressions: Basic Model

Variable	High-School Graduate			Years of Education (max = 14)			Teenage Out-of-Wedlock Birth			Economically Inactive		
	Coef.	t-st.	t-st. probit	Coef.	t-st.	t-st. tobit	Coef.	t-st.	t-st. probit	Coef.	t-st.	t-st. probit
Constant	.74	16.3**	2.6**	11.44	58.8***	52.6***	0.12	2.0**	−2.2**	.21	2.4**	−2.7***
Female	.04	2.3**	2.4**	.28	3.9**	4.4***	.06	2.1**	1.7	.07	2.5**	2.5***
African-American	.09	4.0**	3.9**	.34	3.7**	4.0***	−.01	0.3	0.2	.09	2.2**	2.2**
Father a High-School Graduate or More	.09	4.0**	4.3**	.62	6.5**	6.2***	−.12	4.5**	4.2**	−.07	1.7*	1.7*
Mother a High-School Graduate or More	.08	4.0**	3.6**	.49	5.7	5.0***	−.06	1.4	1.9*	−.05	1.5	1.4
Any Religion	.02	0.7	0.8	.26	1.9*	1.5	$-.04^{-1}$	0.5	2.4**	−.02	0.3	0.5
Average Posttax Family Income ÷ Poverty Line[a]	.01	1.0	1.6*	.16	5.9**	5.8***	$.01^{-1}$	0.3	0.3	−.01	0.4	0.5
Number of Years Family Head Disabled[a]	−.02	6.1**	4.9**	−.05	3.3**	2.9***	$.09^{-2}$	0.3	0.8	.01	1.0	0.9
Number of Years Mother Worked[a]	.01	2.3**	2.0**	.01	0.7	0.8	.02	4.5**	3.4**	−.01	2.4**	2.3**
Number of Years Lived with One Parent[a]	−.01	3.1**	2.8**	−.04	2.9**	3.0***	.02	2.9**	1.9**	$.04^{-1}$	0.7	0.6
Average Number of Siblings[a]	−.02	2.6**	2.6**	−.07	2.7**	2.3***	$-.03^{-1}$	1.1	1.5	$.02^{-2}$	0.2	0.2
Number of Years Lived in SMSA[a]	$-.02^{-1}$	0.8	0.9	$-.09^{-2}$	0.1	0.3				.01	2.5**	2.7**
R-squared (chi-square)	.11	(197)		.20	(45.1)		.14	(136)		.09	(71)	

NOTES: Regressions include controls for whether both parents are in the sample as of 1968, and whether the child's grandfather was foreign-born.
Negative superscript values indicate decimal point is to be shifted that many places to the left.
For extended definitions of variables, means and standard deviations, see Appendix A, Table A.1.

[a] During ages 6–15.

* Significant at 10 percent level.
** Significant at 5 percent level.

TABLE 4.16 Multiple Regressions: Modified Model

Variable	High-School Graduate Coef.	t-st.	t-st. probit	Years of Education (max = 14) Coef.	t-st.	t-st. tobit	Teenage Out-of-Wedlock Birth Coef.	t-st.	t-st. probit	Economically Inactive Coef.	t-st.	t-st. probit
Constant	.65	10.0**	0.4	11.63	41.8***	37.2**	0.36	4.2	0.8	.43	3.3	−0.4
Female	.04	2.3**	2.4**	.28	3.8***	4.4***				.08	2.5	2.6
African-American	.07	3.3**	3.3**	.31	3.3***	3.9***	.09	3.1	2.5	.12	2.9	2.9
Average Number of Siblings	−.02	2.6**	2.4**	−.05	2.1**	1.8*	.03	3.3	1.9	.01	0.7	0.6
Father a High-School Graduate or more	.09	3.9**	4.2**	.60	6.2**	5.9**	−.01	0.4	0.2	−.08	1.8	1.8
Mother a High-School Graduate or more	.09	4.2**	3.9**	.45	5.0**	4.5**	−.15	5.3	4.8	−.07	1.8	1.7
Any Religion	.03	0.9	1.0	.31	2.3**	1.9*	−.06	1.4	1.7	−.02	0.3	0.5
Average Family Income ÷ Poverty Line	.01	1.7*	2.3**	.16	5.9**	5.9**	−.02	1.9	3.7	−.01	0.6	0.6
Number of Years Family Head Disabled[a]	−.02	6.2**	5.0**	−.06	3.7**	3.1**	$.03^{-1}$	0.7	0.0	.01	0.8	0.7
Number of Years Mother Worked[a]	.01	2.3**	2.1**	$.02^{-2}$	0.0	0.4	$-.07^{-2}$	0.2	0.6	−.01	2.9	2.7
Average Annual Hours with Parent	.05	1.2	1.2	−.02	1.3	0.8	−.01	2.8	2.1	−.01	1.6	1.4
Number of Years Lived in South[a]	$.05^{-2}$	0.3	0.5	−.01	0.9	1.2	−.01	2.0	2.7	−.01	1.4	1.3
R-squared (chi-square)	.11	(189)		.20	(45.1)		.13	(133)		.09		(67)

NOTE: Regressions include controls for whether both parents are in the sample as of 1968, and whether the child's grandfather was foreign-born.

[a] During ages 6–15.

* Significant at 10 percent level.
** Significant at 5 percent level.

122

comes are different than those observed in the cross-tabulations, where African-Americans tended to have less education than whites. In the multiple regression results, when the effects of all of the background, parental choice, and family circumstance variables are controlled for, African-Americans are estimated to have about .3 years more schooling than are whites. For the teenage out-of-wedlock birth regression, African-American females are more likely to experience such an outcome than are whites, a pattern consistent with the cross-tabulations.

Parental Choices/Opportunities

Father a High-School Graduate. Having a father who is a high-school graduate is positively associated with the probability that the child will graduate from high school; it is also positively associated with the number of years of schooling. The estimated impact is about .6 of a year more education for children whose fathers are graduates, compared with those children whose fathers have not completed high school. Both of these education coefficients are statistically significant. For the teenage out-of-wedlock birth outcome, the education of the father appears to have no significant impact. The father's education is negatively related to the probability that the child will be economically inactive at age 24, and the coefficient is significant.

Mother a High-School Graduate. The effect of the mother's education on children's outcomes is very similar in both sign and magnitude to the effect of father's education, with one important exception. For the teenage out-of-wedlock birth outcome, the impact of the mother's education is large and highly significant; the father's education, while it had the same sign, was not significant.[14] Daughters of mothers who have a high-school diploma are significantly less likely to give birth as an unmarried teenager than are the daughters of mothers who have failed to graduate.

Religion. The variable measuring religion in our data does not record the intensity of religious involvement, but simply whether or not respondents indicate that they have a religion and are willing to identify it. Our findings on the effect of having a religion are mixed: religion does not appear to be significantly associated with the probability of high-school graduation, but it is positively though not quite significantly associated with the number of years of education that the child attains. The effect of this variable on the years of education completed is about .3 of a year (holding constant all of the other variables in the model). Reporting a religion is negatively related to the probability that a girl will have a teenage out-of-wedlock birth, and is statistically significant. While the sign on the coefficient of the religion variable is as expected in the economic inactivity model, it is insignificant.

Average Posttax Family Income over Child's Ages 6–15. In all four models shown in each of Tables 4.15 and 4.16, the sign on this economic resource variable is as expected: family economic resources are related to desirable outcomes. However, the levels of statistical significance vary widely. For the high-school graduation variable, family resources have an independent and marginally significant effect. However, this variable is very strongly related to the number of years of completed education, and the t-statistic is quite high. This is as expected, as family resources would be likely to have more of an effect on continuing schooling beyond high school than on high-school completion. The results suggest that for each additional $1000 of average annual family income, a child receives an additional .16 of a year of schooling. The relationship of family economic resources to the probability of a teenage nonmarital birth is statistically significant (except in one of the specifications using the linear probability model). Not surprisingly, its relationship to economic inactivity is small and not significant.[15]

Family Circumstances

Number of Years Family Head Is Disabled, Ages 6–15. Growing up in a family in which the head of the household is disabled is likely to require additional resources in terms of care for the parent, medical care, and time. It also implies that the head of the family will not be contributing to the earnings and other economic resources of the family as would an able-bodied family head. All of these effects imply a reduction in the resources available to the child. (An exception to this may be increased time that the disabled parent might be able to spend with the child.) Our results are consistent with the view that reduced economic resources will have a negative effect on children's outcomes.

Children with a disabled parent who is the head of household are less likely to graduate from high school and, on average, they will have fewer years of schooling (relative to otherwise identical children whose family head is able-bodied). However, the effect of this variable on the number of years of completed education is not large—.05 years of schooling per year the head is disabled, or a maximum of one-half year less schooling if the parent were disabled over the entire period when the child is 6–15. There appears to be no association between having a disabled head and either the probability of a teenage birth or the probability of being economically inactive at age 24.

Number of Years Mother Worked, Ages 6–15. The number of years that a mother works while her child is aged 6–15 could create two offsetting effects on the child's ultimate attainment. First, time spent in the labor force implies a reduction in the time that the mother would have available for child-related activities. Second, work time yields earned income, and hence economic resources that could be used to benefit the child. A third possible effect of the mother's work could be its role-model impact on the child.

Our results suggest a significant and positive association between the number of years a mother works and the probability that the child will graduate from high school. However, the mother's work variable has no significant relationship to the level of completed schooling of the child. The first of these relationships suggests that the economic resources or the role-model effect of mother's work may dominate; the second suggests that the reduction in time spent with children may offset these positive effects.

While there is no statistically significant association between the number of years a mother works and the probability her daughter will give birth as a teenager out of wedlock, the mother's work variable is negatively and significantly associated with the probability that the child will be economically inactive at age 24. This last result again suggests that the role-model effect of the mother's economic activity may have an important effect.

Number of Years Living with One Parent, Ages 6–15. A second indicator of parental time is the number of years that the child lived with a single parent when the child was 6–15. As with the results found in the cross-tabulations, the effect of this factor varies as expected with our four outcome variables. Children who live more years with one parent are significantly less likely to graduate from high school and are predicted to complete fewer years of schooling. For each additional year spent living in a one-parent family, the expected decrease in completed schooling is .04 of a year—or nearly one-half a year of completed schooling if all 10 years were spent living in a one-parent family.

The time that a girl lives with one parent is positively and significantly related to the probability that the girl with have an out-of-wedlock birth as a teenager. While this independent variable is positively related to the probability that the child will be economically inactive when he or she reaches the age of 24, the coefficient is not significant.

The substitute for the variable measuring years lived with one parent in Table 4.16 is the variable measuring time spent with parents. This is an average of hours per year when the child is aged 6–15. The amount of time that parents spend with the child is significantly related to the probability the child will have a teenage out-of-wedlock birth. For each addition of 100 hours per year of parental child-care time, the daughter has a 1 percent lower probability of giving birth as a nonmarried teen. This child-care time variable is also significantly associated (at the 10 percent level) with a reduced probability of being economically inactive at age 24. Here again, for every addition of 100 hours per year the parents spend with a child, the probability of economic inactivity is reduced by 1 percent. This parental time input variable is not significantly associated with the education level of the child.

Average Number of Siblings, Ages 6–15. The parental reproductive choice regarding completed family size is reflected in the number of siblings in the family of a child. A larger number of siblings in the family may indicate a dilution of the time spent by parents with any given child. While the evidence on this dilution effect is not strong, prior research has often found that children who grow up in large families tend to have lower achievement levels than children who are raised in small families. Our measure of this variable reflects the average number of siblings with whom a child lived when he or she was aged 6–15.

The estimates suggest a negative and significant relationship between the number of siblings and educational attainment. This relation is consistent with the asserted trade-off between the quantity of children that parents have and the quality of these children. The estimates indicate that each sibling with whom a child lives when that child is 6–15 is associated with about .6 fewer years of schooling, controlling for all of the other variables included in the model.

There is also a significant association between number of siblings and the probability that the girls in our sample will have a teenage nonmarital birth. While both the OLS and the probit results indicate a significant relationship, the t-statistic is smaller in the more appropriate probit model. One interpretation of this result is that the reduced parental attention given to children with many siblings may have a negative effect on outcome. Another possible interpretation is that children who grow up in large families may accept large family size and childbearing as a norm or value.

Finally, while the number-of-siblings variable is positively associated with a higher probability of economic inactivity, the coefficient is not at all significant.[16]

Number of Years Living in SMSA, Ages 6–15. The last variable included in our basic estimates—the number of years that the parents chose to live in a large urban area when the child was 6–15—is a measure of the cost of living in the area in which the child grew up and/or a measure of the prevailing attitudes and values in the area. In the basic estimates for the four primary outcome variables, this areal variable has no significant effect on either of the educational attainment outcomes, but in both cases the relationship is negative. The SMSA variable appears to be negatively related to the teenage out-of-wedlock birth outcome for the girls in our sample, but the coefficient has marginal statistical significance. Only in the case of the economic inactivity outcome does the SMSA variable have a statistically significant effect: growing up in an SMSA is positively and significantly associated with the probability of being inactive at age 24.

The alternative specification replaces this variable with years lived in the South while growing up. The pattern of results for this variable is similar to those for the SMSA variable for the education outcomes. The signs in both equations are negative, but in neither model is the variable statistically significant. Growing up in the South is negatively related to the probability of having a nonmarital teenage birth, and the coefficient is statistically significant. This result may reflect the different values and norms prevalent in the southern region of the country, or the lower expected welfare benefits there, or greater religious intensity, or perhaps a lower cost of living. A southern upbringing is also related to a lower probability of being economically inactive, but the coefficient is not significant.

The Basic Model Plus Parental Choices/Opportunities Creating Children's Stress

As suggested in earlier chapters, one set of factors thought to be important in explaining the success of young adults is their exposure to, or their avoidance of, stress-producing events or circumstances. In this section, we describe the results from a series of models that add five variables designed to measure the effect of stressful parental decisions on events that occurred during the childhood years (ages 6–15) of the individuals in our sample. The stress variables include:

- Number of years that a parent was unemployed
- Number of parental separations
- Number of parental marriages or remarriages
- Number of geographical moves
- Whether the family was ever on AFDC

We are interested in the relationship between each of these variables and our primary outcome variables, but also whether their inclusion in the model substantially alters the signs and significance levels of the already-included variables. The results of these estimations are reported in Table 4.17.

The first stress variable—the number of years a parent was unemployed—is likely to cause stress through a variety of channels. These include the loss of income, reduced self-esteem for the parent as well as the child and other family members, and stress due to budgeting and uncertainty regarding future income. Given all of these potential influences, it is perhaps surprising that this factor does not appear to play a significant role in influencing any of our outcome variables.

The second stress variable—the number of parental separations—is also likely to influence adversely the child's well-being in a number of ways, including the stress of the separation itself (and the associated insecurity and ill feelings) and the likely reductions in income and parental time. This stress variable is significantly and positively associated with the probability that a daughter will have a teenage out-of-wedlock birth, but has no statistically significant effect on the schooling or economic inactivity outcomes. The estimated impact of this variable on the childbearing outcome is not large—the probability of having a teenage out-of-wedlock birth increases by .1 percent with each separation.

The third measure of stress—the number of marriages or remarriages of the parent with whom the child is living when he or she is aged 6–15—may in fact signal increased stability (especially financial stability) in family life, and another adult to provide attention and guidance. On the other hand, a parental marriage or remarriage may create additional family stress as it often brings into the household an additional person or persons who may compete for the time of the child's parent, add demands for resources, and change the child's daily pattern. In the case of nonmarital births, the remarriage may suggest to the child a rejection of the single-parent role by the parent, and this may convey both a new norm as well as information on these two marital status options. In the case of years of education, the interpretation may be that the income variable measures family income but the part earned by the step-parent is not available to the child. Our estimates suggest that the positive influence seems to dominate for the teenage out-of-wedlock birth outcome, but for years of completed education the negative effect appears to dominate. There is no significant effect of this factor for either the high-school completion or economic inactivity outcomes.

The fourth measure—the number of location moves—is negatively associated with both the probability of high-school graduation and with years of schooling, as we observed in the cross-tabulations. On average, we estimate that for each location move when the child is aged 6–15, the child will complete .09 fewer years of school. For the teenage out-of-wedlock birth outcome, we found a generally positive, but nonlinear, relationship between having such a birth and the number of moves in the cross-tabulations; in the regression results we observe a positive relationship that is not statistically significant. The number of geographical moves is not significantly associated with economic inactivity.

The last stress variable—whether or not the family ever received welfare while the child was aged 6–15—reflects the presumption that being on welfare has stigma effects, thereby increasing the child's stress and feelings of limited opportunities. The variable may also measure attitudes or norms held by the family, and it is related to assertions regarding the intergenerational transmission of welfare recipiency, suggesting that children of welfare recipients are themselves likely to be welfare recipients. The presumptions lying behind this view concern the impact of the additional information about the welfare system that recipiency conveys, the reduced level of information of and contacts with the labor market for those who are recipients, and a reduced stigma associated with receiving welfare.

It seems likely that this last variable would have the strongest tie to the teenage nonmarital birth outcome, which would be consistent with the pattern observed in the cross-tabulations presented in the first section of this chapter. In our regression results, however, we find no significant relationship between the teenage nonmarital birth outcome and whether or not the child's family ever received welfare. The welfare recipiency variable also has no significant relationship with the two schooling outcomes, suggesting that rather than welfare per se, it is

TABLE 4.17 Multiple Regressions Including Stress Variables

Variable	High-School Graduate			Years of Education (max = 14)		
	Coef.	t-st.	t-st. probit	Coef.	t-st.	t-st. tobit
Constant	.80	17.3**	3.5**	11.68	58.7**	52.3**
Female	.03	1.9*	2.0**	0.26	3.6**	4.1**
African-American	.08	3.6**	3.3**	.31	3.3**	3.9**
Average Number of Siblings[a]	−.01	2.0**	1.9*	−.06	2.4**	1.9*
Father a High-School Graduate or More	.08	3.6**	3.8**	.60	6.2**	6.0**
Mother a High-School Graduate or More	.08	4.1**	3.9**	.50	5.8**	5.3**
Any Religion	.01	0.2	0.4	.19	1.4	1.1
Average Posttax Family Income ÷ Poverty Line[a]	$.04^{-1}$	0.6	1.2	.16	5.7**	5.5**
Number of Years Family Head Disabled[a]	−.02	5.0**	4.4**	−.04	2.2**	1.8*
Number of Years Mother Worked[a]	.01	2.4**	2.4**	.01	0.6	0.6
Number of Years Lived in SMSA[a]	$−.02^{-1}$	0.9	1.1	$−.02^{-1}$	0.2	0.6
Number of Years Lived with One Parent[a]	−.01	1.8*	−1.8*	−.03	1.8*	1.8*
Average Number of Years Head Unemployed[a]	0.01^{-1}	0.0	0.6	−.02	1.2	1.3
Number of Parental Separations[a]	.02	0.6	0.5	.12	1.1	1.0
Number of Parental (Re)marriages[a]	$.03^{-1}$	0.1	−0.5	−.26	2.1**	2.1**
Number of Household Location Moves[a]	−.03	5.8**	4.9**	−.09	4.4**	3.8**
Family Ever Received AFDC = 1[a]	−.04	1.4	0.9	−.05	0.5	0.5
R-squared (chi-square)	.13		(229)	.22		(45.1)

NOTE: Regressions include controls for whether both parents are in the sample as of 1968, and whether the child's grandfather was foreign-born.

[a] During ages 6–15.

* Significant at 10 percent level.
** Significant at 5 percent level.

Teenage Out-of-Wedlock Birth			Economically Inactive		
Coef.	t-st.	t-st. probit	Coef.	t-st.	t-st. probit
0.07	1.2	-2.6**	.18	2.1**	-3.0**
			.08	2.5**	2.5**
.07	2.2**	1.8**	.08	2.0**	2.1**
.02	2.9**	2.0**	$-.01^{-1}$	0.1	0.1
$-.01$	0.2	0.2	$-.06$	1.6*	1.6*
$-.12$	4.6**	4.5**	$-.05$	1.4	1.4
$-.04$	0.9	1.5	$-.01$	0.2	0.3
$-.01^{-2}$	0.2	2.2**	$-.03^{-1}$	0.2	0.3
$-.04^{-2}$	0.7	-0.3	$-.02^{-2}$	0.0	0.1
$.07^{-2}$	0.2	0.3	$-.01$	1.7*	1.8*
$-.02^{-1}$	0.8	1.3	.01	2.3**	2.5**
.01	1.8*	1.4	$.01^{-1}$	0.1	0.1
$-.02$	0.0	0.4	.01	1.2	0.8
.11	3.4**	3.3**	$-.02$	0.4	0.4
$-.07$	1.7*	1.1	.03	0.5	0.6
.01	1.3	1.4	.01	0.7	0.9
.02	0.6	-0.3	.08	1.8*	1.7*
.15		(154)	.10		(78)

those factors that lead a family to receive welfare that are significant factors in influencing the education and childbearing outcomes of the children in our sample.

Interestingly, however, growing up in a family that received welfare is positively—but not quite significantly—associated with the probability that the child will be economically inactive at age 24. This relationship is consistent with the intergenerational welfare transmission perspective, suggesting that growing up in a family that receives welfare increases the probability that a child will be economically inactive and, possibly, a welfare recipient.

Finally, we ask whether the inclusion of the stress variables in the model has an effect on the other coefficient estimates. With the exception of the variables for years lived with one parent and religion, there are only small changes in the signs and significance levels of the other included variables. The coefficient on the variable for years lived with one parent remains marginally significant in the schooling equations, but it becomes insignificant in the teenage nonmarital birth estimations once the full set of five stress-related variables are added to the model. This variable was not significant in any of the estimations involving the economic inactivity outcome. This pattern suggests that it may be the stress of a separation, rather than years living with one parent, that has the stronger tie to the probability of a teenage nonmarital birth.

The Basic Model Plus Neighborhood Attributes

Another set of factors that have received increased attention as potentially important determinants of individual behaviors and outcomes are neighborhood factors: those characteristics of neighborhoods related either to low income, ghetto patterns, or to affluence and high achievement. Clearly, neighborhoods are not truly exogenous factors: parents choose where to live within the set of constraints regarding income and assets, job opportunities, housing values, and the location of family and friends. Moreover, the influence of neighborhoods may interact with the family's choices and circumstances as the characteristics of those in the neighborhood reinforce or are at odds with those of the family. Conversely, the influence of neighborhoods on children may be independent of the parents' characteristics and choices as children grow up, attend schools, and are exposed to the norms, values, and experiences of those in their neighborhood.

We include measures of three neighborhood characteristics in this version of our extended model[17]:

- Average percentage of youths who are high-school dropouts, ages 6–15
- Average percentage of families in the neighborhood that are headed by a female, ages 6–15
- Average percentage of the workers in a neighborhood that are employed in a high-prestige occupation (such as executive and managerial occupations), ages 6–15

The first set of neighborhood characteristics, those related to low income or ghettolike patterns, are expected to influence adversely a child's perceptions of future opportunities, and hence to reduce performance. The positive elements are viewed as demonstrating values and norms associated with attractive outcomes. As indicated above, we take these variables as proxies for community and school quality, and hence the level of social and governmental investment in children. The results are reported in Table 4.18.

The variable measuring the upper-class character of a neighborhood is not significantly related to any of our education and childbearing variables, but is positively and marginally significantly related to the economic inactivity variable. Perhaps this relationship implies that the foregoing of productive activities is a normal good, reflecting the higher incidence of nonwork of the spouses of high-earnings males.

The variable measuring the proportion of high-school dropouts was strongly related to the high-school graduation outcome in the cross-tabulations presented in the first section of this chapter, and the results in the regressions are consistent with this pattern. Even after controlling for the rich set of family and background characteristics, living in an area with a greater proportion of young adults who are high-school dropouts is negatively and significantly related to the probability that an individual will graduate from high school. This neighborhood characteristic is also negatively, but not quite significantly, related to the years of completed schooling. This variable appears to have no significant relationship to the probability of a teenage nonmarital birth or to the probability of economic inactivity at age 24.

The final neighborhood variable—the prevalence of female-headed families—also attempts to capture characteristics of the families in the immediate environment in which children grow up that might influence

TABLE 4.18 Multiple Regressions Including Neighborhood Variables

Variable	High-School Graduate			Years of Education (max = 14)		
	Coef.	t-st.	t-st. probit	Coef.	t-st.	t-st. tobit
Constant	.87	14.8**	3.3**	11.53	47.6**	43.0**
Female	.04	2.4**	2.5**	.28	3.9**	4.4**
African-American	.11	4.2**	3.8**	.48	4.4**	4.8**
Average Number of Siblings[a]	−.02	2.7**	2.5**	−.08	2.9**	2.4**
Father a High-School Graduate or more	.08	3.7**	4.0**	.59	6.1**	5.9**
Mother a High-School Graduate or more	.07	3.5**	3.2**	.46	5.3**	4.8**
Any Religion	.02	0.7	0.9	.26	1.9*	1.5
Average Posttax Family Income ÷ Poverty Line[a]	$.03^{-1}$	0.4	1.0	.14	4.7**	4.8**
Number of Years Family Head Disabled[a]	−.02	5.7**	4.7**	−.05	3.3**	2.8**
Number of Years Mother Worked[a]	$.01^{-1}$	2.3**	2.0**	$.04^{-1}$	0.4	0.5
Number of Years Lived in SMSA[a]	$-.02^{-1}$	0.8	0.8	$.01^{-1}$	0.1	0.2
Number of Years Lived with One Parent[a]	−.01	3.2**	2.9**	−.04	2.8**	2.8**
Average Percentage of Workers in High-Prestige Occupations[a]	$-.01^{-2}$	0.4	0.2	.01	1.4	0.7
Average Percentage of Youths Who Are High-School Dropouts[a]	$-.04^{-1}$	3.9**	3.4**	−.01	1.2	1.7*
Average Percentage of Female Heads[a]	$-.03^{-2}$	0.3	0.1	−.01	1.2	1.2
R-squared (chi-square)	.12		(229)	.21		(45.1)

NOTE: Regressions include controls for whether both parents are in the sample as of 1968, and whether the child's grandfather was foreign-born.

[a] During ages 6–15.

* Significant at 10 percent level.
** Significant at 5 percent level.

Teenage Out-of-Wedlock Birth			Economically Inactive		
Coef.	t-st.	t-st. probit	Coef.	t-st.	t-st. probit
0.06	0.8	$-2.1**$	.14	1.3	$-3.0**$
			.07	2.4**	2.4**
.05	1.4	1.1	.11	2.4**	2.6**
.02	3.0**	1.9*	$.02^{-1}$	0.0	0.1
$-.02^{-1}$	0.1	0.0	$-.08$	1.8*	1.9*
$-.12$	4.2**	4.0**	$-.05$	1.4	1.3
$-.06$	1.5	2.0**	$-.02$	0.4	0.4
$-.02^{-1}$	0.2	2.1**	$-.01$	0.8	1.0
$.08^{-2}$	0.2	-0.2	$.05^{-1}$	0.8	0.6
$.01^{-1}$	0.4	0.9	$-.01$	2.7**	2.6**
$.03^{-1}$	0.9	1.1	.01	2.5**	2.8**
.02	4.4**	3.3**	$.05^{-1}$	0.8	0.6
$.04^{-2}$	0.2	-0.1	$.04^{-1}$	1.6*	1.8*
$.03^{-1}$	1.6	1.3	$.03^{-1}$	1.3	1.4
$.07^{-2}$	0.5	0.4	$-.01^{-1}$	0.7	0.9
.14		(139)	.10		(77)

their choices and attainments. This variable is not significantly related to any of the four outcomes that we analyze in this chapter. The nonlinear nature of the underlying relationship that was identified in the cross-tabulation results presented in the first section suggests the reason for this lack of a statistically significant relationship.[18]

The introduction of these neighborhood variables into the basic regression model causes only a few changes in the signs and significance levels of the other variables. First, in the high-school completion equation, average family income during the individual's childhood years loses the marginal significance that it had in the basic specification. This suggests that when the family-income variable is entered into the model without the neighborhood variables (the base model), its estimated impact is partly capturing the effect of the neighborhood in which the child lived.

Second, the positive coefficient on the race variable in the years-of-schooling model increases when the neighborhood variables are included in the estimation. This suggests that the generally lower rates of college attendance for African-Americans partially reflect neighborhood characteristics, and that once these factors are included in the regression, the effect of race on years of education is even greater than suggested in the base estimates. In the model including the neighborhood characteristics, an African-American person is estimated to have, on net, nearly one-half year more of completed education than a white person.

Finally, the relationship between living in an urban area and having a teenage out-of-wedlock birth changes sign in the specification with neighborhood variables. However, in neither case is the variable statistically significant.

NOTES

1. Because these cross-tabulations focus on the relationship between only a few variables at a time, we view them as only indicative of the potential relationships revealed in the data. Hence, we do not present measures of statistical significance for these estimates. To explore the independent relationships between several determinant variables and our attainment indicators, we present multiple regression estimates later in the chapter. These estimates are accompanied by measures of statistical significance. A table of zero-order correlations between all of those variables discussed in this section and the dependent variables are provided in an appendix to this chapter.

2. Economically inactive is defined only for those age 24 and over as of 1988. A person is economically inactive if he or she is not a full-time student; does not work 1000 hours or more per year, does not attend school part-time and work 500 hours; is not the mother of an infant, or is not the mother of two or more children less than 5 years old; or is not in school part-time and the mother of a child less than 5 years old.

3. The zero-order correlations among these variables (reported in the appendix to this chapter) convey similar information. The correlation coefficient describing the relationship between a dummy variable for African-American and high-school completion is $-.08$ (meaning that being African-American relative to white leads to an 8 percentage point negative difference between the two probabilities of graduating from high school. The coefficient for college attendance is $-.14$, and among females, that for experiencing a teenage out-of-wedlock birth is .26. The zero-order correlation coefficient between the dummy variable for African-American and economic inactivity is .21.

4. Later we explore whether these differences are attributable to racial differences in opportunities, attitudes, or proxies for the level of family and social investment in children, rather than race per se.

5. The data for these results are not shown in the tables.

6. The zero-order correlations between whether a child's mother graduated from high school (versus not graduating) and: (1) the child's own graduation from high school; (2) the child's attending college; and (3) the child's years of schooling are .21, .25, and .31, respectively.

7. The zero-order correlations between the number of location moves and high-school completion is $-.19$; between the number of moves and post-secondary school attendance it is $-.12$. This pattern is consistent with the negative but nonlinear pattern we observe in the cross-tabulations.

8. Persistence in poverty is likely to be correlated with the distance below the poverty line of the family's permanent income; hence, what we interpret as the relationship between poverty persistence and schooling, in fact, may reflect the relationship between the permanent poverty income gap of the family and schooling.

9. One might be concerned that this neighborhood characteristic is endogenous: that the youths in the sample are part of this neighborhood and could themselves be included in the dropout count. For several reasons, this is not a problem. First, only the very oldest of the children in our sample—those who were 5–6 years old in 1968—are 16 or 17 as of 1979, the date of the 1980 Census that provides the measure of the neighborhood characteristics for the 1980–1985 period. Second, there are very few of these youths in any neighborhood relative to the total number of youths in the neighborhood. For both reasons, our neighborhood measures are largely independent of the behavior of the observations in our sample.

10. College attendance is not included in this analysis, as it is conditional on

high-school graduation. Hence, an appropriate analysis would need to model this decision in conjunction with the high-school graduation decision. We present such a sequential decision analysis in Chapter 5. The same logic applies to the receipt of welfare, as it is conditional on eligibility, which requires the presence of a dependent child. For an analysis of this sequential decision, see Chapter 6.

11. The use of ordinary least squares (OLS) analysis in the case of a dichotomous dependent variable is known as a linear probability model. Such models have two potential problems: (1) the fitted values could be outside the 0–1 interval, making problematic the labeling of the predicted values as probabilities, and (2) the residuals from the estimates may be heteroskedastic. The probit estimation procedure eliminates these problems. The underlying assumption of the probit model is that the cumulative distribution of the disturbance term is normally distributed.

12. The potential problem here is that the final level of schooling is not observed for some of the observations in our sample. This is likely to be the case for the younger subjects, some of whom ultimately graduate from college, or for nearly any of those who will eventually enter graduate school.

13. In the case of such right-hand-side censoring, the use of OLS may lead to biased estimates of the parameters. A commonly used alternative is a tobit specification that assumes an underlying normal distribution.

14. The zero-order correlation of the mother being a high-school graduate and the father being a high-school graduate is .47.

15. Parental income could have two offsetting effects on youth inactivity at age 24. Higher parental income implies high parental motivation, drive, and connections, suggesting lower levels of youth inactivity. On the other hand, higher parental income indicates the availability of income sources other than self-earnings for youths, implying a higher probability of youth inactivity.

16. It is difficult to draw out a consistent result regarding the effect of parental time from the coefficient estimates of the three variables reflecting the extent of available time variables. While the time the mother works appears positively to affect outcomes (at least for high-school graduation and economic inactivity), the time spent living with one parent and the number of siblings appear to have negative effects on children's attainments. The substitution of the variable estimating the actual time parents spend with the child for the variable measuring the number of years that the child lived with one parent suggests that the average time parents spend with their daughters is significantly and negatively related to the probability that the daughter will have a nonmarital birth as a teenager. The estimated relationship of the number of years the mother worked to her children's attainments is not affected by this modification to the specification of the model. However, the effect of the number of siblings is somewhat more strongly (and negatively) related to the years of schooling and teenage

births than it is when the years lived with one parent are included. Since the time spent with the child is an estimated value and hence afflicted with measurement error, these results do suggest that parental time plays some role—perhaps an important one—in influencing the probability of high-school graduation as well as teenage nonmarital births.

17. We have added the neighborhood variables to the basic equation. If, instead, the neighborhood variables are added to the specification reported in Table 4.17, the signs and significance of the neighborhood variables are essentially unchanged.

18. As indicated in our discussion in the first section of this chapter, a threshold relationship seems to exist for a number of variables, including this one. A specification of this relationship as linear will not capture this sort of nonlinear pattern.

APPENDIX 4A
SUMMARY STATISTICS

TABLE 4A.1 Correlation Matrix, Full Sample, $N = 1705$

Variable	African-American	Mother a Graduate	Location Moves
Dependent			
Graduated high school*	−.08	.21	−.19
Attend college*	−.14	.25	−.12
Years of education	−.17	.31	−.19
Independent			
African-American*	1.00	−.36	.04
Mother a high-school graduate*	−.36	1.00	−.04
Number of household location moves †	.04	−.04	1.00
Number of parental separations †	.02	.01	.28
Years lived in poverty †	.51	−.37	.12
Number of years lived with one parent †	.41	−.21	.20
Family ever received AFDC †	.40	−.27	.27
Average percentage of female heads †	.63	−.28	.04
Average percentage of youths who are high-school dropouts †	.37	−.31	.08

*Dummy variable that equals one if the person has the described characteristic.
† During ages 6–15.

Parental Separations	Years in Poverty	Years with One Parent	Family Received AFDC	% Female Heads	% Youth Dropouts
−.06	−.21	−.16	−.22	−.13	−.18
−.05	−.24	−.16	−.19	−.15	−.17
−.08	−.27	−.20	−.25	−.19	−.21
.02	.51	.41	.40	.63	.37
.01	−.37	−.21	−.27	−.28	−.31
.28	.12	.20	.27	.04	.08
1.00	.07	.29	.18	.07	.06
.07	1.00	.54	.57	.41	.29
.29	.54	1.00	.56	.44	.18
.18	.57	.56	1.00	.44	.23
.07	.41	.44	.44	1.00	.42
.06	.29	.18	.23	.42	1.00

TABLE 4A.2 Supplementary Correlation Matrix, Females Only, $N = 873$

Variable	All Females $N = 873$ Teenage Out-of-Wedlock Birth	Teenagers Who Had an Out-of-Wedlock Birth $N = 125$ Received Welfare within 3 Years
Independent		
African-American*	.26	.09
Mother a high-school graduate*	−.27	−.03
Number of household location moves †	.11	.09
Number of parental separations †	.17	.12
Number of years posttax family income < poverty line †	.25	.24
Number of years lived with one parent †	.25	.34
Family ever received AFDC †	.24	.27
Average percentage of female heads	.22	.03
Average percentage of youths who are high-school dropouts †	.18	.02
Dependent		
Graduated high school*	−.31	−.07
Attend college*	−.24	−.12
Years of education	−.29	−.08

Supplementary Correlation Matrix, Those Age 24 or More Only, $N = 765$

	Economically Inactive*
Independent	
African-American*	.21
Mother a high-school graduate*	−.19
Number of household location moves †	.06
Number of parental separations †	.05
Number of years posttax family income < poverty line †	.18
Number of years lived with one parent †	.15
Family ever received AFDC †	.15
Average percentage of female heads †	.18
Average percentage of youths who are high-school dropouts †	.14
Dependent	
Graduated high school*	−.13
Attend college*	−.19
Years of education	−.20

*Dummy variable that equals one if person has the described characteristic.
† Ages 6–15.

5

The Determinants
of Educational Attainment:
High School and Beyond

Education has long been viewed as the key to socioeconomic success. People with more education tend to have higher wage rates than those with less education, they obtain more generous fringe benefits associated with employment, are less likely to be unemployed, and tend to be in occupations with greater prestige. But the gains go beyond the labor market. Persons with more education tend to have better health, are better able to obtain the number of children they desire, are more efficient consumers, and appear to raise children who themselves are likely to receive more education. They are also more likely to contribute to the advancement of technology and to adapt to changing situations. For all of these reasons, and many more, the determinants of the level of education are of substantial interest to our society.

A prominent national survey undertaken regularly by the federal government tracks the school completion and educational attainment of young people in the United States. The survey is called "High School and Beyond." That same phrase is in the title of this chapter. However, rather than simply track U.S. students, here we try to understand— indeed, to "explain"—their schooling choices and their schooling attainments. We attempt to identify the factors that underlie these choices, focusing on the role of parental decisions in this process.

It is not hard to justify educational attainment as an important indicator of the success of young people. "Do well in school" has been preached to many generations of American children by their parents. For children from poor families wanting to make it to the middle class, and for middle- and upper-class children who want to do better than their parents, achieving high grades in a good school has been the recipe for labor market and economic success. Moreover, getting good grades in school has been seen as the ticket to more schooling. Indeed, there is evidence that educational attainment plays a larger role in determining labor market and economic success now than it has in the past. Few would be able to identify a more important indicator of the success of a young adult than educational attainment.

Most employers gauge educational attainment by the highest grade level that an individual has attained. Such a choice is likely to be an error for an employer: probably more attention should be focused on the course grades earned, the courses taken, and other learning-related activities. These latter items may be better predictors of how successful a new hire might be than simply the level of the highest grade attained. Like employers, we too measure educational attainment by the number of years of schooling. However, while employers could change their practices, for the purposes of this study, we cannot. Our PSID-based data set contains information that allows us to measure only the years of schooling as an indicator of the educational attainment of the children we study.

We use three indicators of educational attainment in the analyses reported here: whether or not a person graduated from high school; the number of years of schooling completed; and the decision to continue to postsecondary training (e.g., college), having graduated from high school. Each of these variables provides valuable, yet different, information on the decisions of individuals regarding the accumulation of human capital.

In today's society, clearly the first variable—high-school graduation—represents the minimum level of attainment that is necessary for securing entry level jobs that have career characteristics. The second variable reflects the extent of schooling chosen by individuals, measured in years. It provides little information on the determinants of choices made at particular crucial decision points, such as whether or not to drop out of school, or whether or not to continue beyond high school. Finally, the third variable focuses on the explicit decision of whether or not to seek education and training beyond secondary school.

After providing some background information on national trends in educational attainment and the implications of these trends in the first section, we present our estimates of the determinants of the choices of young adults regarding schooling. We then discuss the potential determinants of these choices, followed by our empirical estimates of models designed to explain these decisions. We present results for both the high-school graduation decision and for the number of years of completed schooling. Neighborhood correlates of these choices are presented, as well as the separate effects of parental decisions made at various times during the child's upbringing. In the fourth section, we present estimates of the effects of changes in the relevant explanatory variables on the level of the educational attainment outcomes through a simulation analysis. Finally, in the last two sections, we discuss and present estimates from a model that reflects the potential simultaneous decisions involving high-school graduation and postsecondary schooling.

EDUCATIONAL ATTAINMENT: SOME BACKGROUND

National Patterns of Educational Attainment

Over the postwar period, the level of education attained by the average American has increased steadily. In 1950, for example, the average American 25 years old or older had 9.3 years of education; by 1990, this had increased to 12.7 years. This trend is not surprising: during the 1980s, typical Americans that died had completed their education by the early 1930s, when being a high-school graduate was more the exception than the norm. Moreover, the baby-boom generation—those born after World War II and until the mid-1960s—completed their educations after 1970, when completing high school became both a national goal and a common choice.

This increase in the average level of education in the American population is reflected in an increased rate of high-school completion. In the cohort aged 25–29 in 1960, nearly 40 percent failed to graduate from high school; by 1989, among those aged 25–29 in that year this proportion had fallen to 14.5 percent.

Throughout the postwar period, the level of education of whites exceeded that of African-Americans; similarly, the proportion of whites from any given age cohort who graduated from high school exceeded that for African-Americans throughout this period. During the 1970s and 1980s, however, the difference in the levels of educational attainment between whites and nonwhites narrowed. By 1989, median education was 12.7 for African-Americans aged 25–29, compared to 12.9 for the overall population of that age group. Put another way, about 86 percent of whites aged 25–29 had graduated from high school, compared to about 82 percent of African-Americans in this age cohort. In 1970, twenty years earlier, the two percentages were 76 and 55. In 1970, the median level of schooling for African-Americans aged 25–29 was 12.1, compared to 12.6 for the overall population aged 25–29.

College attendance follows a somewhat different pattern, with a smaller reduction in racial differences. Among high-school graduates aged 18–21, about a third attended college in 1975, including nearly 35 percent of whites but only 25 percent of African-Americans. By 1989, nearly 40 percent of high-school graduates aged 18–21 were in college, including 42 percent of whites and 28 percent of African-Americans.

However, the pattern differs by sex. From 1975 to 1989, African-American female high-school graduates aged 18–21 substantially increased their college enrollment—from 26 to 33 percent. Over the same period, college attendance among comparable African-American males actually decreased, by about .6 to about 23 percent. Among whites the proportion of high-school graduates attending college increased for both sexes, but the increase was far larger for females—a 10 percentage point increase to 43 percent, versus a 3.5 percentage point increase to 40 percent for males.

These gains in the years of schooling say little about how much has been learned by students, or about the value of what has been learned. The spate of recent attention to the secular decline in test scores among America's high-school graduates is troubling in this regard.[1] It is quite possible that while rates of high-school completion—and the number of years of educational attainment—have increased, measured levels of learning and cognitive achievement have not. The indicators of educational success available in our data do not, unfortunately, shed light on actual levels of cognitive achievement; hence, we limit our analysis to the number of years of schooling attained. It is reasonable to expect that the years of schooling attained is correlated with the level of learning that has been achieved.

The Effects of Educational Attainment

As we have noted, the years of schooling completed is commonly taken to indicate the amount of human capital a person has accumulated. The level of the person's human capital, in turn, indicates the value of the labor services that he or she supplies to the market. The higher this value, the higher the probability that he or she will obtain employment.

Conditional on working, the higher the level of human capital, the higher the wage rate that a person can command, and the higher the probability that the person's job will be a career-type job carrying health and pension benefits, not a dead-end job lacking a clear job ladder.

To be sure, experience and specialized skills not learned in standard classrooms (e.g., musical or athletic proficiency) are also human capital, and they also increase the expected value of a person's earnings. Our analysis could be enriched if these aspects of a person's stock of human capital—as well as indications of the person's motivation and drive, and his or her appearance and physical characteristics—were included in our data. Unfortunately they are not.

Labor market success contributes to earnings and occupational status. And, the more success that a person has in the labor market—holding all other things constant—the lower the probability that that person will experience a variety of events or circumstances that are viewed as failures. We expect that the probability that an individual will live in poverty or be a welfare recipient is inversely related to educational attainment and labor market success. We expect the same to hold for the probability that a girl will have a teenage birth out-of-wedlock, or that a young male will be incarcerated.

While the accumulated stock of human capital conveys advantages in the labor market—advantages that can be measured in dollar terms—it also confers other advantages, some of which are not so easily measured. While labor market advantages are reflected in earnings differentials, these other benefits are typically not so valued. For example, holding all else constant, a person's own health status may be positively related to his or her level of schooling. Perhaps schooling fosters healthier lifestyles, more attention to preventive care, or better choices when health problems develop. Similarly, a variety of other positive nonmarket effects of schooling have been distinguished and studied—the quality of a person's children, the efficiency of the consumer choices he or she makes, the lower frequency of criminal activity, and the higher level of community involvement. All of these things, associated as they are with years of schooling, must be figured into any assessment of the success that comes with additional schooling.

One study that cataloged these nonmarket effects of education and assessed the literature on their quantitative importance concluded that the value of these impacts of education, when added to the market-valued benefits, increases the total by at least 50 percent.[2]

The implications of additional years of schooling, then, are substantial. Not only is the probability of labor market success increased by additional schooling, but the expected levels of a variety of other components of a happy and prosperous life are also augmented. Viewed from this broader perspective, then, educational attainment—years of schooling—is perhaps the most pervasive and reliable indicator of individual success in life. It is with this belief that we rely on it so heavily in this study.

What Factors Contribute to Educational Success?

Numerous factors have been mentioned as contributing to the educational attainment of children. In addition to a wide variety of background factors, these involve decisions made by government, by parents, and by children themselves. Before beginning our empirical analysis of the determinants of this aspect of attainment, it is helpful to form a catalog of potentially important factors. Such a list will remind us of the complexity of the process that produces educational success or failure and serve as a check on effects that we have found. No complete enumeration of the determinants of educational success would fail to include the following items:

- The values of a child's parents regarding education and success in school

- The extent of parental nurturing and monitoring of a child's school performance (e.g., the amount of child-care time offered by parents to their children, or the presence of one or two parents)

- Parental choices, such as their own education levels

- The economic resources (e.g., income) of a child's parents, reflecting both their choices regarding earnings relative to the benefits of other uses of time and the opportunities for the purchase of goods and services complementary to schooling

- Parental decisions during a child's formative years that may enhance or erode self-confidence, motivation, or security (e.g., parental separation and geographic moves)

- The quality of the schools attended by a child, reflected in the resources made available to the schools and the quality of their teachers

- The characteristics of the school (e.g., whether it is a private or a public school, and the racial and economic diversity of the students in the school)

- The characteristics of the neighborhood in which a child grows up; in particular the values of neighbors regarding schooling and the evidence that they project regarding the payoffs to education
- The characteristics of the friends and peers selected by the child
- The motivation, drive, and interest in learning possessed by the child
- The abilities of the child such as intelligence or artistic talent
- The characteristics of the labor market in which the child will supply labor services; in particular, the relative payoff in terms of net earnings and economic well-being attributable to additional years of schooling

Although this is a long list, we have clearly not identified all of the relevant factors. Because the factors on our list are interrelated in complex ways, it is extremely difficult to identify reliably the independent effect of any single factor apart from the effects of all of the others.

The results presented below are our attempt to measure the independent influence of those variables for which we have information. Of course, our success in accurately modeling the process of educational attainment depends upon the extensiveness of the information on each child included in our study—information on both governmental and parental investments in the child, and the child's own choices.

THE DETERMINANTS OF EDUCATIONAL ATTAINMENT

Our analysis builds on work by prior researchers who have sought to identify the determinants of educational success, and to measure their effects. Most of these studies employ information on individual children and the families in which they grow up. Our review of this work in Chapter 3 revealed a variety of factors that are consistently related to the schooling attainments of children. Parental education, family income, the number of parents in the child's family, parental expectations, and school and teacher quality and characteristics are among the more important of these factors.

Our study differs in several ways from most previous research on the determinants of educational attainment. First, we attempt to reflect in the structure of our models the view that a child's ultimate educational attainment is the result of conscious decisions made by society (e.g., regarding the community environment in which children live or the quality of the schools that they attend), by their parents, and by the children themselves. In effect, we view adolescents as conscious decision makers who process information on the gains and losses associated with specific options in an effort to enhance their well-being. Beyond the minimum number of years of education mandated by the state, children are viewed as choosing when to stop attending school; that decision determines the number of years of completed schooling attained.

Clearly, an important element in this individual maximizing decision is an appraisal of the labor market situation at the time a choice has to be made. Information regarding job prospects and available wages is, therefore, important in the decision process. At the high-school and college level, for example, the better the *current* job and earnings prospects, the higher the opportunity costs of remaining in school.

Set off against the assessment of current labor market prospects—and hence the opportunity costs of remaining in school—are a forecast of the gains in the *future* from additional schooling. These gains are associated with higher future earnings, or a trajectory implying increasing earnings attributable to schooling. The evaluation of these future gains and costs is made in a world in which there is substantial uncertainty concerning the relative rewards of various options. These gain and loss estimates clearly depend on a variety of characteristics of both the person and the family in which he or she has grown up. For example, having more-educated parents—or parents who work, or parents with high earnings—is likely to be associated with more reliable information on the relative costs and gains of alternative choices regarding educational attainment.

The second way our study differs from previous research is that we view these individual choices as nested in an environment that is determined by choices made by two other sets of decision makers—the society (or, more particularly, the government) and the child's parents. Decisions made by society and parents—for example, the resources devoted to schools attended by the child (in most cases, a government decision) and the amount of child-care time devoted to the child (a parental decision)—also influence individual choices regarding the amount of education to be sought. Similarly, the quality of the schooling provided children in their early years is likely to affect their tastes for schooling and their perception of their success at the education enterprise. Parental monitoring of school performance or expressions of expectations regarding schooling are also likely to influence the ultimate evaluations of gains and costs of incremental schooling made by the child. Additional such factors include the characteristics of the neighborhoods in which children grow up and the influence of parents as role models (suggesting that parental educational attainment is a factor affecting the schooling decisions of children).

The third way our study differs from previous ones is that, as implied in the previous paragraphs, we leaven this perspective on the determinants of education with the insights of other social scientists—sociologists and developmental psychologists—regarding the determinants of children's educational attainment. Hence, we identify parental decisions that create stress during children's formative years and that may alter their decisions regarding additional schooling. Similarly, considerations of the intergenerational transmission of attainments—for example, the effect of parental welfare receipt on children's success—are introduced into the analysis. Where possible, we group those factors from the long list of determinants that we are able to identify in our data into categories reflecting the decisions by society, parents, and children themselves.

The extensiveness of the variables that we have available in our data also distinguishes our effort to understand the determinants of educational attainment from the efforts of many previous researchers. Rather than testing a single hypothesis regarding the determinants of educational attainment, as many studies have done, we are able to introduce a rather full set of variables into the analysis, including variables consistent with several of the hypotheses that have been the subject of other studies. In this way, the independent effects of the full range of economic, family, and neighborhood factors can be measured, along with the basic background characteristics of the individual.

OUR BASELINE MODELS AND EMPIRICAL ESTIMATES

High-School Graduation

We view graduation from high school as indicating attainment of the most basic level of schooling success; hence, our first model specifies this outcome as a dependent variable. Our baseline estimates do not allow for the simultaneous determination of high-school graduation and other factors, nor do they view graduation as conditional upon prior attainments.[3]

Our estimates are based on a probit regression run over the 1705 individuals in our sample; the unweighted data are used for estimation. The dependent variable is equal to 1 if the individual completed high school by 1988, and 0 otherwise. The proportion of our sample who graduated from high school is .842.

Columns 1 and 2 of Table 5.1 show the results from a multivariate probit estimate in which a basic set of background characteristics are

TABLE 5.1 Determinants of High-School Graduation, Full Sample, Probit Estimation, $N = 1705$

Variable	Coefficient	t-statistic	Coefficient	t-statistic
Constant	.54	2.56**	1.29	4.38**
Background				
African-American	.40	3.94**	.25	1.68*
Female	.19	2.43**	−.03	.24
African-American × female			.40	2.40**
Parental Choices/Opportunities				
Any religion	.12	.84		
Catholic			.22	1.25
Jewish			4.12	.01
Protestant			.12	.27
Average number of siblings[a]	−.07	2.56**	−.04	1.37
Number of years lived with one parent[a]	−.03	3.12**	−.03	1.62
Father a high-school graduate or more	.49	4.33**		
Father a high-school graduate			.34	2.76**
Father some college			.62	2.80**
Father a college graduate			.29	1.24
Mother a high-school graduate or more	.34	3.60**		
Mother a high-school graduate			.28	2.85**
Mother some college			.63	2.71**
Mother a college graduate			4.87	.01
Average posttax family income ÷ poverty line[a]	.07	1.59		
Number of years posttax family income < poverty line[a]			−.01	.35
Number of years in poverty × AFDC[a]			−.01	.38
Number of years mother worked[a]	.02	2.00**	.03	2.17**
Number of years lived in SMSA[a]	−.01	.86	−.01	1.05
Number of household location moves[a]			−.13	5.35**
Number of parental separations[a]			.07	.66
Number of parental (re)marriages[a]			−.06	.43
Family Circumstances				
Number of years family head disabled[a]	−.07	4.91**	−.06	3.89**
Firstborn child			.28	2.35**
Head's parents poor			−.03	.30

Variable	Coefficient	t-statistic	Coefficient	t-statistic
Neighborhood Attributes				
Average percentage of female heads[a]			−.16	.34
Percentage of youths who are high-school dropouts[a]			−.02	3.46**
Average percentage of workers in high-prestige occupations[a]			$-.42^{-2}$	.64
Goodness of Fit				
Log likelihood	−644		−608	
Proportion predicted correctly	.845		.853	

NOTE: The model specifications include controls for whether both parents are in the sample in 1968, and whether the child's grandfather was foreign-born.

*Significant at 10 percent level.
**Significant at 5 percent level.

[a]During ages 6–15.

explanatory variables; it is taken from earlier results shown in Chapter 4. The parsimonious set of explanatory variables included in this model (all of which are defined in Appendix A), are grouped into the following categories:[4]

Background
    Female
    African-American
Parental Choices/Opportunities
    Mother a high-school graduate or more
    Father a high-school graduate or more
    Any religion
    Average posttax family income ÷ by poverty line, ages 6–15
    Number of years lived with one parent, ages 6–15
    Number of years mother worked, ages 6–15
    Average number of siblings, ages 6–15
    Number of years lived in SMSA, ages 6–16
Family Circumstances
    Number of years family head disabled, ages 6–15

Columns 3 and 4 of Table 5.1 present a more complete specification of variables in each of the categories. The explanatory variables included in this model are:

Background
  Female
  African-American
  African-American × female

Parental Choices/Opportunities
  Catholic ⎫
  Jewish ⎬ No religion is missing category
  Protestant ⎭
  Average number of siblings, ages 6–15
  Number of years lived with one parent, ages 6–15
  Father a high-school graduate ⎫
  Father some college ⎬ Father less than high-school graduate
  Father a college graduate ⎭ is missing category
  Mother a high-school graduate ⎫
  Mother some college ⎬ Mother less than high-school graduate
  Mother a college graduate ⎭ is missing category
  Number of years posttax family income < poverty line, ages 6–15
  Number of years family received AFDC, if poor, ages 6–15
  Number of years lived in SMSA, ages 6–15
  Number of household location moves, ages 6–15
  Number of parental separations, ages 6–15
  Number of parental (re)marriages, ages 6–15

Family Circumstances
  Number of years family head disabled, ages 6–15
  Head's parents poor
  Firstborn child

Neighborhood Attributes
  Average percentage female heads, ages 6–15
  Average percentage youths who are dropouts, ages 6–15
  Average percentage of workers in high-prestige occupations, ages
    6–15

The results of this basic model of Columns 1 and 2—described in
Chapter 4—can be summarized as follows:

- When a rich set of background and family and community circumstance factors is taken into account, African-American and female children are significantly more likely to graduate from high school than their race-gender counterparts
- Children who grow up in large families are significantly less likely to graduate

- Children who grow up in a single-parent family have a significantly lower probability of graduating

- Mother's and father's educational attainment is significantly related to graduation chances

- Economic resources (average income relative to the family's poverty line and whether or not the mother worked) appear to increase the child's chances of graduation

- Growing up in a family in which the head is disabled is significantly and negatively associated with the probability of graduating from high school

Most of the basic relationships seen in Column 1 are sustained in the richer specification of Column 3.[5] A few of the statistically significant coefficients in Column 1 become insignificant when additional family-based characteristics are included as explanatory variables. For example, when a variable is introduced that indicates whether or not the child is the first born in the family, it is positively and significantly related to the probability that the child will graduate from high school; however, then the variable indicating the total number of siblings loses its statistical significance. Similarly, the variable indicating the number of years that the child lived with one parent becomes statistically insignificant when the richer set of variables is included.

A somewhat different picture of the role of economic resources is conveyed in the richer specification. The primary income variable included in the equation is changed to indicate the number of years the family had income below the matched poverty line, rather than the continuous income measure. This specification is chosen to test the hypothesis that very low incomes may have a particularly adverse effect on educational attainment. In this specification, the father's and mother's education in their four-value form are viewed as measures of permanent income.

Although family income relative to the poverty line was marginally significant in the simple specification, the richer model that included poverty status and the receipt of welfare benefits[6] fails to predict that these circumstances are significantly related to graduation chances. The parental education variables, however, viewed as indicators of permanent income, suggest that income does play a significant role, although the coefficient on the highest level of schooling is not statistically significant.

The Column 3 specification reveals a number of additional insights into the factors affecting decision of children to complete high school. First, it appears that it is the completion of high school by parents (or perhaps having some postsecondary training) that plays the strongest role in explaining the choices of children regarding high-school graduation. While having a college degree is positively related to the probability that a parent's children will choose to graduate from high school, it is not significant.

Second, the number of geographic location moves made by the family while the child was growing up is strongly and negatively related to the chances that the child will choose to remain in high school until graduation. Geographic moves may make schooling more stressful in terms of both the education process itself—with changing curriculum and expectations—and the need to form new friends.

The estimates for the neighborhood variables suggest that the child who grows up in a neighborhood that has a high proportion of youths who are high-school dropouts will have a higher probability of dropping out of high school than a child growing up in a neighborhood with few dropouts: the t-statistic exceeds 3.0. Although the variable indicating the prevalence of female-headed families in the neighborhood has the expected sign, it is not significant. The variable indicating the prevalence of workers in high-prestige occupations in the neighborhood has an unexpected negative sign, though it too is not significant.[7]

We undertook tests of joint significance for the primary categories of variables distinguished in Column 3 of Table 5.1. For purposes of this test, we grouped the variables into the following categories: (1) race, gender, and religion; (2) parental education; (3) family stress (SMSA, moves, separations, remarriages, and disabled head); (4) family position (firstborn, number of siblings); (5) economic circumstance (years in poverty, years on AFDC, years mother worked); and (6) neighborhood attributes.[8] The race/gender/religion variables, as a group, are jointly significant at the 1 percent level, as are the parental-education, family-stress, family-position, and neighborhood attributes. The economic-circumstance variables are not jointly significant.

Completed Years of Education

Graduating from high school represents the most basic level of education required for success in today's economy. A more full-blown indicator is the number of years of schooling that an individual completes. Table 5.2 presents our empirical estimates of this educational outcome; the specifications and the categories of variables are the same as those

TABLE 5.2 Determinants of Years of Education, Full Sample, Tobit Specification, $N = 1705$

Variable	Coefficient	t-statistic	Coefficient	t-statistic
Constant	11.40	52.63**	12.36	44.91**
Background				
African-American	.41	4.03**	.27	1.83*
Female	.35	4.35**	−.03	.28
African-American × female			.66	4.22*
Parental Choices/Opportunities				
Any religion	.24	1.48		
Catholic			.37	2.20**
Jewish			−.14	.36
Protestant			.15	1.03
Average number of siblings[a]	−.07	2.30**	−.09	3.23**
Number of years lived with one parent	−.04	3.03**	−.04	2.62**
Father a high-school graduate or more	.66	6.22**		
Father a high-school graduate			.49	4.37**
Father some college			.83	5.20**
Father a college graduate			1.13	5.86**
Mother a high-school graduate or more	.46	4.96**		
Mother a high-school graduate			.40	4.27**
Mother some college			.66	3.90**
Mother a college graduate			1.27	4.93**
Average posttax family income ÷ poverty line[a]	.21	5.75**		
Number of years posttax family income < poverty line[a]			−.06	2.53**
Number of years in poverty × AFDC[a]			.04	1.69*
Number of years mother worked[a]	.01	.79	.01	.98
Number of years lived in SMSA[a]	−.00	.31	−.00	.10
Number of household location moves[a]			−.10	3.91**
Number of parental separations[a]			.14	1.19
Number of parental (re)marriages[a]			−.24	1.79*
Family Circumstances				
Number of years family head disabled[a]	−.05	2.87**	−.04	2.61**
Firstborn child			.11	1.08
Heads parent's poor			−.02	.21

TABLE 5.2 (*continued*)

Variable	Coefficient	t-statistic	Coefficient	t-statistic
Neighborhood Attributes				
Average percentage of female heads[a]			$-.75^{-2}$	1.59
Percentage of youths who are high-school dropouts[a]			$-.83^{-2}$	1.52
Average percentage of workers in high-prestige occupations[a]			$.42^{-2}$	.69
Goodness of Fit				
Log likelihood		-2686		-2645

NOTE: The model specifications include controls for whether both parents are in the sample in 1968, and whether the child's grandfather was foreign-born.

*Significant at 10 percent level.
**Significant at 5 percent level.

[a]During ages 6–15.

in Table 5.1 so as to facilitate comparison. Column 1 of Table 5.2 indicates the relationships estimated in the simple model analyzed in Chapter 4; Column 3 presents the results from our full specification.

The estimates in Table 5.2 are based on a tobit specification, again run over the 1705 children in our sample. Because some of the observations in the sample were still in school in the last year in which they are observed (1988), their completed years of education cannot be observed. Hence, we have created a variable that is the actual number of years of education completed by the children, unless they have completed more than 14 years.[9] Those observations with more than 14 years of schooling, or with 14 years of schooling and still in school, are assigned a value of 14 for the years of education completed. As a result, the dependent variable is truncated at 14 years, suggesting that ordinary least squares regression may yield biased estimates of the relationships at issue.

The Table 5.2 relationships convey much the same story as those in Table 5.1 regarding the determinants of the educational choices of children. In our discussion, we will indicate the additional—or different—insights revealed by Table 5.2 relative to Table 5.1.

The signs of all of the variables in the basic specification of Column

1 of Table 5.2 are the same as their counterparts in Table 5.1. In most cases, the significant relationships appear stronger in Table 5.2 than they do in Table 5.1. Two changes are noteworthy. First, although the income level of the family while the child was growing up was marginally significant in the high-school graduation probit, it is strongly significant (t-statistic = 5.75) in the equation for the years-of-schooling. This pattern is not unexpected; schooling through the 12th grade is essentially costless to the student and his or her family, while years of education beyond 12 typically require tuition and higher levels of foregone earnings. Family economic resources would seem to be more important determinants of student choices regarding these additional years of schooling.

Second, while the number of years that the mother worked was positively and significantly related to the probability that the child would graduate from high school, it loses its significance as a determinant of the number of years of completed education.

Several important differences are present in the results of the richer specification presented in Column 3 of Table 5.2. All of these differences occur in the family position, child-care time, parental educational orientation, and economic resource categories of variables.

First, while the dummy variable for being born first was significant in the high-school graduation model, the number of siblings is significant in the models of years of schooling completed. Although coming from a large family does not appear to affect adversely the chances of achieving the minimal level of educational attainment—graduating from high school—it does seem to reduce the number of years of education actually attained. With more children in a family, there are likely to be fewer economic resources available to any one of them for pursuing education beyond the high-school level.

Second, while the coefficient of the number of years the child lived with a single parent was not statistically significant in the high-school graduation model, it is significantly and negatively related to the number of years of schooling actually attained by a child. Perhaps this reflects less time invested in the child—or smaller resources in terms of assets or time spent in gathering information on higher education, or fewer ties to grandparents who might help support college. Third, the pattern of influence of the parental education variables differs substantially between the two models. Having a parent who graduated from college did not appear to be significantly related to the probability of graduating from high school; conversely, parents with a college education appear to have a very strong positive and significant relationship to the total number of years of education completed by a child. This may represent the importance of parental role models, the permanent income of the family, the effectiveness of parents in child-rearing, or simply the inherited characteristics of the child.

While the number of years that the mother worked was significantly and positively related to the child's probability of graduating from high school, it is not a statistically significant variable in our estimate of the determinants of the years of education completed. Conversely, the number of years in poverty appears to affect adversely and significantly the number of years of schooling completed, although it was not significantly related to the probability of high-school graduation. The receipt of welfare if the family was poor has a positive though not quite significant relationship to the years of education attained, again suggesting a positive link between economic resources and years of schooling.[10]

This pattern with regard to economic resources complements the finding regarding the number of siblings: family economic resources seem to be important factors in understanding how much schooling a child will attain, but not in predicting whether or not the child will complete high school. The results on parental college completion are consistent with this result as well.

Finally, in terms of neighborhood attributes, we find that the coefficient of the youth dropout variable is marginally significant, as is the coefficient of the variable indicating the prevalence of female-headed families in the neighborhood. For the completed years of education outcome, then, the adverse characteristics of the neighborhoods in which children grow up—a prevalence of youths who are high-school dropouts and of families headed by a female—appears to affect adversely the level of education that they attain.[11]

We again ran tests of joint significance on the groups of variables indicated above. All six of the groups of variables are jointly significant at the 1 percent level, with the exception of the family economic circumstance and neighborhood variables. The set of economic resource variables are significant at the 10 percent level and the neighborhood variables are significant at the 5 percent level. The patterns of significance observed in Table 5.1 are, in general, present in Table 5.2 as well.

In these estimates, then, we have modeled the determinants of children's educational attainment, giving special attention to those parental choices and opportunities most likely to influence the choices of children regarding educational attainments. Hence, our focus is on the availability of family economic resources to an individual child (the years the family lived in poverty, the number of siblings with whom family resources must be shared, and the educational level—and hence the earnings capacity—of the parents), the role-model effect of the level of educational attainment of the child's parents, and the stressful childhood events and circumstances that are likely to inhibit the aspirations of children and their educational decisions.

As expected, we find that economic resources play a more significant role in influencing the overall years of education completed than they do in influencing the probability of graduating from high school. The reason is likely to be the differential financial resources required to pursue schooling beyond the secondary level, including both direct costs (tuition, room, and board) and indirect costs (foregone earnings).

While our estimates include a rich specification of the parental choice/opportunity factors influencing children's decisions, there are a variety of other factors that we are unable to measure but that may, in their own right, significantly influence these decisions. The quality and socioeconomic/racial composition of the children's schools are clearly a relevant determinant, as are the economic opportunities available in the areas where children live and the macroeconomic performance affecting the labor markets in which they operate. Attitudes and expectations of the parents of the children, as well as the monitoring efforts that they give to their children's activities, are also likely to play some role, as will the inherent mental powers and physical characteristics of the children. Finally, the neighborhoods in which children live and the peers with whom they associate will influence the decisions about education that they make over their life course. With the exception of the characteristics of the neighborhoods in which children live, the rest of these considerations must remain as unobserved variables, given the information available in our data.

Time-Related Estimates

The estimates presented in Tables 5.1 and 5.2 show the effects of a variety of background, family position, economic circumstance, parental education, parental child-care time, family stress, and neighborhood factors on youths' educational decisions, but they reveal little about the differential impacts of the occurrence of the time-related variables. Does

TABLE 5.3 Estimates of Time-Related Determinants of Educational Attainment

Determinants	High-School Graduation		Years of Education	
	Coefficient	t-statistic	Coefficient	t-statistic
Years Lived with One Parent, Ages 6–8	−.07	1.12	−.04	.64
Years Lived with One Parent, Ages 9–11	.03	.33	−.02	.19
Years Lived with One Parent, Ages 12–15	−.02	.25	−.05	.53
Years in Poverty, Ages 6–8	−.02	.38	.03	.67
Years in Poverty, Ages 9–11	.03	.37	−.14	1.90*
Years in Poverty, Ages 12–15	−.04	.64	−.06	.85
Years Mother Worked, Ages 6–8	.04	1.20	.05	1.45
Years Mother Worked, Ages 9–11	−.07	1.31	−.07	1.36
Years Mother worked, Ages 12–15	.11	2.33**	.06	1.24
Number of Location Moves, Ages 6–8	−.21	4.81**	−.14	3.12**
Number of Location Moves, Ages 9–11	−.00	.02	.00	.05
Number of Location Moves, Ages 12–15	−.15	2.46**	−.14	2.33**
Years Family Head Disabled, Ages 6–8	−.03	.58	−.02	.40
Years Family Head Disabled, Ages 9–11	−.90	1.55	−.01	.10
Years Family Head Disabled, Ages 12–15	−.65	1.30	−.11	2.12**

NOTES: The variables shown are those time-related variables that are significant in either Column 3 of Table 5.1 or Column 3 of Table 5.2. The number of parental remarriages variable is not included (see text). Other predictor variables in the high-school graduation and years of education models are those listed in Column 3 of either Table 5.1 or Table 5.2.

* Significant at 10 percent level.
** Significant at 5 percent level.

the time during childhood that the family is poor or changes geographic location have an impact on educational attainment? Does child-care time or growing up in a family with a disabled head have a larger effect if these circumstances occur in adolescent years than if they occur in early childhood?

In Table 5.3, we present results on the impact of various events and circumstances at different points during the childhood years. We break up the childhood period over which we observe the individuals in our sample—ages 6–15—into three segments of three or four years each:

- Ages 6–8—Primary-school years
- Ages 9–11—Pre-adolescent years
- Ages 12–15—Adolescent years

Then, for each of these three childhood periods, we measure the effect of those economic, child-care time, and stress variables that can be identified with the child's age. These period-specific measures enable us to estimate the effect of the various parental decisions and circumstances occurring at various points during the childhood years. For example, does a geographic move have a greater adverse effect on a child's attainment if it occurs during the adolescent years, or (as is suggested by some) a more serious effect if it occurs early in the child's life—say, during the primary-school years?

Column 1 of Table 5.3 presents the results of these time-related variables for the full specification of the high-school graduation model of Column 3 of Table 5.1; Column 3 presents analogous results for the full specification of the years of completed years of education model of Column 3 of Table 5.2. We show the time-related results for those child-care time, economic circumstance, and stress variables that are statistically significant in *either* the high-school graduation or the years of completed schooling estimates (Column 3 of Tables 5.1 and 5.2).[12] These include the number of years living with one parent, years living in poverty, years of mother's work, location moves, and years living with a disabled family head. The estimates shown are from models that include all of the other predictor variables shown in Column 3 of Tables 5.1 and 5.2.[13]

The years spent living with one parent can be regarded as a proxy for the amount of parental time available to the child while he or she is growing up. Although this variable had a negative and significant effect on the number of years of completed education (and a marginally significant negative effect on the probability of graduating from high school), there does not appear to be any particular period during childhood when this effect is especially strong. Although the coefficients are persistently negative, none of the period-specific coefficients are statistically significant.

The number of years spent living in poverty was negatively related to both the probability of graduating from high school and the number of years of completed schooling, and was a statistically significant explanatory variable in the latter model. When entered into the model in time-period-specific form, the coefficients are, again, persistently negative, but in only one case—that of poverty during the pre-adolescent period, ages 9–11—is the coefficient statistically significant.

The number of years the mother worked while the child was growing up was positively related to the probability that the child would graduate from high school, and is statistically significant. It is also positively related to the completed years of schooling of the child, and is marginally significant. When the specific-period effects are estimated, the variable has a positive sign in the early and late childhood periods for both dependent variables, and a t-statistic in excess of 1.2 in all cases. This variable is statistically significant in the adolescent years in the high-school graduation model. For both educational outcome variables, the extent of the mother's work during the pre-adolescent period of ages 9–11 is negatively related to educational attainment, and for both of the outcome variables, the t-statistics are greater than 1.3.

The number of geographic moves during childhood had a large and negative effect on educational outcomes in both Tables 5.1 and 5.2. This variable maintains its strong negative effect when the timing of the geographic moves are considered. Interestingly, disrupting the child's physical location when he or she is young (8 years or less) or an adolescent (ages 12–15) has large, negative, and significant effects on both the probability of graduating from high school and the number of years of completed schooling. The latter effect is especially consistent with the common impression that disrupting children's peer group, school, and physical location while they are in high school is detrimental to school performance. The large and significant effects in the youngest age period are consistent with the view of child-development experts who stress the importance of events during the early years of life.

Finally, the years that a child spends living with a disabled parent is uniformly negative in all of the childhood periods. The effects are stronger when this stressful circumstance occurs during the last of the periods, when the child is an adolescent. This negative effect during the adolescent period is statistically significant in the years of education model.

SIMULATED EFFECTS

The probit and tobit coefficients of Tables 5.1 and 5.2, together with their t-statistics, show which of the independent variables are statistically significant correlates of the probability of completing high school and the number of years of completed schooling—our educational attainment variables. However, these coefficients give little indication of the extent to which changes in these outcomes are associated with changes in the independent variables.

In Table 5.4, we present *predicted* values of the two educational outcome variables associated with *assumed* values of the independent vari-

TABLE 5.4 Simulated Effects of Changes in Explanatory Variables: Predicted Value of Attainment Variable and Percentage Change from Population (Base) Value of Attainment Variable

Variable	Probability of Graduation	Percentage Change from Base	Years of Completed Schooling	Percentage Change from Base
Base	.88		13.0	
Mother/Father are High-School Graduates	.93*	6.4	13.6*	4.3
Family in Poverty 0 Years[a]	.88	0.5	13.0*	.3
Not on welfare, if poor[b]	.88	.2	13.0	−.2
On welfare, if poor[c]	.88	−.1	13.0	.1
Family Lived 0 Years with One Parent	.89	1.1	13.1*	.6
Four Family Location Moves	.83*	−5.9	12.8*	−1.8
Zero Family Location Moves	.91*	4.2	13.1*	1.1
Grew Up in "Bad" Neighborhood[d]	.80*	−9.0	12.5	−4.0
Grew Up in "Good" Neighborhood[e]	.91*	3.9	13.3	2.1
Mother Worked 10 Years	.90*	2.1	13.0	.4
Mother Worked 0 Years	.85*	−3.0	12.9	−.5
Parent is Disabled 10 Years	.77*	−11.8	12.6*	−3.0
Parent is Disabled 0 Years	.89*	1.7	13.0*	0.3
One more Sibling	.87	−.8	12.9*	−.7

[a] If family is poor in any year, income equal to the poverty line is assigned.
[b] If family is poor in any year, welfare = 0 is assigned.
[c] If family is poor in any year, welfare = 1 is assigned.
[d] Proportion in neighborhood of households headed by a female and proportion of youths who are dropouts set = 40; proportion of those who work in neighborhood who are in high-prestige occupations set = 0.
[e] Proportion in neighborhood of households headed by a female and proportion of youths who are dropouts set = 0; proportion of those who work in neighborhood who are in high-prestige occupations set = 40.

*Based on a coefficient that is statistically significant at 5 percent level.

ables taken one at a time, *ceteris paribus*. In obtaining the numbers in Column 1, we use the full specification of the probit equation described in Column 3 of Table 5.1 to estimate the probability of graduating from high school for each individual in our sample, when the stipulated independent variable is assigned the value indicated in the stub of the table, while the level of each of the other variables is kept at its actual level. The value reported in the table is, in each case, the weighted average over the individuals of these predicted values (multiplied by their population weights).[14] Hence, the values in Column 1 of Table 5.4 show how the predicted probabilities differ from .88, the base probability for the national population, obtained when the actual value of all of the independent variables for each weighted individual are used in the simulation. An analogous procedure is used for the predicted years of completed schooling found in Column 3, again using the full specification of the tobit equation in Column 3 of Table 5.2.

The values shown in Columns 1 and 3 of Table 5.4 can be used to infer the quantitative effect on the probability of graduating from high school—and the number of years of completed schooling—associated with changes in the values of the independent variables, taken one at a time. In Columns 2 and 4, we present the percentage changes from the base value in each of the models attributable to the changed values of the independent variables indicated in the table. Only a few of these effects are noted here, as their interpretation in the table is straightforward.

In the high-school graduation model, some of the simulated changes in the independent variables yield rather large changes in the probability of graduating from high school. For example, if all of the parents of the children had been high-school graduates while the children were growing up, we estimate that 93 percent of the children would have graduated from high school, compared to the actual value of 88 percent—an increase of 6.4 percent. Large changes in outcomes are also observed for simulated changes in the number of location moves, years living with a disabled parent, and the neighborhood variables. Our results suggest that if all the children in our sample had grown up in the worst-quality neighborhoods, only 80 percent of them would have graduated from high school, a decrease of 9 percent. Similarly, were the family of every child to have moved four times during the childhood years, we estimate that the high-school graduation rate would have been 6 percent less than the national base rate of 88 percent.

Most of the patterns revealed in Columns 1 and 2 of the table are also seen in the simulations for the completed years of schooling model. Again, the largest percentage effects are associated with the variables for the parental education, location moves, years lived with a disabled parent, and neighborhood quality. The percentage changes simulated in this model are substantially smaller than those in the high-school graduation model. The changes in the independent variables that we have simulated shift the entire national distribution of years of completed education either up or down, with the effect of the shift on the mean (in percentage change terms) being less than the effect on the high-school completion outcome.

A BIVARIATE PROBIT ESTIMATE OF HIGH-SCHOOL AND POSTSECONDARY EDUCATION CHOICES

The estimates that we have presented in the last three sections have sought to explain two related educational outcomes—high-school graduation and the number of years of completed schooling—by means of single-equation estimation techniques. Our aim has been to include as extensive a set of family-based characteristics as possible in order to minimize the chances of biases resulting from the omission of important unobserved variables. This approach, however, neglects the fact that in making education choices, decisions at later stages of the process are contingent on—or conditioned by—outcomes at earlier stages. For example, the decision to undertake postsecondary schooling is, with few exceptions, conditional on graduating from high school. Given this, estimates of the postsecondary schooling choice—or the decision of how many years of schooling to complete—made without considering the high-school graduation outcome could be biased.

The Nature of the Model

Here we attempt to model the decision of individuals to undertake postsecondary schooling, recognizing that the high-school graduation outcome is prior to, and influences (or conditions), the decision to continue schooling beyond high school. In this sense then, the two decisions are mutually interdependent, or simultaneous. The decision of whether to opt for postsecondary schooling depends on whether or not the child has graduated from high school; at the same time, whether the child chooses to stay in school until a high-school diploma is earned depends upon his or her expectations regarding whether or not postsecondary schooling will be chosen. Hence, our approach is, first, to estimate the relationship of a number of background, parental choice/opportunity, family circumstance, and neighborhood variables to the high-school graduation outcome, and then to measure the separate effects of those variables most pertinent to the postsecondary schooling decision on that conditional choice. Our model is a simultaneous model, in that the decision regarding high-school completion is influenced by the likelihood that continuing schooling beyond high school would be chosen, if matriculation occurs. Through such a modeling approach, consistent estimates of the postsecondary schooling decision can be obtained by correcting for the process whereby some young people complete high school and others do not. In addition, through this approach, the influence of the various factors that are particularly pertinent to each stage of the process can be identified.

Our model also attempts to use as explanatory variables those factors that are prior to or distinct from the education choices being modeled. In this we are only partially successful. In some sense, nearly all observed characteristics of the family in which a child grows up—for example, whether the family is headed by one or two parents, or the parents' income level—may reflect some underlying drive (or value, or motivation) that could also influence how much education the child will choose. In this case, empirical modeling of decisions becomes intractable. However, in practice, some observed variables are more suspect than others, and the effort of the researcher must be to purge the more questionable of these variables of their "endogeniety" with the dependent variables.[15]

A formal statement of the bivariate probit econometric model that we employ is presented in Appendix B at the end of the volume.

Estimating Procedures

The bivariate probit model is estimated using full information maximum likelihood techniques. We estimate simultaneously the decision of the individual to graduate from high school and the decision to continue schooling beyond the postsecondary level, conditional on the high-school graduation decision. The high-school graduation outcome is a variable equal to 1 if the child has completed 12 years of schooling. The decision to continue schooling beyond secondary school is a variable equal to 1 if the individual has observed years of schooling in excess of 12.

The sample of 1705 children described in Appendix A forms the basis of our estimate. Of these children, 1437 (84 percent) have graduated from high school; of these 1437 children, 618 (43 percent of the high-school graduates, 36 percent of the sample) have opted for schooling beyond high-school matriculation.

As in our prior estimates, the explanatory variables have been grouped into four categories: (1) background factors, (2) parental choices/opportunities, (3) family circumstances, and (4) neighborhood or community attributes.

We present the results from two variants of the bivariate probit model. First, we present a very parsimonious model that employs a subset of the explanatory variables used in our estimates shown in Tables 5.1 and 5.2. These variables reflect parental choices/opportunities, family circumstances, and neighborhood attributes over the entire childhood period, ages 6–15, and emphasize those that appeared to be significantly related to the education outcomes in Tables 5.1 and 5.2.

Second, we expand this model by recognizing that parental choices/opportunities, family circumstances, and neighborhood attributes that occur close to the time at which the child makes the decision whether or not to opt for postsecondary schooling are more likely to effect that decision than the occurrence of these factors during the early childhood years. Hence, in that part of the bivariate model focusing on the postsecondary schooling choice, we measure the number of years during which a particular parental decision or circumstance could occur over the child's ages 16–18 (rather than ages 6–15).

ESTIMATES FROM THE BIVARIATE PROBIT MODELS

A Parsimonious Specification Using Childhood Variables

In Table 5.5, we present the results of the bivariate probit estimation that employs a subset of those explanatory variables found to be significantly related to educational attainments in Tables 5.1 and 5.2. We view this estimate as a transition to our more full-blown model and as a test of the potential interdependence (simultaneity) of the high-school graduation and postsecondary schooling choices.

Consistent with our investment-in-children choice framework, we included in the high-school graduation component of the model: (1) parental choices reflecting their own educational attainments, (2) the number of siblings of the child, (3) the time the mother spent working, and (4)

TABLE 5.5 Bivariate Probit Estimates: High-School Graduation and Subsequent Postsecondary Schooling: Parsimonious Model

Variable	High-School Graduation $N=1705$		Postsecondary Schooling $N=1437$	
	Coefficient	t-statistic	Coefficient	t-statistic
Constant	1.24	7.28**	−.71	4.17**
Background				
African-American	.24	1.84*	−.04	.32
Female	−.03	.21	.11	1.19
African-American × female	.40	2.33**	.41	2.68**
Parental Choices/Opportunities				
Catholic	.14	1.22		
Average number of siblings[a]	−.07	2.55**	−.05	1.93*
Father high-school graduate	.34	2.72**	.28	2.59**
Father some college	.64	2.95**	.49	3.45**
Father a college graduate	.40	1.70*	.65	3.89**
Mother a high-school graduate	.27	2.63**	.16	1.70*
Mother schooling beyond high school	.78	3.37**		
Mother some college			.22	1.50
Mother a college graduate			.46	2.27**
Average family income ÷ poverty line[a]			.11	4.25**
Number of location moves[a]	−.11	4.99**	−.01	.21
Number of years lived with one parent[a]	−.04	2.75**		
Years mother worked[a]	.03	2.62**		
Family Circumstances				
Years family head disabled[a]	−.06	4.26**		
Neighborhood Attributes				
Average percentage of youths who are dropouts[a]	−.02	3.74**		
Goodness of Fit				
Rho	−.41	1.69*		
Log likelihood	−1488.7			

NOTE: The model specification also includes a control variable for whether both parents are in the sample in 1968.

*Significant at 10 percent level.
**Significant at 5 percent level.

[a]During ages 6–15.

the years the child lived with one parent, (along with the standard gender and race variables). In addition, we included the two family-circumstance and neighborhood variables that appeared to be related to this choice in Table 5.1. In the postsecondary schooling segment of the model, we added the income variable of the parents but eliminated some of the other variables that did not appear significantly related to years of schooling in Table 5.2.

The Rho test for the simultaneity of this parsimonious bivariate specification is marginally significant (t-statistic = 1.69, Wald test = 2.86).[16] This provides some, though limited, evidence that these two decisions of the child are, indeed, interdependent or simultaneous. The decision of whether to complete high school is taken in light of expectations regarding schooling beyond high school, and vice versa.[17]

In Table 5.5, we find that the race and gender background variables are significantly related to both of the educational outcomes, consistent with our findings in the second section of this chapter. The t-statistic on the race variable is marginally significant in the high-school graduation model (Column 4, Table 5.1) as well as in the high-school graduation segment of this bivariate model. The Catholic variable maintains its positive sign, but it is also statistically insignificant in the bivariate specification[18] of the model. Parental education is significantly related to both the high-school graduation decision and to the choice of postsecondary schooling. Unlike the earlier results, the mother's schooling is significant in the postsecondary schooling decision; the effects of the father's schooling dominate those of the mother's schooling in both choices.[19]

The number of siblings is negatively related to both education decisions; whereas this variable is significant in only the years-of-education specification of Table 5.2, here it is statistically significant in both components of the specification. The negative effect of more siblings in the decision to pursue postsecondary schooling would appear to reduce the probability of graduating from high school. The effect of family income on the probability of pursuing postsecondary schooling remains significantly and positively related to the probability of attending college after graduating from high school. The signs and significance levels of the remaining variables are as expected.

A Full Specification Using Decision-Proximate, Time-Specific Variables

The bivariate probit estimate that we present in Table 5.6 is full-bodied and indicates the effect of our time-specific explanatory variables

TABLE 5.6 Bivariate Probit Estimates: High-School Graduation and Subsequent Postsecondary Schooling: Full-Specification Using Decision Proximate Variables

Variable	High-School Graduation N = 1705		Postsecondary Schooling N = 1437	
	Coefficient	t-statistic	Coefficient	t-statistic
Constant	1.31	5.85**	−.80	4.01**
Background				
African-American	.29	2.17**	−.06	.48
Female	−.02	.15	.10	1.03
African-American × female	.38	2.24**	.41	2.72**
Parental Choices/Opportunities				
Catholic	.17	1.43		
Average number of siblings[a]	−.07	2.41**	−.04	1.25
Father high-school graduate	.34	2.62**	.29	2.71**
Father some college	.64	2.61**	.45	3.16**
Father a college graduate	.38	1.59	.60	3.66**
Mother a high-school graduate	.27	2.65**	.17	1.81*
Mother schooling beyond high school	.77	3.30**	.31	2.27**
Average posttax family income ÷ poverty line[a]	.02	.60		
Average posttax family income ÷ poverty line, 16–18			.06	2.02**
Family ever received AFDC[a]	−.07	.59		
Number of years lived with one parent[a]	−.03	2.28**	.02	.57
Number of years lived in SMSA[a]	−.01	1.27	.04	1.37
Number of household location moves[a]	−.11	4.64**	−.09	1.56
Number of parental separations[a]			−.11	.74
Number of parental (re)marriages[a]			.15	.77
Number of years mother worked[a]	.03	2.28**		
Family Circumstances				
Number of years family head disabled[a]	−.07	4.15**	−.02	.55

172

Variable	High-School Graduation $N=1705$		Postsecondary Schooling $N=1437$	
	Coefficient	t-statistic	Coefficient	t-statistic
Neighborhood Attributes				
Average percentage of youths who are high-school drop-outs[a]	−.01	3.41**		
Average percentage of workers in high-prestige occupa-tions[a]			−.01	2.99**
Average percentage of female heads[a]			−.00	.57
Goodness of Fit				
Rho	−.46	2.09**		

NOTE: The model specification includes a control variable for whether both parents are in the sample in 1968.

*Significant at 10 percent level.
†Significant at 5 percent level.

[a]During ages 6–15.

measured prior, but proximate, to the relevant decisions. In this speci-fication, the time-specific variables in the high-school graduation deci-sion segment of the model are measured over the child's ages 6–15; those included in the postsecondary schooling choice segment are mea-sured over the child's ages 16–18—just prior to the college-going choice.

In addition to the variables included in the parsimonious specifica-tion, we add parental decisions regarding family disruption and forma-tion, geographic location moves, living in an SMSA, and neighborhood variables indicating the prevalence of high-status occupation workers and families headed by a female.

The estimates from this expanded model are substantially richer than those of the parsimonious model. In this case the value of Rho is statis-tically significant—in this case, at the 5 percent level—indicating that the decisions of youths regarding whether or not to complete high school and whether, having graduated from high school, to pursue post-secondary schooling are made simultaneously. Apparently, expectations regarding schooling after high school significantly affect the decision of whether or not to graduate from high school.[20]

Having compared the results of the parsimonious specification with those in Tables 5.1 and 5.2, we here compare the results of our extended model with those shown in Table 5.5. The estimates of the effects of the background variables in Table 5.6 are nearly identical with those in Table 5.5. While the variables indicating parental educational choices show much the same pattern of effect in the two tables, the measured effect of the number of siblings changes between the two estimates. While this variable is significantly related to both of the education outcomes in Table 5.5, it is significantly related only to the high-school graduation component of the model reported in Table 5.6. While the number of location moves was insignificant in postsecondary schooling component of the parsimonious model (Table 5.5), in Table 5.6, location moves—in this case, measured over the ages of 16–18—is marginally significant (t-statistic = 1.56).

Finally, the percentage of the employed persons with high-status occupations in the neighborhood in which the youth lived while growing up is positively and significantly related to the probability of choosing postsecondary schooling in the Table 5.6 results. This variable is not significantly related to either the high-school graduation decision or to the number of years of education, shown in Tables 5.1 and 5.2.

CONCLUSION

In this chapter we have attempted to identify the family-based decisions and circumstances and the community characteristics that economists and other social scientists have identified as potential determinants of the educational success of children. We measured educational attainment in two ways: first, whether or not a child graduated from high school; and second, the number of years of schooling that the child completed. Both a parsimonious model of determinants, and then a more full-blown model that incorporated a very extensive set of potential determinants of educational success, were estimated.

We have summarized the findings of our estimations throughout the chapter. Here we present a heuristic overview of the main results. The overall story that our estimates tell runs something as follows:

> When a very extentive set of family and neighborhood variables are included in the analysis, both gender and race appear to influence the num-

ber of years of schooling attained; *ceteris paribus,* being African-American and female are associated with a higher probability of graduating from high school, and with a larger number of years of schooling completed. Growing up in a Catholic family also has a positive effect. The amount of parental time available while growing up—including the presence of two parents in the home—is positively related to educational attainment. However, where the child fits in the family pecking order also affects educational opportunities and attainments; being firstborn and having fewer siblings appears to increase the probability of graduating from high school, as well as the amount of education attained. Both the educational level of the parents—especially having a college degree—and the economic resources available to the family (proxied by the number of years that the family was in poverty) are positively related to educational progress. And, significantly, the stresses encountered by a child while growing up—especially the number of geographic moves that are experienced and the presence of a disabled family head—seem to inhibit the number of years of schooling that a child achieves. Children who grow up in a neighborhood with poor role models—such as a very high proportion of high-school dropouts among the youths living there, or a high fraction of the families headed by a female—tend to have lower levels of educational attainment than children who grow up in neighborhoods with a higher proportion of high-school completers, or more intact families.

NOTES

1. As noted in Chapter 1, average SAT scores declined from about 1970 to the early 1980s, then increased moderately to 1985. The scores remained at about the 1985 level until 1989, and then decreased slightly until the early 1990s. Recent years have recorded a modest increase in the average math score. We note, however, that the proportion of high-school graduates who have taken the test has increased fairly steadily since 1977, with only a slight dip in 1990.

2. See Haveman and Wolfe (1984).

3. However, in results presented below, we estimate the probability of graduation from high school as simultaneous with the decision to attend postsecondary school. In this model, attending college is viewed as an educational outcome, the occurrence of which occurs after graduating from high school, but is potentially causal to the graduation decision.

4. For the event (or occurrence) variables measured over ages 6–15, we code the variables for each year from the child's age from 6–15, assigning a value of 1 if the event/circumstance occurred or existed in that year, and 0 otherwise. Then, we totaled the number of events or occurrences over the 10-year period.

5. It has been suggested that the underlying process determining educational attainment may differ between African-Americans and non-African-

Americans, and the significant coefficient on the race variables indicates that race plays an important role in determining educational attainment. We conducted a test for structural differences in the slope coefficients of models equivalent to those shown in Column 3 run over the African-American and non-African-American subsamples. We used a test of omitted variables where the variables omitted in the full sample specification are the independent variables interacted with race (see Engle [1984], pp. 776–826). Using the full specification shown in Column 3 of Table 5.1, the test indicated that the null hypothesis of no structural difference could not be rejected at a 10 percent significance level. Nevertheless, we show the results of this model separately for African-Americans and non-African-Americans in Appendix 5.A to this chapter.

6. The variable for welfare benefits is only given a positive value for any year *if* the child lives in a family whose income is below the poverty line *and* receipt of welfare income is reported for the family.

7. In results not shown here, we tested the conjecture that neighborhood effects are nonlinear, with larger effects associated with prevalence that exceeds some threshold. From the cross-tabulations in Chapter 4, the ratio of 40 percent seemed to indicate a breaking point, and we adopt that level in a set of spline estimations. In the full specification, the youth dropout prevalence variable was negatively related to the probability of high-school graduation up to the 40 percent level, but was not significant. It was significant beyond 40 percent (t-statistic = 2.18), indicating that neighborhoods in which the youth population contains a very large proportion of dropouts have a deleterious effect on the probability of high-school graduation for children who grow up in them. Similarly, the prevalence of female-headed families in the neighborhood was not significant at levels less than 40 percent, but was significant at the 10 percent level (t-statistic = 1.78) when the proportion of households headed by a woman exceeded 40 percent. We also tested the hypothesis that neighborhood characteristics have significantly different effects on African-Americans than on non-African-Americans, but none of the nonwhite neighborhood interaction terms were statistically significant.

8. These specifications were tested using the likelihood ratio test, which compares the restricted model to the unrestricted model: this ratio is distributed chi square with degrees of freedom equal to the number of restricted variables.

9. We chose 14 years since the youngest age group in the sample was 21 years old as of 1988 and hence may still have been in school. If they attended school without any interruptions they will have 15 or 16 years of education by 1988. The choice of 14 years as the upper truncation is consistent with an interruption of a year or two.

10. Interpretation of these results is not straightforward, and requires that the coefficients of years in poverty and years on AFDC if the family was poor be combined in order to understand the pattern being described. These

results suggest that, overall, the influence of being poor is negative with regard to years of education. If, however, welfare is received if the family is poor, the negative association is somewhat reduced: combining the coefficients yields a negative $-.02$ if the family is poor and receives welfare, as compared to $-.06$ if the family is poor but does not receive welfare.

11. The conjectures regarding the threshold effect of neighborhood characteristics and their differential effects by racial group were also tested using the specification for the number of years of schooling completed. For this educational outcome, none of the coefficients of the extreme values of the neighborhood characteristics were significant. Similarly, the effects of the neighborhood characteristics did not appear to differ significantly by racial group.

12. The exception to this statement is the parental remarriages variable, which was marginally significant only in Table 5.2.

13. With the exception of the SMSA and remarriages variables, the time-related variables not shown in Table 5.3 were entered into the equations with the same three age categories. The effects of the non-time-related variables—e.g., gender, race, parental education, and so on—are not shown in Table 5.3. The signs and significance levels of these variables when included with the time-related variables show very little change from those reported in Tables 5.1 and 5.2.

14. By calculating the weighted-average prediction, our simulated values represent the predicted values for the nation as a whole rather than for our sample observations.

15. One could argue that deep-seated underlying—and unobserved—factors such as drive, constitution, motivation, creativity, mental capacity, or energy influence nearly everything that we observe about parental choices, as well as influencing the educational decisions of their children. These factors, for example, could determine the choice of parental educational levels, whether the parents of the children were immigrants, the number of siblings of the child, whether or not the family lives in a city or on a farm, whether the parents decide to stay together or to split up, or whether the parents decide to change geographic location often or not. Indeed, some argue that these factors are correlated with both race and outcomes such as education. While such possibilities cannot be totally ruled out, the modeling problem soon becomes infeasible if one attempts to model all of these potential interdependencies.

16. The Wald test-statistic has a critical value of 2.7 for the 10 percent level and 3.84 for the 5 percent level of significance.

17. Expanded versions of this model, including virtually all of the variables in Tables 5.1 and 5.2, had Rho statistics of the same sign as that shown in Table 5.5, but they were not statistically significant.

18. Note that the specification of religion in the two models is somewhat different. In this bivariate specification, Catholic is the lone religion variable,

with all other responses being the omitted category. In Tables 5.1 and 5.2, three religion variables were entered, with "no religion" being the omitted category.

19. In the bivariate probit specification for high-school graduation, the postsecondary schooling decision of the child's mother is collapsed into one category. In Tables 5.1 and 5.2, some college is distinct from being a college graduate. However, the small number of mothers with a college degree constrains our ability meaningfully to measure the potential effect of this category.

20. A possible alternative explanation is that there are unmeasured variables involving tastes, abilities, or motivation that simultaneously affect both the high-school graduation decision and the choice of whether or not to attend college. In the absence of data measuring these characteristics, we do not test this explanation.

APPENDIX 5A
RACE-SPECIFIC RESULTS
FOR THE HIGH-SCHOOL GRADUATION
AND YEARS OF EDUCATION MODELS

In the third section and Tables 5.1 and 5.2 of this chapter, we report the results of our estimation of the determinants of the probability of graduation from high school and the number of years of completed education. These base estimates indicate that the race of the individual has a statistically significant impact on both of the variables: African-Americans tend to have both a higher probability of graduating from high school and a greater number of years of completed education after controlling for the other factors indicated in the tables.

Although our statistical tests indicated that the slope coefficients on the nonrace variables did not differ significantly by race, because a few of the variables show different results by race we show race-specific results analogous to those in Tables 5.1 and 5.2 in this appendix.

Tables 5A.1 and 5A.2 present results on the determinants of high-school graduation analogous to those in Table 5.1 for both African-Americans and non-African-Americans; Tables 5A.3 and 5A.4 present race-specific results for the years of completed schooling variables, analogous to those in Table 5.2.

Comparing the high-school graduation results in Tables 5A.1 and 5A.2 with those in Table 5.1, only a few race-specific differences appear. For the female and firstborn variables, the coefficient is positive and significant for both the total sample and for African-Americans; however, it is positive but not significant for non-African-Americans. For number of years the mother has worked, the coefficient is positive in all cases; it is significant in the pooled sample and non-African-American estimate, but not in the African-American model.

Generally similar results regarding the determinants of completed years of schooling are also shown for the African-American and non-African-American estimates in Tables 5A.3 and 5A.4, as compared to those in Table 5.2. As with the high-school graduation results, the female variable is positively and significantly related to the number of years of completed schooling for both the pooled sample and for African-Americans; while the coefficient is positive in the non-African-American estimates, it is not significant. Not surprisingly, given the small number of African-American Catholics in our data, this variable—although positively related to years of schooling—is not statistically sig-

TABLE 5A.1 Determinants of High-School Graduation, African-American Probit Estimation   N = 779

Variable	Coefficient	t-statistic	Coefficient	t-statistic
Constant	.91	2.46**	1.36	2.72**
Background				
Female	.37	3.30**	.36	3.08**
Parental Choices/Opportunities				
Any religion	.14	.57		
Catholic			.29	.81
Protestant			.19	.78
Average number of siblings[a]	−.09	2.46**	−.05	1.20
Number of years lived with one parent[a]	−.04	2.46**	−.03	1.27
Father a high-school graduate or more	.57	2.78**		
Father a high-school graduate			.52	2.23**
Father some college			4.86	.02
Father a college graduate			−.35	.54
Mother a high-school graduate or more	.31	2.25**		
Mother a high-school graduate			.19	1.27
Mother some college			.76	1.56
Mother a college graduate			3.90	.00
Average posttax family income ÷ poverty line[a]	.07	.71		
Number of years posttax family income < poverty line[a]			−.03	.92
Years in poverty × AFDC[a]			−.00	.19
Number of years mother worked[a]	.02	1.30	.02	1.12
Number of years lived in SMSA[a]	−.02	1.15	−.01	.78
Number of household location moves[a]			−.16	4.47**
Number of parental separations[a]			.21	1.32
Number of parental (re)marriages[a]			−.01	.07
Family Circumstances				
Number of years family head disabled[a]	−.05	2.51**	−.04	1.86*
Firstborn child			.40	2.11**
Head's parents poor			−.05	.34
Neighborhood Attributes				
Average percentage of female heads[a]			−.00	.63

Variable	Coefficient	t-statistic	Coefficient	t-statistic
Average percentage of youths who are high-school dropouts[a]			−.01	1.70*
Average percentage of workers in high-prestige occupations[a]			.01	.61
Goodness of Fit				
Log likelihood		−319		
Proportion predicted correctly			.825	

*Significant at 10 percent level.
**Significant at 5 percent level.

[a]During ages 6–15.

nificant for African-Americans; for both non-African-Americans and the pooled sample, the coefficient of Catholic religion is both positive and significant or nearly so. The results for parents completing college also differ somewhat by race; the coefficients are positive in all cases, but are not significant for African-Americans. Minor differences are also observed between the races for the years spent with one parent (negative in all three estimates, but not quite significant for non-African-Americans), the number of remarriages (negative and significant for non-African-Americans and the pooled sample; not significant for African-Americans), and the number of years living with a disabled head (negative in all estimates; not significant only in the case of African-Americans).

TABLE 5A.2 Determinants of High-School Graduation, Non-African-American Sample Probit Estimation, $N = 926$

Variable	Coefficient	t-statistic	Coefficient	t-statistic
Constant	.55	2.00**	1.23	3.12**
Background				
Female	−.00	.02	.02	.13
Parental Choices/Opportunities				
Any religion	.16	.86		
Catholic			.18	.81
Protestant			.18	.92
Average number of siblings[a]	−.05	1.10	−.03	.61
Number of years lived with one parent[a]	.03	1.27	−.01	.21
Father a high-school graduate or more	.42	3.15**		
Father a high-school graduate			.27	1.74*
Father some college			.61	2.47**
Father a college graduate			.34	1.25
Mother a high-school graduate or more	.39	3.05**		
Mother a high-school graduate			.37	2.62**
Mother some college			.61	2.18**
Mother a college graduate			4.92	.01
Average posttax family income ÷ poverty line[a]	.06	1.23		
Number of years posttax family income < poverty line[a]			−.01	.20
Years in poverty × AFDC[a]			−.00	.03
Number of years mother worked[a]	.02	1.34	.04	1.86*
Number of years lived in SMSA[a]	−.00	.19	−.01	.41
Number of household location moves[a]			−.11	3.10**
Number of parental separations[a]			−.14	.80
Number of parental (re)marriages[a]			−.03	.17
Family Circumstances				
Number of years family head disabled[a]	−.11	4.83**	−.11	4.26**
Firstborn child			.15	.97
Head's parents poor			−.08	.64
Neighborhood Attributes				
Average percentage of female heads[a]			.02	1.34

Variable	Coefficient	t-statistic	Coefficient	t-statistic
Average percentage of youths who are high-school dropouts[a]			−.02	3.41**
Average percentage of workers in high-prestige occupations[a]			−.01	1.28
Goodness of Fit				
Log likelihood		−278		
Proportion predicted correctly			.883	

*Significant at 10 percent level.
**Significant at 5 percent level.

[a] During ages 6–15.

TABLE 5A.3 Determinants of Years of Education, African-American Tobit Specification

Variable	Coefficient	t-statistic	Coefficient	t-statistic
Constant	11.72	32.01**	12.83	26.68**
Background				
Female	.66	5.99**	.65	5.96**
Parental Choices/Opportunities				
Any religion	.35	1.45		
Catholic			.28	.81
Protestant			.32	1.28
Average number of siblings[a]	−.10	2.97**	−.11	3.01**
Number of years lived with one parent[a]	−.03	1.96**	−.04	2.23**
Father a high-school graduate or more	.39	2.47**		
Father a high-school graduate			.38	2.16**
Father some college			.61	1.57
Father a college graduate			.84	1.26
Mother a high-school graduate or more	.34	2.66**		
Mother a high-school graduate			.26	1.92*
Mother some college			.68	2.36**
Mother a college graduate			.33	.30
Average posttax family income ÷ poverty line[a]	.18	1.90*		
Number of years posttax family income < poverty line[a]			−.05	2.02**
Years in poverty × AFDC[a]			.04	1.47
Number of years mother worked[a]	.01	.77	.01	.68
Number of years lived in SMSA[a]	−.00	.30	−.00	.19
Number of household location moves[a]			−.10	3.00**
Number of parental separations[a]			.11	.73
Number of parental (re)marriages[a]			−.09	.46
Family Circumstances				
Number of years family head disabled[a]	−.02	1.09	−.02	.87
Firstborn child			.16	1.00
Head's parents poor			−.06	.45
Neighborhood Attributes				
Average percentage of female heads[a]			−.01	1.84*

Variable	Coefficient	t-statistic	Coefficient	t-statistic
Average percentage of youths who are high-school dropouts[a]			−.01	1.21
Average percentage of workers in high-prestige occupations[a]			−.01	.67
Goodness of Fit Log likelihood		−1259		

*Significant at 10 percent level.
**Significant at 5 percent level.

[a]During ages 6–15.

TABLE 5A.4 Determinants of Years of Education, Non-African-American Sample Tobit Specification, $N = 926$

Variable	Coefficient	t-statistic	Coefficient	t-statistic
Constant	11.42	39.97**	12.21	32.98**
Background				
Female	.02	.15	.02	.21
Parental Choices/Opportunities				
Any religion	.17	.91		
Catholic			.31	1.50
Protestant			.10	.54
Average number of siblings[a]	−.03	.67	−.07	1.47
Number of years lived with one parent[a]	−.04	1.62	−.04	1.25
Father a high-school graduate or more	.72	5.25**		
Father a high-school graduate			.54	3.52**
Father some college			.81	4.18**
Father a college graduate			1.11	4.84**
Mother a high-school graduate or more	.61	4.51**		
Mother a high-school graduate			.56	4.03**
Mother some college			.77	3.42**
Mother a college graduate			1.42	4.80**
Average posttax family income ÷ poverty line[a]	.19	4.62**		
Number of years posttax family income < poverty line[a]			−.09	1.69*
Years in poverty × AFDC[a]			.05	.86
Number of years mother worked[a]	.01	.65	.01	.75
Number of years lived in SMSA[a]	.01	.68	−.00	.19
Number of household location moves[a]			−.09	2.49**
Number of parental separations[a]			.20	1.13
Number of parental (re)marriages[a]			−.40	2.08**
Family Circumstances				
Number of years family head disabled[a]	−.09	3.16**	−.07	2.61**
Firstborn child			.09	.69
Head's parents poor			−.01	.10
Neighborhood Attributes				
Average percentage of female heads[a]			−.01	.61

Variable	Coefficient	t-statistic	Coefficient	t-statistic
Average percentage of youths who are high-school dropouts[a]			−.01	.72
Average percentage of workers in high-prestige occupations[a]			.01	.79
Goodness of Fit				
Log likelihood		−1379		

*Significant at 10 percent level.
**Significant at 5 percent level.

[a] During ages 6–15.

6

The Determinants
of Teenage Out-of-Wedlock Births
and Welfare Recipiency

In this chapter we focus on that aspect of success in young adulthood associated with nonmarital childbearing while a teenager. Because a common pattern for unmarried teenage mothers is to seek and obtain welfare benefits subsequent to having a birth, we also examine this outcome. As with the analyses in prior chapters, we emphasize the parental choices/opportunities, family circumstances, and neighborhood attributes that effect the decisions made by teenage women.

Implicit in our analysis is the presumption that the state of unmarried teenage motherhood represents lack of success. The high correlation between being a teenage unmarried mother and a wide variety of indicators of low achievement (e.g., failing to complete high school, being on welfare, being poor, and being out of the labor force) provides the basis for this presumption. That many, if not most, teenage nonmarital pregnancies are "unexpected" or unplanned[1] (and hence, many births as well) indicates the likely importance of lack of family planning information. We first discuss some of the facts regarding national developments in the patterns of teenage nonmarital births and subsequent welfare recipiency, and their implications. We also summarize several of the most prominent speculations regarding the underlying causes of these developments. Next we present the basic conceptual framework that guides our empirical analyses, and then present some of our empirical estimates. Our baseline estimates are discussed in the third section as a prelude to the estimates from a two-stage simultaneous model of the determinants of teenage nonmarital births and subsequent welfare

188

recipiency. The fourth section presents both that model and the estimates from it. Various tests of the robustness of the estimates are presented, and simulated estimates of the effects of changes in some of the explanatory variables on the probability of these two related outcomes are shown. The last section concludes.

TEENAGE NONMARITAL BIRTHS
AND WELFARE RECIPIENCY:
SOME BACKGROUND

The Facts

During the postwar period, the average age at which women experience their first birth has drifted up, in part caused by the increase in the age of first marriage. Consistent with these trends, the number and rate (per 1000 women) of births to teenage women has also decreased. For example, in 1955 the teenage birth rate stood at over 90; by 1975 it had fallen to 56, and in the early 1980s it hovered in the low 50s.

However, from 1986 to 1990, the number of teenage births in the United States increased from 472,000 to 518,000, an increase of nearly 50,000 births. After reaching a low of 51 in 1986, birth rates to American teenagers have increased steadily, and stood at 58 in 1989. This post-1986 increase is recorded for both young teenagers (ages 15–17), and older teenagers; for the younger group, the increase from 1986 to 1989 was from 31 to 37; for the older group it was from 81 to 86.

While the bulk of the teenage births are to white women—about two-thirds—this percentage has been falling over time. By 1989, although African-American women aged 15–19 composed 15.7 percent of this female age cohort, they accounted for 35 percent of the teenage births. Indeed, teenage births account for nearly one-quarter of all births to African-American women.

Substantial shifts have occurred in the pattern of teenage births between married and unmarried women. In 1970, 70 percent of the teenage births were to married women; by 1989, two-thirds of teenage births were out of wedlock. For African-Americans, the unmarried teenage birth rate stands at about 80, and has been falling since 1970; the rate for unmarried white teenagers is about 20, and it has doubled since 1970.

The teenage birth rate in the United States is high in comparison to that of other developed, industrialized countries. Our neighbor, Canada, for example, has a teenage birth rate less than one-half of that of the United States, as does the United Kingdom. The teenage birth rate in the Northern European countries stands at about one-third of that in the United States.

Some Implications

Few social issues have attracted as much attention in the popular press as the high level and rapid increase in the number of births to teenagers who are not married, and the reason for this is not hard to discern. Children born to unmarried teenage mothers do not have an even start in life. They are more likely to grow up in a poor and mother-only family, live in a poor or underclass neighborhood, and experience high risks to both their health status and potential school achievement. For those who value equal opportunity as a social goal, the high rate of births to unmarried teenagers is viewed with great apprehension.

The teenage mothers, too, appear to be harmed by the experience of having a birth out of wedlock. The probability that these mothers will be receiving welfare benefits within a short period after giving birth is high: well over one-half of them do so. Moreover, a relatively small percentage of teenage unmarried mothers finish high school. Lone teenage mothers clearly prejudice economic and marriage opportunities that they might otherwise have had, and in any case they experience a sudden end to their own childhood.

The high level and recent growth in the number of teenage nonmarital births also has implications for public policy. Among recipients of AFDC benefits who are less than 30 years old, three-quarters first gave birth as a teenager, in most cases out of wedlock. About $22 billion is paid annually through AFDC, food stamps, and Medicaid to teenage mothers. Each family that began with a birth to a teenager will cost the public an average of about $17,000 in some form of support over the next 20 years (see Center for Population Options [1990]).

Although the implications of the unmarried teenage birth rate that we have noted above seem consistent with both casual observation and common sense, it is not necessarily the experience of the birth of a child to an unmarried teenager that is responsible for the observed patterns of poverty, the failure to complete high school, and welfare recipiency. It could be that the girls who give birth out of wedlock would have these poor outcomes even if they had not had the birth; maybe they have family backgrounds or personal characteristics that foster low attainments. The experience of a birth to an unmarried teenager may be but another manifestation of this poor outlook for future success. This position has been suggested by a number of researchers (Luker, 1991; Nathanson, 1991); moreover, a recent study comparing sisters (hence, controlling for family background) who become mothers at different ages concluded that there were but negligible differences between teenage and nonteenage mothers in a wide variety of outcomes (see Geronimous and Korenman, 1992). For a variety of reasons, however, the results from this study do not appear robust, and a recent critique of this study (and reanalysis of its model) concludes that "the socioeconomic effects of teen motherhood do not disappear, nor, indeed, are they small" (Hoffman, Foster, and Furstenberg, 1993).

The Causes

The prevalence of teenage nonmarital births (and the subsequent receipt of welfare), particularly among African-Americans, is a social phenomenon worth understanding. Yet, like so many other social developments, its determinants are complex, and attempts to attribute causation lead into murky waters.

Perhaps the broadest assessment of the potential causes of this outcome, and recent increases in its prevalence, is found in the report of the National Academy of Sciences Panel on Adolescent Pregnancy and Childbearing, *Risking the Future* (Hayes, 1987). The causal factors identified by the authors of this report include the following:

• The increased prevalence of early, nonmarital sexual activity
• The decline of parental authority and responsibility
• More general changes in social norms regarding contraception, feminism, and patterns of work and family structure
• Constraints on the availability of abortion services
• Increased poverty and decreases in employment opportunities for those with few skills and low education in the 1980s (especially among African-American women)
• The decline in attractive marriage opportunities for African-American women (related to the increase in joblessness among minority youths)
• Increasing pessimism and disillusionment among poor and minority youths
• Changes in the racial and demographic characteristics of the population

- Changes in the costs (e.g., foregone earnings opportunities) or benefits (e.g., welfare benefit availability) of having a child out of wedlock as a teenager

While the Panel Report did not attempt to quantitatively assess the independent contribution of any of these factors to the teenage nonmarital birth outcome, a number of research studies have taken up this challenge. The tack taken by most of these studies is to rely on detailed survey information on teenage girls to assess the relationship of a variety of potentially causal factors to the probability that these girls will give birth out of wedlock.

In Chapter 3, we presented a review and critique of these studies, concluding that race seemed to play an important independent role (suggesting a cultural or perhaps a neighborhood effect). Similarly, a variety of parental choices or circumstances (such as whether the girl grew up in a disrupted family, whether she had parents with little education, and whether or not she had a parent or sibling who was an unmarried childbearer) were significantly related to the probability that she would give birth out of wedlock, as were the availability and accessibility of contraceptive and abortion services (for whites).

THE DETERMINANTS
OF TEENAGE NONMARITAL BIRTHS
AND WELFARE RECIPIENCY

In this section, we present our approach to assessing the impact of those factors that are related, and potentially causal, to the teenage nonmarital birth-subsequent welfare receipt phenomenon. We present a verbal description of how we proceed, and the rationale for it; a formal presentation of the model is placed in Appendix B. We then present and discuss our empirical estimates.

Our Approach: A Heuristic Description

In Chapter 4 we presented a number of cross-tabulations and simple correlations between factors that have been suggested as contributing to the prevalence of teenage nonmarital births and subsequent welfare receipt, and the probability of occurrence of these events. We found what we expected to find. Girls who were African-American, who had mothers with low education levels, who lived in large urban centers, who had no religion, who had numerous siblings, who were poor, who lived in bad neighborhoods, who grew up in disrupted families, and who grew up in families that had been on welfare were more likely to have a teenage nonmarital birth (and be a welfare recipient subsequently) than were girls that did not have these characteristics.

While these zero-order correlations are interesting, they may not be reliable indicators of potential causal linkages. If African-American teenage girls from poor families are more likely to have a nonmarital birth than white teenagers from nonpoor families, is race the causal factor, or is it the level of family income? Or is it neither of these factors, but rather some third (or fourth or fifth) factor—say, growing up in a mother-only family—that is an important causal influence? Moreover, could these other factors be causal to the poverty status of the girl's family, or to other family attributes that are related to this outcome?

Our approach to understanding the causes of teenage nonmarital reproductive behavior is to focus on the parental choices and community environment in which girls grow up, seeking to identify those effects that are likely to be playing a causal role in children's development. Some of these relevant factors derive from economic theory about social (governmental), parental, and individual decisions. We have discussed this point of view in some detail in Chapter 3, and it guides our research approach here. Other factors are suggested by the research of sociologists and developmental psychologists, and still others have been regularly verified in empirical research, even though they do not have a firm theoretical basis.

While parental choices that reflect investments in children are our central focus, we also explicitly consider the potential effects of other aspects of their environment (for example, the characteristics of their neighborhoods), as well as the character of work, earnings, and other income opportunities that are open to them (the labor market, the marriage market, and the availability of public transfer income).

Some Theoretical Considerations

An economic approach to individual reproductive behavior and work-welfare status views people as rational individual decision makers seeking to make themselves as well off as possible. It presumes that they have weighed the benefits and costs associated with the options available to them, and have made the choices that we observe, constrained by circumstances or limitations that affect their available choices. In this context, then, a girl observed to have a nonmarital birth is interpreted as having made a deliberate choice for this option. For example, given the constraints that she faces and the information that she possesses, having become pregnant, carrying the child to term is superior to seeking an abortion. Similarly, subsequent to giving birth, she may stay living with her parents or she may set up an independent living unit; she may get married or not; she may get a job, or choose to receive welfare. All of these options are seen as potential choices for the girl, and given the constraints that she confronts and the information available to her, the choices that she makes are seen as the best set of decisions from her point of view.[2]

As we emphasized in Chapter 3, information plays an important role in understanding such choices. While individuals are viewed as making their decisions after weighing the advantages and disadvantages associated with each option, it is often the case that many of the gains and losses associated with each option are perceived incompletely and asymmetrically. As a result, the decision actually observed may be quite different from the decision that would have been made had more complete information been available. Moreover, without sound information, luck may play a substantial role in explaining outcomes.

The case of teenage girls considering whether or not to give birth out of wedlock would seem to be a classic case of an option for which the costs are systematically understated, while at the same time the benefits are exaggerated. With poor information, both the costs of raising a child as a lone mother—costs of money and time—and the opportunity costs associated with the foregone earnings and marriage possibilities attributable to the nonmarital birth, are likely to be understated. On the other hand, the potential psychological benefits of having a child of one's own may be exaggerated. If the information available to teenagers is poor and asymmetrical, their decisions about whether or not to conceive and bear a child out of wedlock are likely to be biased toward that option.

There would seem to be little doubt that the reliability of these individual calculations depends on the characteristics of the girl's parents and the investments that her parents and community have made in her. For example, girls whose mothers and fathers have chosen more education for themselves are likely to have more access to reliable information on childbearing costs and the foregone earnings and marriage opportunities associated with a nonmarital birth, than are girls whose parents have less education. Moreover, the more-educated parents are more likely to communicate this information to the girl. Similarly, a child who has benefited from parents who have chosen to devote substantial time to caring for and interacting with their children is likely to have more reliable information on the relevant costs and benefits of reproduction, work, and welfare decisions than children with small allocations of parental time.[3] Much the same can be said for girls who are raised in a family in which parents work (and are familiar with labor market processes) or who receive welfare (and are familiar with those arrangements). The role of information in the economic model, then, provides the basis for including parental education, parental child-care time, and parental work effort in any list of parental choices or family-based determinants of the girl's nonmarital birth outcome.

Any full-blown version of the economic model will also admit the relevance of stigma costs in the reproductive choices made by teenage girls. Those girls whose mother gave birth out of wedlock—or who have a sister who was a lone teenage mother—are likely to view this event differently than other girls do, and are likely to have quite different assessments of the stigma costs attached to bearing a child out of wedlock; these assessments will influence the probability of this event occurring. Similarly, girls living in a neighborhood in which there are many teenagers who have given birth out of wedlock, and in which there are many female-headed families, are likely to face lower stigma costs than other girls. Religious affiliation is also likely to influence the perceived level of stigma associated with bearing a child out of wedlock.

This view of the economic model is a rather encompassing one, and it can easily accommodate a variety of factors that are emphasized by other social scientists. Psychologists, for example, emphasize the role that stressful events during childhood play in determining a girl's self-esteem and efficacy, and hence her ultimate success. In this view, parental separations, divorces, or remarriages that occur while the girl is growing up will influence her choices. Changes in the geographic location of the family could play the same role. While stressful events are seen as having a negative effect on children's outcomes, "stress mediators"—for example, the self-esteem and coping ability of the mother, or the nurturing environment of the girl's family—are cited as potential offsets to these adverse influences.

While all social scientists accept the influence of parental choices and family circumstances on the choices made by children, sociologists have recently emphasized the potential effect of the characteristics of the neighborhood in which children grow up on their choices.[4] The conceptual basis for this view derives in part from the concept of role models and their effect on children's aspirations and self-perception. For example, a child who grows up in a neighborhood in which few adults work is likely have a less strong commitment to the labor force than a child who grows up in a neighborhood dominated by the work ethic. Similarly, a girl who regularly observes teenage nonmarital births, lone parents, and welfare recipiency in her neighborhood will be more likely to opt for such an outcome than a girl who finds such events rare and foreign.

Our analysis, then, starts with the economic model in which teenage girls make rational choices—choices that serve their best interests—on the basis of their appraisal of the gains and costs associated with the options that they face. These choices are, in turn, influenced by the level of parental investments that have been made in them; these investments are, in turn, determined by the decisions made by parents and the opportunities that are open to them. We rely on an extended version of this economic framework that incorporates the role of imperfect and asymmetrical information in affecting a girl's appraisal of the available options. Finally, we leaven this framework by including the insights of other social scientists regarding the importance of stressful events, sociopsychological factors, and neighborhood attributes in affecting behaviors and choices.

Although our approach is rather full-bodied, incorporating a wide variety of potential determinants of the choice of teenage girls regarding nonmarital childbearing, we have omitted a number of potentially important factors. We have not mentioned the male partners of teenage girls, and they clearly play a role in determining the level of sexual activity in which the girl engages, the contraceptive practices prevalent in this activity, whether the girl marries either prior to or after pregnancy occurs, or whether she chooses to carry to term any pregnancy. We have excluded them from our analysis because the data set that we have available has no information on them. Similarly, the availability and accessibility of family planning services that are present in the girl's community are not included in our framework: although they are relevant to the outcome that we are observing, our data contain no information on these community-based factors.[5]

OUR BASELINE MODELS
OF TEENAGE OUT-OF-WEDLOCK BIRTHS
AND EMPIRICAL ESTIMATES

In Table 6.1 we recount the results of a multivariate probit estimate of the correlates of the out-of-wedlock birth decision of the teenage girls in our sample. The purpose of these estimates is to give bearing to our full bivariate probit estimate, which follows.[6]

These estimates are based on our (unweighted) sample of 873 females, all of whom had passed their 21st birthday by 1988. The dependent variable is equal to 1 if the girl had a birth between the ages of 13 and 18 and was unmarried, and 0 otherwise. The proportion of our sample who had given birth out of wedlock is .14.

Columns 1 and 2 of Table 6.1 show the results of the parsimonious specification, and are taken from Chapter 4. We group the independent variables into the same categories used in Chapter 5. Columns 3 and 4 of Table 6.1 present a richer specification of the multivariate probit model.[7]

The results of the basic model were discussed in Chapter 4. They suggest that African-American teenagers are more likely to have a teenage out-of-wedlock birth than are other teenagers, a result that is consistent with the raw data and cross-tabulations. In terms of parental education—and the likely transmission of more accurate information regarding the cost and benefits of a teenage birth—the evidence suggests that the mother's education is a large and powerful influence. Daughters of mothers who have a high-school diploma are significantly less likely to give birth as an unmarried teenager than are the daughters of mothers who have failed to graduate. The father's education, while it has the same sign, is not significant. Reporting a religion is negatively related to the probability of a teenage out-of-wedlock birth and is statistically significant.

The resources available to a family—or chosen by the family, in some cases—are also a significant determinant of the probability of a teenage birth. Average family income has a negative association with the probability of a teenage birth and is highly significant. The number of years that a child lives with a single parent (a proxy for the extent of parental time investment) is positively related to the probability that the daughter will have a teenage nonmarital birth. Similarly, if a child has more siblings, she is likely to receive less parental attention and parental investment, and she is more likely to have a teenage nonmarital birth.

TABLE 6.1 Determinants of Teenage Out-of-Wedlock Birth, Full Sample, Probit Estimation, $N = 873$

Variable	Coefficient	t-statistic	Coefficient	t-statistic
Constant	−0.79	−2.2**	−1.02	1.7*
Background				
African-American	0.26	1.7*	0.20	1.0
Parental Choices/Opportunity				
Any religion	−0.40	1.9*		
Catholic			−0.56	1.8*
Jewish			−3.10	0.0
Protestant			−0.30	1.3
Average number of siblings[a]	0.07	1.9*	0.09	2.2**
Number of years lived with one parent[a]	0.06	3.4**	0.03	1.4
Father a high-school graduate or more	−0.03	0.2		
Father a high-school graduate			−0.03	0.2
Father some college			−0.39	0.8
Father a college graduate			−0.15	0.3
Mother a high-school graduate or more	−0.62	4.2**		
Mother a high-school graduate			−0.63	4.0**
Mother some college			−0.77	2.1**
Mother a college graduate			−4.12	0.0
Average posttax family income ÷ poverty line[a]	−0.23	2.4**	−0.17	1.7*
Mother's age at first birth			−0.02	1.0
Mother had out-of-wedlock birth			0.04	0.2
Number of years mother worked[a]	0.01	0.8	0.01	0.7
Number of years lived in SMSA[a]	0.02	1.5	0.01	0.8
Number of household location moves[a]			0.06	1.4
Number of parental separations[a]			0.52	3.2**
Number of parental (re)marriages[a]			−0.28	1.4
Parents ever received AFDC[a]			−0.06	0.4
Family Circumstances				
Number of years family head disabled[a]	−0.01	0.3	−0.01	0.3
Head's parents poor			−0.19	1.4
Firstborn child			−0.16	0.9

198

Variable	Coefficient	t-statistic	Coefficient	t-statistic
Neighborhood Attributes				
Average percentage of female				
heads[a]			0.01	0.9
Government Choices				
Maximum welfare benefits				
in state[a]			0.05 E-2	1.1
Goodness of Fit				
Log likelihood	-291		-279	
Porportion predicted correctly	0.853		0.858	

NOTE: The model specifications include controls for whether both parents are in the sample in 1968, and whether the child's grandfather was foreign-born.

*Significant at 10 percent level.
**Significant at 5 percent level.

[a]During ages 6–15.

None of the other variables included in these estimates are statistically significant.

Columns 3 and 4 present the results of our richer specification. This model is designed to test specific questions related to teenage out-of-wedlock birth, such as the intergenerational transmission of welfare and the role of the generosity of welfare benefits on teenage out-of-wedlock births. To do so, we include in our specification: the state generosity of welfare benefits, the proportion of female-headed families in the neighborhood in which the girl grew up, whether the mother had an out-of-wedlock birth, her age at her first birth, and whether the family received welfare at any time while the girl was 6–15.

In terms of these added explanations, we find no evidence of a significant role of intergenerational transmission of welfare on the probability of a teenage nonmarital birth. None of the variables for parental receipt of welfare—parental receipt of welfare, the proportion of female-headed families in the area, the mother having had a nonmarital birth or her having a birth as a teenager (based on her age at first birth), nor the state generosity of welfare benefits—are even marginally significant. There is a suggestion that family stress plays a significant role in teenage nonmarital births: daughters who experienced more parental separations are significantly more likely to have such a birth. None of the other variables added to the simple exploration are significant. Turning to those variables (or close substitutes) included in the more limited estimate reported in Columns 1 and 2, we find only a few changes. In extended estimates, race is not a significant determinant of such births. Apparently it is other factors associated with the experiences of African-American versus non-African-American girls that have a significant impact on the probability of a nonmarital teenage birth.

The results on religion suggest that being a Catholic is negatively and significantly associated with a nonmarital birth; indeed, the sign on all three religions is consistent with the overall negative association between a teenage nonmarital birth and religion. Turning to education, the results are again consistent with the simpler version—daughters of mothers with more education (high-school graduates and above) are less likely to have a teenage nonmarital birth.[8] The father's education has the expected negative sign but continues to be not at all significant. The results for family income again confirm the important role of family resources in influencing the outcomes of young adults; and daughters with more siblings are more likely to have a teenage nonmarital birth than those with smaller families.

Overall, then, these extended results suggest that the mother's higher education, family size, family income, religion, and the separation of the child's parents are significantly associated with the probability of a teenage nonmarital birth. However, factors associated with intergenerational transmission of welfare are not significantly associated with this outcome, nor are the years that the mother works, the father's education, and other measures of family circumstance.

A BIVARIATE PROBIT ESTIMATION
OF TEENAGE OUT-OF-WEDLOCK BIRTHS
AND WELFARE RECIPIENCY

The bivariate probit model that we estimate characterizes the interdependent nature of the reproductive and welfare receipt decisions confronting unwed teenage girls.* Our goal is to understand the relative importance

* A version of the bivariate probit model yielding estimates of the out-of-wedlock birth and welfare choices, but based on a somewhat different sample and specification, is in An, Haveman, and Wolfe (1993). In a few instances, the magnitude of coefficient estimates and t-statistics differ between the two versions.

of a wide variety of social and parental choices/opportunities, family circumstances, and labor market and welfare receipt opportunities on the childbirth decision of unmarried teenage girls, and then the subsequent decision of whether or not to receive welfare. The model reflects the fact that the decision to receive welfare is conditional on having carried a pregnancy to term. Similarly, the girl's decision regarding the birth depends on her assessment of the available income support from welfare should she have a child, and the probability that she will be a recipient.

The Nature of the Model

Our model treats the welfare receipt and the nonmarital birth decisions of an unwed teenage girl as simultaneous: the decision of whether or not to have a birth is influenced by her assessment of the likelihood that she will receive welfare if the birth occurs, and vice versa. Estimation of such a simultaneous model will enable us to obtain consistent estimates of the determinants of welfare receipt by correcting for the process by which some teenage girls choose to become lone mothers while others do not. Moreover, by distinguishing the two choices in this interdependent way, the various determinants of each of the choices can be analyzed. In particular, the importance of available AFDC benefits in the decision to give birth out of wedlock as a teenager can be tested.[9] A formal statement of the econometric model that we use is presented in Appendix B at the end of the book.

Estimating Procedures

We fit our model using full information maximum likelihood techniques. More specifically, we run a bivariate probit model estimating whether or not the girl was observed to experience an out-of-wedlock birth during her teenage years (ages 13 to 18), and, if a nonmarital birth was observed, whether or not the girl received AFDC benefits at any time within the subsequent three postbirth years.[10] The dependent variable in the teenage out-of-wedlock birth equation is a dummy variable equaling 1 if the girl gave birth while unmarried between the ages of 13 and 18; the dependent variable for the receipt of AFDC benefits subsequent to a teenage out-of-wedlock birth is a dummy variable equaling 1 if the teenage mother received AFDC benefits in any of the three years after giving birth out of wedlock.[11]

In our sample of 873 girls, 125 (14.3 percent) gave birth out of wedlock while a teenager. Of the 125 girls experiencing a teenage out-of-wedlock birth, 91 (73 percent) received welfare within the subsequent three years. Among the 425 African-American females in our sample, 100 (24 percent) experienced a teenage out-of-wedlock birth by age 18. Of these, 67 (67 percent) received welfare within three years.[12]

We group the independent variables employed in our analysis into the four categories described in Chapter 5: (1) background information on the child, (2) measures of parental choices/opportunities, (3) family circumstances, and (4) neighborhood or community attributes. We totaled the number of times each time-related event occurred in the child's family from ages 6 to 15. Variables for time-related events include number of household moves, number of parental separations, number of parental (re)marriages, years living in SMSA, and years living in the South. The state maximum AFDC benefits, the food stamp benefit, and the Medicaid expenditures variables used in the estimates are in 1976 dollars and are averaged over the relevant years.[13] In the teenage out-of-wedlock birth equation, the average of these benefits is taken over the years the child was between the ages of 6 and 15; for the receipt of AFDC benefits by the family of the teenage mother, the value is the average over the years from age 6 until the birth of the child. The economic circumstance variable is the welfare ratio (posttax family income divided by the poverty line of the girl's family) averaged over the years the girl was between 6 and 15 years old, also in 1976 dollars.

Estimates from the Bivariate Probit

Table 6.2 shows the maximum likelihood estimates for the teenage out-of-wedlock birth and subsequent welfare receipt equations, estimated from our bivariate probit model. Our specification of these equations (and the definition of our categories of variables) has been guided by the economic framework described in Chapter 2 and insights from both social science literature and prior empirical research.

Consistent with the intergenerational welfare (or lifestyle) transmission literature, we have included a number of variables related to the choices of the girl's mother regarding welfare participation and childbearing in the out-of-wedlock birth equations. These include whether the mother gave birth out of wedlock, her age at her first birth, the number of children to whom she has given birth, and whether she had been a welfare recipient while the girl was growing up. For similar reasons, welfare recipiency and her age at her first birth were included in the daughter's welfare recipiency equation. (The inclusion of the

TABLE 6.2 Bivariate Probit Results: Teenage Out-of-Wedlock Birth and Receipt of Welfare Benefits after Teenage Out-of-Wedlock Birth

Variable	Out-of-Wedlock Birth $N=873$		Receipt of Welfare Benefits after Teenage Out-of-Wedlock Birth $N=125$	
	Coefficient	t-statistic	Coefficient	t-statistic
Constant	−1.15	−1.65	−0.28	−0.20
Background				
African-American	0.30	1.66*	0.58	1.21
Parental Choices/Opportunities				
Any religion	−0.39	−1.65*		
Average number of siblings[a]	0.07	1.74*		
Mother a high-school graduate	−0.65	−3.93**	−0.20	−0.37
Mother's age at first birth	−0.01	−0.31	−0.01	−0.40
Mother had out-of-wedlock birth	0.04	0.24		
Numbers of years lived in South, ages 14–17			−0.90	2.08**
Average occupational status of head[a]			0.08	0.66
Average posttax family income ÷ poverty line[a]	−0.21	−2.14**	−0.68	2.53**
Family ever received AFDC[a]	−0.01	0.03	0.20	0.63
Number of years lived in SMSA[a]	0.02	1.07		
Number of household location moves[a]	0.07	1.61	0.12	1.60
Number of parental separations[a]	0.54	3.65**		
Number of parental (re)marriages[a]	−0.41	−1.75*		
Prior Child's Choices/Attainments				
Split-off from family			−0.15	0.54
Lost a grade level			0.94	1.30
Neighborhood/Community Attributes				
Bad neighborhood in 1976	0.01	1.10		
Average county unemployment rate[a]	−0.002	0.04		
Maximum welfare benefits in state[b]	0.0004	0.94	0.001	0.99
Goodness of Fit				
Rho	0.67	2.05**		
Log likelihood	−338			

*Significant at 10 percent level.
**Significant at 5 percent level.

[a]During ages 6–15.
[b]Ages 6–15 in birth equation; 3 years after birth in recipiency equation.

mother's education and race in the specification can also be justified on similar conceptual grounds.)

The mother's welfare participation is positively related to the daughter's receipt of welfare, but it is not at all statistically significant. Other background variables, race, and the mother's education are related as expected to the probability of an out-of-wedlock birth and are statistically significant. Using a likelihood ratio test, this group of variables is statistically significant at the 1 percent level.

To reflect the economic circumstances of the family and the information about the connections to the world of work and welfare receipt that economic resources convey, a second grouping of linkages was included in both equations. These include the average welfare ratio of the girl's family when she was growing up and her parent's receipt of welfare benefits. Inclusion of the occupation of the head of the family and having a religious affiliation in the welfare receipt equation are justified on the same grounds. As expected, the average welfare ratio is negatively related to both the probability of having a teenage nonmarital birth and the subsequent receipt of welfare and is statistically significant in both cases.

Several variables were included in the specification to reflect the effect of parental decisions that could have caused stress during the child's upbringing. These include geographic moves and parental separations and remarriages; the first of these is included in both equations, the latter two only in the birth equation. In addition to the stress that a geographic move places on adolescents, such an event may also separate them from traditional sources of economic support (e.g., extended family, employment, or connections), hence making the receipt of welfare benefits subsequent to a nonmarital birth more likely. Parental remarriages are changes in family circumstances that, while stressful, are likely to decrease the probability of out-of-wedlock births because of role-model or stability effects. The inclusion in the birth equation of years living in an urban area is justified on similar grounds.

The geographic moves and parental separations variables both enter with expected positive signs in these equations; the remarriages variable is negative and significant in the birth equation.[14] The parental separation variable is statistically significant in the first equation; geographic moves is nearly significant in the second. The remarriage variable has the expected negative sign in the birth equation and is statistically significant at the 10 percent level.

The final set of linkages relates to the opportunities available to the teenager in both the labor market and in the welfare market. To capture these potential effects, we include the unemployment rate in the county where the girl lives, the generosity of welfare benefits in her state, and the proportion of female-headed households in her neighborhood in the out-of-wedlock birth equation. All neighborhood/community variables have the expected sign, but none are statistically significant. In the welfare receipt equation, both living in the South and state welfare generosity are included to test for the effect of available public support and services on welfare recipiency. Living in the South during the period close to that when most of the out-of-wedlock births occurred had a negative and statistically significant effect on the probability that the girl received welfare subsequent to a nonmarital birth—probably capturing the limited availability of benefits and services in this region.[15]

Whether the girl had lost a grade in school or had split off from her family after the birth were also included in the welfare recipiency equation to capture the availability of short-run nonwelfare opportunities; the sign of the lost grade is as expected; that of splitting off is negative; neither variable is statistically significant.

Finally, race (reflecting cultural and value differences, and expected to affect the probability of both out-of-wedlock births and welfare recipiency), the mother's education (reflecting the mother's productivity in raising her children, her attitudes toward teenage births and welfare recipiency, and her contraceptive knowledge, and also expected to affect both out-of-wedlock birth and welfare recipiency probabilities), and religion (reflecting the counsel of virtually all religions regarding out-of-wedlock sexual relationships, and hence expected to affect the probability of nonmarital births but not subsequent welfare recipiency) are entered into the model. These variables have the expected effects in the out-of-wedlock birth equation and are statistically significant. Those entered in the welfare recipiency equation are not statistically significant.

The exclusion of the human capital variables from the bivariate probit model rests on the judgment that parental earnings capacity per se is not a direct determinant of daughter's reproductive and welfare recipiency behavior (although family economic status, proxied by the welfare ratio, may convey an indirect effect of parental labor market capabilities on behavior). The exception to this is the mother's education, which serves as a proxy for parental knowledge of, advice on, and monitoring of her daughter's sexual and contraceptive behavior, consistent with numerous findings and hypotheses of both economists and sociologists.[16] Although growing up in a single-parent family is likely to have an effect on teenage reproductive and other behaviors, it is excluded from the bivariate probit model, as the effect of family structure is captured by the parental separation and remarriage variables.

In addition, we tested the sensitivity of the bivariate probit specification in several ways. First, we tested the results using alternative starting values for the bivariate probit. The results are identical. Second, we replaced our income values with a variable equal to the number of years that the family of the girl was poor during her ages 6–15. This poverty variable is significant and positive in the equation for receipt of welfare: it is positive but not significant in the teenage birth equation. The coefficient of the other variables are consistent with those in the reported equation.

The test for the simultaneity of the bivariate probit model is positive and significant (t-statistic = 2.05, Wald test = 4.20), providing evidence in favor of this simultaneous specification of the model that treats the decisions as sequential—first, the probability of giving birth out of wedlock as a teenager and second, conditional on giving such a birth, whether to apply for and receive welfare benefits.[17]

Our finding that race is a significant correlate of the probability of a teenage nonmarital birth is consistent with prior research and suggests that the model be run separately for African-Americans and non-African-Americans. However, in testing our model for differences between non-African-Americans and African-Americans, we cannot reject the hypothesis that the subsamples were structurally the same, even at the 20 percent confidence level.[18]

Related to this is the lack of statistical significance of the coefficient of the state welfare generosity variable in the out-of-wedlock birth equation. This finding is consistent with other literature for African-Americans, but not for whites.[19] To test for this difference, we reestimated the bivariate probit model, adding a variable interacting race and welfare generosity. The t-statistic for the coefficient on the welfare generosity variable increases substantially, but remains statistically insignificant; the sign on the interaction variable is negative, suggesting a smaller influence on African-Americans than non-African-Americans, but the coefficient is not statistically significant. This result then is consistent with the direction, but not the significance, of racial differences found in other work.

The model works well in predicting teenage out-of-wedlock births.

Although the actual percentage of the sample of observed individuals that gave birth out of wedlock as a teenager is .143, our model applied to individual data predicts an identical average probability. The model also accurately predicts the receipt of benefits. The actual percentage receiving benefits (among those experiencing a teenage out-of-wedlock birth) is .73; our predicted average probability after correcting for selectivity is .73. The model accurately predicts the out-of-wedlock birth outcome for 86 percent of the observations and the welfare recipiency decision for 79 percent of the observations.

Simulated Impacts of Explanatory Variables

Table 6.3 presents our estimates of the effect on the national probabilities of both the teenage nonmarital birth decision, and the subsequent decision to receive AFDC benefits, of assumed changes in a number of family-based factors. The variables selected are those that might be responsive to policy: welfare generosity, geographic moves, parental separations, reduced poverty, and increased mother's education.

Increasing the educational attainment of parents has the largest effect in reducing the prevalence of teenage out-of-wedlock births. We estimate that if all mothers of teenage girls had completed high school,[20] the probability their daughters would have a teenage out-of-wedlock birth would be reduced by nearly one-half.[21] This estimate should be interpreted cautiously, as it neglects the unmeasured factors that explain the level of education attained by mothers—things such as motivation, aspirations, and intelligence. It does, however, suggest important payoffs to increasing education, beyond those of market productivity and wages.

Table 6.3 also shows the simulated effects of increasing the income of the families of the daughters in our sample. We simulate income increases in two ways. In the first simulation, we increase the average income-to-needs (welfare) ratio of each family by 20 percent. Second, we increase the income of any family in poverty in any year (that is, any family with a welfare ratio below 1) by an amount that is sufficient to raise them above the poverty line in that year. Then, with the new income level, we recalculate the average welfare ratio of the family and simulate the effect on the probability of a teenage nonmarital birth and subsequent welfare recipiency. In effect, this simulation shows the estimated results of eliminating poverty among the families in which the

TABLE 6.3 Simulated Effects of Changes in Explanatory Variables: Predicted Value of Attainment Variable and Percentage Change from Population (Base) Value of Attainment Variable

Variable	Teenage Out-of-Wedlock Birth		Receipt of Welfare Benefits	
	Probability of Teenage Out-of-Wedlock Birth	Percentage Change from Base	Probability of Receipt of Welfare Benefits	Percentage Change from Base
Base	0.080		0.720	
20 Percent Increase in Average Ratio of Income to Poverty Line[a]	0.071	−10.3	0.663	−7.9
Zero Years Income < Poverty Line[a]	0.077	−2.6	0.694	−3.7
All Mothers are High-school Graduates	0.042	−47.7		
Number of Household Location Moves + 1[a]	0.087	+9.6	0.741	+2.9
Number of Household Location Moves − 1[a]	0.074	−6.7	0.704	−2.3
Number of Parental Separations + 1[a]	0.164	+105.9		
Number of Parental Separations − 1[a]	0.058	−26.7		

NOTE: Simulation estimates based on specification in Table 6.2 and include variables with t-statistics of at least 1.6.

[a] During ages 6–15.

daughters grow up. For both simulations, an increase in income—holding all other factors constant—reduces the probability of both teenage out-of-wedlock births and the receipt of welfare benefits conditional on such a birth. However, in all cases, the response to the income change is relatively small.

A variable that shows a major impact on the probability of a teenage out-of-wedlock birth is the number of parental separations. Our simulations suggest that if all parents of teenage girls in the sample were to separate one additional time while the daughter is 6–15, the probability their daughter would have a teenage out-of-wedlock birth more than *doubles!* The reverse—a reduction in separations by 1—has a smaller influence, since only families that had at least one separation are affected by the simulated reduction.

Finally, geographic moves are predicted to have influence on both teenage out-of-wedlock births and receipt of welfare benefits, although the magnitude is relatively small. The effect of an increase in the number of location moves by 1 for all girls in the nation during their ages 6–15 is about a 10 percent increase in the probability that they will have an out-of-wedlock birth and a 3 percent increase in the probability of welfare receipt conditional on having an out-of-wedlock birth.

CONCLUSIONS

In this chapter we have presented estimates of the correlates of teenage nonmarital births and welfare recipiency for our sample of young women. Controlling for the large number of determinants included in the model, being African-American is positively associated with the probability of a teenage nonmarital birth. This is consistent with prior research and suggests that the model be run separately for non-African-Americans and African-Americans. However, in testing our sample for differences between non-African-Americans and African-Americans, we cannot reject the hypothesis that structure of relationships within the two subsamples was the same even at the 20 percent confidence level.

The negative sign of the coefficient of the predicted average income-to-needs ratio of the family in which the girl was raised indicates that the teenage out-of-wedlock birth decision is associated with the economic resources that are available to the family, even when controls for a substantial number of other variables are introduced. Parental education, which is itself an important determinant of the investment in children, is one of these important variables. The educational background of the mothers of the young women in our sample is negatively and significantly related to the probability that their offspring will have an out-of-wedlock birth.

The sign of the coefficient of the religion variable is negative and significant, and this result is also consistent with other research. The number of siblings of the teenager (a measure of reduced investment in children) is positively and significantly related to the chances that she will have a nonmarital birth.

The variables indicating stress in the family—separation/divorce, remarriage, or change in geographic location—all have a statistically significant effect or nearly so on the probability that the teenager will have a nonmarital birth, and all of the signs of these variables are expected. Those family changes indicating disintegration or dislocation tend to increase the probability of having a birth out of wedlock as a teenager; the change suggesting restabilization (the remarriage of a single mother or father) reduces the probability of having a nonmarital birth.

A girl who lived in a family that had ever received AFDC benefits (by age 15) does not appear to have a higher probability of having a teenage out-of-wedlock birth. The generosity of the welfare benefits in the state in which the girl resided while she was growing up has a positive sign, but it is not statistically significant.

Our estimates of the determinants of the probability that a teenager who has given birth out of wedlock will receive AFDC benefits subsequent to giving birth suggest that being African-American increases this probability, but it is not significant. The income of the family in which the girl grew up has a negative effect on the probability that she will choose to go on welfare, and it is significant. A measure of wealth—the prestige of the head of household's job—has the expected sign, but it is not significant.

There is little evidence that having a mother who has received AFDC benefits before the daughter gave birth increases the probability that the nonmarried daughter will choose welfare recipiency. The generosity of the welfare benefits in the state that the girl resides shows no relationship to being a welfare recipient, but a variable for living in the South, which has the lowest welfare benefits in the nation, is negative and statistically significant.

The family stress variable, geographic moves, is positively related to the probability that the girl will choose welfare recipiency, but the coefficient of this variable is not quite statistically significant. Finally, a variable indicating whether the teenage mother lost a grade in school has the expected sign, but its coefficient is also not significant.

The simulations highlight the potentially important role of parental education and separations on teenage behavior. They suggest that policies that are successful in reducing the incidence of female high-school noncompletion could reduce the teenage out-of-wedlock birth rate for the next cohort of young women. Finally, they suggest that parental separations and geographic moves appear to create family-based stresses that may increase teenage out-of-wedlock births—even after controlling for a wide variety of other potentially important factors such as income, race, region, years lived with one parent, and parental education.

NOTES

1. According to the Alan Guttmacher Institute (1992), 7 in 10 births to teen-agers are from unplanned pregnancies.

2. See Chapter 3 for a more complete discussion of the strengths and weak-nesses of the economic choice framework as a basis for understanding children's outcomes.

3. See Chapter 2 for a discussion of the possible effects of the number of siblings on the amount of parental child-care time available to children.

4. See the discussion of neighborhood effects in Chapter 3.

5. Chapter 3 describes research by Lundberg and Plotnick (1990) based on state information merged to a large survey data base.

6. We proceed directly from the baseline estimates to our bivariate probit model because of the close interdependence of the teenage nonmarital birth and subsequent welfare recipiency decisions. We do not present estimates of a baseline model of welfare recipiency, as this decision is so closely tied to the prior existence of a teenage nonmarital birth for the girls in our sample.

7. The additional variables used in the estimates in this chapter are defined as follows:

- Mother's age at first birth: ($\bar{x} = 22.0$; $\sigma = 5.0$)
- Mother had an out-of-wedlock birth: ($\bar{x} = .16$; $\sigma = .37$)
- Years lived in the South while the child was aged 14–17: ($\bar{x} = .48$; $\sigma = .5$)
- Occupation of head the year the daughter gave birth (1 = professional, managerial; 2 = white collar; 3 = high-skill blue collar; 4 = low-skill blue collar; 5 = unemployed): ($\bar{x} = 3.28$; $\sigma = 1.45$)
- Split-off from family (dummy variable = 1 if daughter split-off from family within 3 years of giving birth): ($\bar{x} = .33$; $\sigma = .47$)
- Lost a grade level (= 0 if the daughter completed 12th grade by age 18): ($\bar{x} = .58$)

8. The impact is significant for high school and some college, but not for college graduates. This is likely to reflect the small number of daughters in our sample with mothers who are college graduates.

9. There is a further issue underlying our model that should be noted. To meet the econometric requirements for obtaining estimates of effects that

are unbiased, the variables chosen to explain the choices made must have values that are independent of these choices, i.e., the independent variables must be uncorrelated with the error terms of the equations explaining the two choices. If one or more substantively important variables in our model do not meet this requirement, instrumental variable techniques may be called for. It could be argued that a number of our independent variables should be "instrumented" because they might be subject to endogeniety problems, including: the ratio of family income to needs, religion, number of siblings, mother's age at first birth, parental education, whether or not the mother gave birth out of wedlock, whether or not the girl lost a grade in school, parental welfare recipiency, parental occupation, parental separations, remarriages and geographic moves, and the quality of the family's neighborhood. We experimented with instrumental variable estimates for some of the variables that are most likely to be endogenous (e.g., the ratio of family income to needs), but the results were not substantively different from those reported here. Hence, because the model becomes both difficult to identify and increasingly cumbersome as instrumental variables are introduced, we chose not to instrument these variables.

10. Only 12 females in the sample gave birth prior to age 15, and only one prior to age 14.

11. Determination of the receipt of AFDC benefits in the PSID is difficult due both to the lack of individual data related to transfer recipiency and to the lack of reporting accuracy in distinguishing transfer income from various programs. Our measurement of AFDC recipiency for those women who gave birth as teenagers is based on responses to several questions in the survey:

- Type of transfer income from individual responses = TYPE

- Relationship of the individual to the household head = RELHEAD

- Head and wife's AFDC income = HWAFDC

- Head and wife's other welfare benefits = HWOWE

If TYPE equals AFDC for the girl, or TYPE equals other welfare only, or TYPE equals both AFDC or other welfare in any of the three years after the girl experienced a teenage out-of-wedlock birth, the girl is assumed to be an AFDC recipient. In addition, if RELHEAD is "head," "wife," "child," or "grandchild," and either HWAFDC or HWOWE is positive, the girl is assumed to be an AFDC recipient. We thank Greg Duncan for helping us define this variable.

12. For 874 African-American girls aged 15 to 19 in the PSID, Duncan and Hoffman (1989) found that 34 percent (unweighted) experienced a teenage out-of-wedlock birth. Of the 295 girls that experienced an out-of-wedlock birth in that sample, 68 percent received AFDC benefits in the subsequent two years.

13. These variables are defined more completely in Appendix A.

14. In the birth equation, these variables measured over time are formed from annual values while the girl was aged 6–15; in the welfare-receipt equation these time-specific variables are tied more closely to the period during which the young mother is making the decision of whether or not to receive welfare.

15. The four neighborhood/community/state variables are jointly significant at the 1 percent level.

16. See Duncan and Hoffman (1990a), Lundberg and Plotnick (1990a), Hogan and Kitagawa (1985), and Moore and Caldwell (1977). The last of these studies concludes: "It has also been maintained that the education of the mother . . . affects the probability of conception among teenagers, since young women with better educated mothers should be more knowledgeable about sex, reproduction, and contraception. Our analysis confirms this argument. . . . This variable does not seem to be a proxy for social class, however, since the education of the father or father substitute was not found to be related to pregnancy." [p. 166]

17. Estimating two separate probit equations, one for out-of-wedlock births on the entire sample and one for welfare recipiency conditional on such a birth ($N = 125$), shows similar results. There are no exceptions in terms of signs and significance in the out-of-wedlock birth equation. For the recipiency equation, the t-statistics for lost a grade level become positive and statistically significant, and the number of location moves becomes statistically insignificant. The similar pattern reassures us of the robustness of our results.

18. We also attempted to run this test for the SEO and random subsamples. We had difficulty obtaining convergence of the random subsample, but a slightly modified specification suggested we could reject the hypothesis of identical structures at the 5 percent level.

19. See Plotnick (1990), Lundberg and Plotnick (1990b), and Duncan and Hoffman (1989).

20. In this simulation, we increase the education level of all of the mothers with less than 12 years of education to 12 years, while allowing the values for all mothers with education levels of 12 or more to remain unchanged. All of the other variables in the equation are unchanged. The predicted value for each observation is then multiplied by the population weight; hence, the base value of .08 for the teenage nonmarital birth outcome is the predicted national probability with all independent variables set at their actual levels.

21. We do not simulate the influence of the mother's increased education on the probability that daughters would, subsequent to a nonmarital birth, receive welfare benefits, as the coefficient of this relationship in the estimated equation is not at all significant.

7

The Determinants
of Economic Inactivity

"Be not Solitary, be not idle"
Richard Burton 1640

Not surprisingly, a variety of behaviors or indicators of success of young adults are highly correlated.[1] These include dropping out of school, teenage nonmarital pregnancy, drug and alcohol abuse, and criminal or delinquent activity. Many of the young adults exhibiting these characteristics tend to live in the nation's central cities. Of these success indicators, teenage pregnancies have increased in recent years (since 1986), while the high-school dropout rate is little changed after declining for two decades. Accurate data on the prevalence of the other behaviors is difficult to obtain, although the rates of substance abuse remain shockingly high, and an unprecedently large number of minority male youths are incarcerated.

Teenage women who give birth out of wedlock are less likely to finish high school—and more likely to become welfare recipients—than are those teenagers who do not have an unmarried birth. Indeed, nearly one-half (48 percent) of AFDC recipients in 1988 had not completed high school. And, if teenage mothers become welfare recipients by the time the child is 3 years old, they face a high risk of being on welfare for a long spell.

Similarly, those persons without a high-school diploma are far more likely to be nonemployed or unemployed than those with more education. In 1970, the ratio of unemployment for those without a high-school diploma to those who graduated from high school was 1.6; by 1988 it had increased to 1.8. Moreover, among youths who work, the wage rates and earnings of those who have chosen to stop attending

214

high school before graduating are substantially lower than are those of high-school graduates—and the gap is growing.

In this chapter, we treat economic inactivity as a young adult as an outcome, and study the social and parental choice correlates of this status. As in the preceding chapters, we emphasize explanatory variables that reflect the social and parental investments in children.

Our definition of economic inactivity is presented in detail in Appendix A at the end of the book and in Chapter 4. We define a person to be economically inactive if he or she is not occupied with work, schooling, or child-care activities for more than about one half-time. In particular, we define persons to be inactive if they are *not* in any of the following categories:

- Attending school full-time
- Working at least one-half time
- Attending school and working at least part-time
- Having primary responsibility for caring for *either* an infant *or* two or more children aged less than 6 years of age
- Combining child-care time with either part-time schooling and/or part-time work

This definition, then, is based on a rather broad concept of economic activity, which is not limited to either labor-force participation or full-time schooling. Since many recent graduates of high school or college may find themselves economically inactive for some period of time—a transition period—we concentrate on economic inactivity when age 24.

In the first section of this chapter, we provide some further background on the issue of economic inactivity. In what ways has it increased or decreased over the last three decades? What is known about the long-run consequences of such idleness? In the next section we present our basic analysis of the determinants of economic inactivity, using our detailed data on 765 youths aged 24 or more in 1988. As in Chapters 5 and 6, we first concentrate on explanatory variables reflecting parental choices/opportunities and family circumstances. We then add stress and neighborhood variables, taken to reflect social or community investments in children. For this analysis, the primary neighborhood variable of interest is the adult unemployment rate, since it is most directly related to the youth's decision to choose to be economically active (or, conversely, to choose not to go to school, to work, or to engage in child-care activities).

In the third section we undertake some further explorations of some of the relationships found in the previous section, emphasizing the roles of parental education, the timing of parental decisions, the role of parental welfare recipiency, and neighborhood effects. The next section presents the results of simulations based on the estimated models.

Since the rate of economic inactivity is much higher among high-school dropouts than among those with more schooling, we estimate a simultaneous model of completing high school and economic inactivity. The results of this analysis are presented in the fifth section of the chapter. Finally, we draw some conclusions from our research.

ECONOMIC INACTIVITY: SOME BACKGROUND

The problem of declining work effort—or joblessness—has become an increasingly important social policy issue, especially as it concerns particular race and ethnic groups, and particular age groups. African-Americans—especially young African-Americans—have experienced high jobless and unemployment rates over the entire postwar period, and these rates, adjusted for the macroeconomic performance of the economy, have been growing over time. The rate of joblessness—having zero weeks worked in a year—for other minority youths has followed the same pattern.

Similarly, there is substantial concern regarding the rates of nonemployment of young women. In their case, it is a concern that dependence on welfare benefits has replaced their own work effort as the source of income and economic well-being. For both young males and females, the concern is that increasing joblessness is associated with the growth of nonproductive activities—illegal activities or welfare dependence—that are substitutes for working and earning.

Aggregate statistics indicate that there is basis for concern regarding youth joblessness. For example, using the Current Population Survey, Danziger and Wood (1992) found that the proportion of all African-American non-Hispanic men aged 18–64 who reported zero weeks worked in the prior year grew from .178 in 1979 to .204 in 1989, an increase of nearly 15 percent. For African-American non-Hispanic men aged 18–19 (20–24) (25–29), the percentage increases over the decade were 6.5 (26.8) (12.8) percent. By 1989, the jobless rates for these three groups stood at 40.7 percent, 25.1 percent, and 12.3 percent, respectively. These rates do not adjust for school enrollment or child care of an infant or of multiple children.

TABLE 7.1 Inactivity Rates, Persons Aged 21–25, 1973 and 1988

	Males		Females	
	1973	1988	1973	1988
White				
Inactive	10.2	9.7	11	8.1
In school	19.3	20.2	13.3	17.2
Nonwhite				
Inactive	15.8	19.7	12.2	11.7
In school	12.8	14.8	9.5	12.0

SOURCE: 1973 and 1988 CPS tapes.

By our own calculations from the Current Population Survey (CPS), the percentage of nonwhite (including African-American, Hispanic, Oriental, and other nonwhite groups) males aged 21–25 with no reported work in the prior year increased by nearly 50 percent from 1973 to 1988. However, the jobless patterns noted for nonwhite males do not hold for either young white males or females. For all of these groups, the proportion that reported no work activity either remained steady over the 1973 to 1988 period or decreased.

It should be noted that these statistics on joblessness may be misleading. The basic issue, we suggest, concerns the alternative activities in which youths might be engaged if they are not working in the formal labor market. Clearly, if attending school is the activity that is being substituted for market work, the problem of joblessness would fade in importance.

In an attempt to correct this problem, we defined a crude indicator of ''inactivity'' to use with CPS data. A person is economically inactive if he or she does not work 1000 hours per year, is not in the military, and is not in school (and, for females, is not the mother of a child less than 5 years old).

In Table 7.1, we present our tabulations on the rates of economic inactivity so defined for nonwhite and white youths aged 21–25 over the 1973 to 1988 period. The 1988 inactivity rates are substantial for all of the groups, ranging from 8.1 percent for white females to 19.7 percent for nonwhite males. For nonwhite males, the inactivity rate over this period has risen sharply from 15.8 percent to 19.7 percent, or by one-fourth. However, for all of the other groups the inactivity rate has fallen over the period. We have also shown the percentage of youths in these groups who are in school in the two years. Interestingly, for all of the groups the rate of school attendance has increased over the period, with the greatest absolute and percentage increase recorded for females.

BASIC ANALYSIS OF DETERMINANTS OF ECONOMIC INACTIVITY

Nearly one-quarter of our (unweighted) sample of young adults who are 24 or more years of age are economically inactive at the age of 24. This includes 29 percent of females and 20 percent of males. Thirty-five percent of young African-Americans are inactive, compared with 16 percent of youths from other races.

Of course, the characteristics of those who are inactive differ substantially from those of the active group of youths. Of those who are economically inactive, 33 percent have a mother who did not complete high school; of those economically active, 17 percent had a mother who dropped out of high school. And, although only 16 percent of young adults who grew up in a family that never lived in poverty were inactive, the incidence of inactivity was 24 percent for the entire sample, and nearly one-half (47 percent) for those who grew up in a family that was persistently poor when they were aged 6–15. While informative, these basic statistics tell us little about the independent effect of any one of these variables, holding the other determinants of economic inactivity constant. For this sort of information, we require multivariate statistical analysis.

The first two columns of Table 7.2 show the results from a sample model of the determinants of economic inactivity at age 24 for our sample. These estimates are similar to that presented in Chapter 4 and serve as a beginning point of our analysis. The second pair of columns present a more full-blown specification.

The results in Columns 1 and 2 of Table 7.2 are consistent with the simple calculations of the incidence of inactivity by gender and race we noted above: females and African-Americans are more likely to be economically inactive than are whites and males; the coefficients on these variables are positive and statistically significant. The educational choices of the parents also have an effect; children of high-school graduates are less likely to be inactive at the age of 24 than young adults whose parents failed to graduate from high school. The coefficients of the parental education variables are statistically significant at the 10

TABLE 7.2 Determinants of Economic Inactivity at Age 24, Sample of Observations Ages 24 Years or More, Probit Estimation, $N = 765$

Variable	Coefficient	t-statistic	Coefficient	t-statistic
Constant	−.28	0.60	−.01	0.0
Background				
African-American	.30	2.23**	.35	2.43**
Female	.26	2.51**	.27	2.56**
Parental Choices/Opportunities				
Any religion	−.13	0.59	−.11	0.51
Average number of siblings[a]	.01	0.21	−.00	0.09
Number of years lived with one parent[a]	−.01	0.25	−.03	1.03
Average annual hours with parents[a]	−.36^{-3}	1.31	−.56^{-3}	1.94**
Father a high-school graduate	−.25	1.67*	−.26	1.65*
Mother a high-school graduate	−.24	1.83*	−.25	1.82**
Average posttax family income ÷ poverty line[a]	−.05	0.94	−0.6	1.13
Number of years mother worked[a]	−.04	2.69**	−.04	2.55**
Number of years lived in SMSA[a]	.04	2.76**	.04	2.89**
Number of household location moves[a]			.05	1.40
Number of parental separations[a]			−.04	0.26
Number of parental (re)marriages[a]			.09	0.50
Average number of years head unemployed[a]			.04	1.33
Family ever received AFDC[a]			.30	1.95**
Family Circumstances				
Number of years family head disabled[a]	.01	0.72	−.01	0.50
Firstborn child	−.07	0.49	−.11	0.73
Neighborhood Attributes				
Average county unemployment rate[a]			−.02	1.41

NOTES: The model specifications include controls for whether both parents are in the sample in 1968, and whether the child's grandfather was foreign-born.

* Statistically significant at 10 percent level.
** Statistically significant at 5 percent level.

[a] During ages 6–15.

percent level for a two-tail test and the 5 percent level for a one-tail test. The two variables are jointly significant at the 5 percent level.

Parental decisions related to earnings and income are not related to the probability of a young adult's being economically inactive. The coefficient of the family income variable has a negative sign, but is not statistically significant. This may be the result of two offsetting effects—those with more income may have successful role models who are active in the labor market; on the other hand, additional income available in the family may reduce the pressure on a young adult to be economically active. However, children whose mothers chose to work in the paid labor market are less likely to be economically inactive. As the mother's work variable is continuous, the greater the number of years that the mother worked, the lower the probability that the youth will be economically inactive. This may reflect the role-model effect of the mother's choice—a set of attitudes regarding labor market participation that the mother is able to convey to the child.

In the simple model, neither of the variables measuring the amount of time parents spend with children while they are growing up—average parental time spent and years lived with one parent—are significantly associated with the probability that their child will be economically inactive at the age of 24. However, the negative coefficient of the variable measuring the average time parents spend with a child while he or she is growing up does suggest that more parental time may be associated with a reduced probability of inactivity.[2]

The number of siblings of the child appears unrelated to economic inactivity, as does the birth order of the child. The only other variable with a statistically significant effect on the probability of inactivity is the number of years that the parents choose to live in an SMSA or urban area. We interpret this to suggest that economic activity norms differ between urban and nonurban areas, perhaps related to the greater availability of informal work in rural areas.

In the last two columns of Table 7.2, we present the results from the more full-blown version of the model—one in which a set of parental choices creating stress for the child and a neighborhood attribute are added to the variables in the simple model.

The variables included in the simpler model of Columns 1 and 2 are but little changed in the fuller specification. The coefficients on both the father's and mother's education-choice variables remain statistically significant at the 10-percent level, two-tail test. The time parents spend with the child while growing up is now significant at the 5-percent level.

All of the measured influences are in the expected direction and suggest that parental choices leading to more resources (income, time, and human capital) reduce the probability that the youth will be economically inactive.

The additional parental choice/opportunity and neighborhood variables included in the equation add to our understanding of the determinants of economic inactivity: having lived in a family that received welfare benefits, a family with more geographical moves, and a family in which the head was unemployed are associated with an increased probability of being economically inactive, and all are at least marginally significant. The positive and significant association of the family welfare benefit receipt variable and young adult inactivity is consistent with estimates found in the intergenerational transmission of welfare literature. Growing up in an environment in which welfare is an important source of income may encourage dependence on income sources other than own-earnings.[3]

The number of location moves during childhood is positively associated with inactivity, although it is only marginally significant. Having a parent who is unemployed more years—suggesting limited labor market success of the parent and potentially negative attitudes toward the labor market—may explain the positive and marginally significant coefficient on this variable.

Surprisingly, the unemployment rate of the neighborhood in which the youths live is negatively associated with the probability that they will be economically inactive at age 24 and has a t-statistic of 1.41. There are, of course, differences in the acceptability of various types of economic activity: for example, working or going to school, as opposed to child care as an unmarried mother. Perhaps a higher county unemployment rate discourages job seeking and encourages greater reliance on welfare benefits or parental income.[4]

How well do these models fit? The simple model has a chi-square value of 73.4 for 15 degrees of freedom and predicts correctly the status of 76.2 percent of the sample, including 98 percent of those who are economically active. The expanded model does somewhat better, correctly predicting the activity status of 77 percent of the sample, including 97 percent of those active. The chi-square value is 84 for 21 degrees of freedom.

Since the prevalence of economic inactivity differs by gender and race, we also ran tests to see if the same structural models apply to African-Americans and other racial/ethnic groups, and to females and males. In both cases we could not reject the hypothesis that the same models apply to both subgroups, even at the 10 percent level.[5]

FURTHER EXPLORATIONS
OF THE DETERMINANTS OF INACTIVITY

The estimates in Table 7.2 represent our basic analysis of the determinants of the economic inactivity of youths when they are age 24. In this section, we explore a few variants of these specifications.

Beyond the parental choice of a high-school education, is there an effect of the mother's and father's schooling beyond that level on the probability of inactivity? Table 7.3 presents results using the fuller specification of Table 7.2, substituting three dummy variables: high-school graduation = 1, some college = 1, and college completion = 1 for the single dummy indicating high-school graduation for each parent.

Youths with fathers who have schooling beyond the high-school level are significantly less likely to be economically inactive than those whose fathers have a high-school diploma or less. This result could reflect a role-model effect of the father or the father's connections to job opportunities that come with additional schooling. The results for the effect of the mother's schooling are somewhat puzzling, however. The primary impact of the mother's schooling appears to be the choice of whether or not to graduate from high school. The children of mothers with a high-school diploma are less likely than other youths to be economically inactive at age 24.[6] Having a mother with at least some postsecondary education appears to have no effect on the activity level of the child, relative to not having a high-school diploma.

Second, does the timing of parental decisions or family circumstances make a difference in influencing the probability that a child will be economically inactive at age 24? We use the same age breakdowns as used in preceding chapters: 6–8, primary school; 9–11, pre-adolescent; and 12–15, adolescent years. Since the sample on which this analysis is based is smaller than that used for education, we also specify these time-related variables using only two periods—primary school (6–8) and adolescence (12–15). Both sets of results are reported in Table 7.4.

These results suggest a number of possible influences of parental choices made during, or family circumstances in, various periods of childhood on the probability of a youth being economically inactive. Three of the factors seem important when they occur when a child is

TABLE 7.3 The Association Between Parent's Level of Education and Child's Economic Inactivity

	Father		Mother	
Level of Schooling	Coefficient	t-statistic	Coefficient	t-statistic
High-School Graduate	−0.21	1.3	−0.29	2.1*
Some College	−0.52	2.0*	0.16	0.6
College Graduate	−0.69	2.3*	0.15	0.4

NOTE: The specification of this equation is otherwise the same as Columns 3 and 4 of Table 7.2.

*Statistically significant at 5 percent level, two-tail test.

young, and values are malleable and norms rather easily established. These factors include having a mother who works while the child is aged 6–8 (an experience that may suggest the importance of work); having the parent who is head of the household experience unemployment while the child is young; and living in a large urban area while a young child, which may lead to a less strong expectation of work while a young adult. In all of these cases, the signs are as expected and the coefficients either significant or marginally significant.[7]

Third, is there a connection between the parent's decision to receive welfare benefits when the child is 15 years or younger and the probability that the child will be economically inactive when a young adult? The results reported in Table 7.2 suggest a positive link—living in a family that received welfare while the child is growing up is reported in that table to be positively and significantly associated with an increased probability of economic inactivity. The time varying results do not indicate such a relationship; indeed, the signs on the years on AFDC variable are mixed, suggesting no clear association. However, it is possible that the duration of welfare receipt—as contrasted to whether the family received welfare at all—may be associated with economic inactivity of the child at age 24. One might speculate that long-term AFDC participation by the family in which children live might encourage them to be dependent on welfare, and hence inactive. On the other hand, such long-term dependence might generate aversion to welfare and a commitment to employment or schooling.

In Table 7.5, we explore this issue in a number of ways, using both subgroups of the population and alternative measures of welfare dependence. In terms of subgroups, Table 7.5 shows the effect of welfare

TABLE 7.4 Estimates of Time-Related Determinants of Economic Inactivity at Age 24

Variable	3 Time Periods		2 Time Periods	
	Coefficient	t-statistic	Coefficient	t-statistic
Average Annual Hours with Parents				
6–8	$-.09^{-4}$	0.1	$-.02^{-3}$	0.2
9–11	$-.05^{-3}$	0.3		
12–15	$-.11^{-3}$	0.8	$-.01^{-2}$	1.2
Number of Years Mother Worked				
6–8	$-.12$	2.3**	$-.08$	2.0**
9–11	.09	1.1		
12–15	$-.09$	1.3	$-.05$	0.8
Number of Years Lived in SMSA				
6–8	.31	3.6**	.20	3.1**
9–11	$-.34$	2.0**		
12–15	.07	0.6	$-.12$	1.5
Family Ever Received AFDC				
6–8	$-.01$	0.1	.01	1.4
9–11	.03	0.3		
12–15	$-.05$	0.5	$-.05$	1.2
Number of Household Location Moves				
6–8	.04	0.6	.05	0.8
9–11	.06	0.8		
12–15	.05	0.5	.07	0.8
Average Number of Years Family Head Unemployed				
6–8	.08	1.1	.11	1.6*
9–11	.12	1.0		
12–15	$-.07$	0.7	$-.01$	0.1

NOTE: The variables shown are those time-related variables that have t-statistics in excess of 1.3 in either Column 2 or 4 of Table 7.2. Other predictor variables are those listed in Column 3 of Table 7.2.

*Statistically significant at 10 percent level.
**Statistically significant at 5 percent level.

**TABLE 7.5 Estimates of Family Welfare Participation
and Economic Inactivity at Age 24**

	Coefficient	t-statistic
Family Received AFDC		
Full sample	.30	1.95**
Female sample	.38	1.81*
Male sample	.13	0.60
African-American sample	.34	1.74*
Non-African-American sample	.01	0.00
Years Family Received AFDC		
Full sample	$.08^{-2}$	0.30
Female sample	−.02	0.40
Male sample	.01	0.30
African-American sample	.01	0.40
Non-African-American sample	−.09	1.27
Spline Estimation		
Years family received AFDC	.27	3.0**
Years family received AFDC beyond 2 years	−.35	3.1**

NOTE: The probit equations are otherwise identical to those of Columns 3 and 4 of Table 7.2, with the following exceptions: in female (male) subsample equations, the (male) female variable is excluded; in the non-African-American (African-American) subsample equations, race is excluded.

*Statistically significant at 10 percent level.
**Statistically significant at 5 percent level.

recipiency on youth inactivity using race- and gender-specific samples. In terms of alternative measures of welfare dependence, we have included a variable measuring the number of years that the family received AFDC benefits (rather than a dummy variable for receipt of benefits); and as an alternative, we created a spline function with two components—number of years on AFDC and number of years on AFDC in excess of two.

The results suggest that the significant and positive effect on the youth's inactivity of the family ever receiving welfare benefits carries over to the African-American and the female sample; the event of receiving welfare does not appear to have an effect on the probability of inactivity for males and non-African-Americans.[8] When the continuous variable—years a family received AFDC—is used, the signs on the coefficients are mixed; however, none of them are significant. The spline function also tests for duration, in this case in a noncontinuous fashion. Here, we break duration into two continuous segments, with the discontinuity occurring at two years. The results suggest that a short duration on welfare is positively and statistically associated with a greater probability of being economically inactive; years beyond this have no further positive influence and rather may have a slightly negative association with the probability of economic inactivity.[9]

Taken together, these estimates suggest that if the family in which children grow up ever receives welfare, the children have a higher probability of being inactive when young adults. However, if the family ever received welfare, longer-term recipiency is not associated with a higher probability of economic inactivity (and, if anything, a lower probability). The absence of a duration effect is seen in both the insignificant coefficient of the years-family-received-AFDC variable, and in the negative and significant coefficient of the extended recipiency variable in the spline specification.

Finally, we inquired as to whether the attributes of the neighborhood in which children grow up are related to the probability that they will be economically inactive at age 24. To do this, we substituted three neighborhood variables (dummy variables for 40 percent or more of the households headed by a female, for 40 percent or more of the workers in high-prestige occupations, and for 40 percent or more of the youths as high-school dropouts) for the adult unemployment rate in the full specification of Table 7.2.[10] Only the female-headed household variable is marginally significant. The negative sign on the coefficient of this neighborhood variable may suggest that growing up in a neighborhood that is intensive in its use of welfare benefits is related to "economic activity" in the form of the care of young children.

SIMULATION RESULTS

Our results in Tables 7.2–7.5 suggest a strong relationship between a number of variables reflecting parental choices/opportunities, family circumstances, and neighborhood attributes during childhood and the probability that a youth will be economically inactive at age 24. However, because the coefficients shown in the tables are estimates from maximum likelihood models, the quantitative relationship between the explanatory and dependent variables cannot be readily discerned.

In Table 7.6 we report a series of simulations designed to reveal the

TABLE 7.6 Simulated Effects of Changes in Explanatory Variables: Predicted Value of Attainment Variable and Percentage Change from Population (Base) Value of Attainment Variables

Variable	Probability of Economic Inactivity	Percentage Change from Base
Base	.18	
Parental Education		
Both parents are high-school graduates	.13	−26.5
Neither parent is a high-school graduate	.26	46.4
Number of Years Mother Worked*		
0	.24	35.2
3	.21	−14.6
10	.13	−25.5
Average Annual Hours with Parents*		
300 hours/year	.28	53.3
1200 hours/year	.15	−17.3
Number of Years Lived in SMSA*		
0	.12	−34.3
3	.14	−20.7
10	.21	18.3
Number of Household Location Moves*†		
0	.16	−9.0
4	.21	−16.2
Average Number of Years Family Head Unemployed*‡		
0	.17	−4.4
3	.20	11.1
10	.27	52.7
Family Ever Received AFDC*		
No	.17	−8.1
At least one year	.19	6.3

NOTE: Simulation estimates based on specification in Table 7.2.

* Variable records events during, or circumstances averaged over, child's ages 6–15.
† Variable has t-statistic of 1.4 in Table 7.2.
‡ Variable has t-statistic of 1.3 in Table 7.2.

effect of changes in the explanatory variables on the probability of economic inactivity. In the simulations, individual variables that are statistically significant in the results shown in Columns 3 and 4 of Table 7.2 are changed, one at a time for each observation, with the remainder of the variables being held constant. The resulting expected probability of inactivity is calculated for each observation, and this value is then multiplied by the observation's weight. The results shown in Table 7.6 are weighted averages over these values for individuals in the sample. By using the population weights in this simulation exercise, our simulated values represent predictions for the nation as a whole.

The explanatory variables with the largest simulated effect on the overall probability of economic inactivity include a number of parental choices and opportunities while the child was aged 6–15: parental choices regarding their own education and work effort, the amount of time parents spend with their children while they are growing up, and the extent of parental unemployment.

At the mean of all of the explanatory variables, the expected national probability of inactivity is .18. However, if the level of parental time spent with children was stipulated to be one standard deviation below the mean of about 950 hours per year, the expected probability of inactivity would rise to .28, an increase of over 50 percent. Similarly, if the level of parental time was increased by one standard deviation from the mean, the expected probability of inactivity would fall to .15, a decrease of about 17 percent.

Effects of a similar magnitude are shown for the parental unemployment and parental education variables. If a child's parent was never unemployed while the child was growing up, the expected probability of economic inactivity at age 24 would be .17. However, if the parents were unemployed during 3 of the 10 years that the child was aged 6–15, the expected probability of inactivity rises to .20, an increase of about 11 percent.

When we simulate that both parents are high-school graduates—as opposed to the mean proportions of the fathers and the mothers—the expected probability of inactivity falls from .18 to .13, a decrease of one-quarter.

The extent to which the mother decides to work while the children are young also appears to have a strong effect on their level of activity at age 24. If the mother is assumed to work for 3 of the 10 years, the probability of youth inactivity is .21, a value that is 15 percent above the base level of .18. However, if the mother had not worked at all during the child's growing up period (holding the amount of parental child-care time constant), the probability that the child would be inactive at age 24 increases to .24, an increase of about one-third.

Finally, large effects on the probability that the child will be economically inactive are also recorded for parental decisions to change geographic locations, to live in a large urban area, and to become welfare recipients. Almost no response is estimated from changing the income of all families in poverty up to the poverty line.[11]

As noted above, the coefficient on the included neighborhood variable is not significant. However, accepting the estimated coefficient as the best point estimate, our simulation suggests that moving from an adult unemployment rate two standard deviations below the mean to an unemployment rate two deviations above the mean (from a rate of 2.5 to 12.6) would decrease the probability of being inactive from .20 to .14.

A BIVARIATE PROBIT ESTIMATION
OF HIGH-SCHOOL GRADUATION
AND YOUTH ECONOMIC INACTIVITY

In Chapter 5 we studied the determinants of educational attainment among youths, on the presumption that educational success is an important indicator of ultimate lifetime achievements. Our estimates in this chapter focus on one aspect of attainment beyond the years of schooling—engaging in productive activity at age 24. If our presumption in Chapter 5 is correct, there is likely to be a relationship between these outcomes.

Table 7.7 is a simple cross-tabulation of the relationship between educational attainment and economic inactivity for the 765 youths in our sample. The relationship is as we expected—those youths with greater schooling attainments have a substantially higher probability of being economically active when they are 24.

While this relationship is clear in our data, it says little about how these two variables are related in the actual decision process of the youth. Does the level of schooling completed influence the probability of economic inactivity at age 24? Do youths make a joint decision regarding schooling and economic inactivity? If youths at, say, age 16 have a high expected probability of being inactive in their mid-twenties, do they tend to choose fewer years of schooling? In this section, we explore the nature of the relationship between these outcomes. Are our results modified if we model the decisions made by the youth as a si-

**TABLE 7.7 Cross-Tabulation of Economic Inactivity,
by Years of Education** *N* = 765

	Percent Economically Inactive Age 24
Level of Education	
Not a high-school graduate	36
High-school graduate	22
Years of Education	
<10	40
11	33
12	29
13	21
14+	15

NOTE: The correlation between inactivity and high-school graduation is −.12; with years of education it is −.20

multaneous system—do similar unmeasured factors such as motivation, tastes, or events during childhood simultaneously influence both of these decisions?

The model that we estimate is a bivariate probit model that specifies first whether the youth graduated from high school and, then, whether he or she was economically inactive at age 24. (The econometric structure of this model is presented in Appendix B.) The test for simultaneity yielded by this estimate provides information on the nature and extent of the relationship between these variables.

Due to the sample size, we use a parsimonious specification of the model. We include as explanatory variables those that were found to be significantly related to the education outcome in Table 5.1 and to the economic inactivity variable in Table 7.2. Among the neighborhood characteristics, we include variables that we expected to be most closely associated with each of the outcomes, such as the proportion of the youths in the child's neighborhood who were dropouts (in the education component of the model), and the adult unemployment rate in the child's neighborhood (in the economic inactivity component).

Our results are presented in Table 7.8. The estimated value of Rho—the test statistic for the simultaneity of the estimates—is −.56. Although this value is relatively large, suggesting that simultaneity may be present among these decisions, it is not statistically significant at the

TABLE 7.8 Bivariate Probit Estimate:
High-School Graduation and Economic Inactivity at Age 24

Variable	High-School Graduation ($N=765$)		Economically Inactive at Age 24 ($N=765$)	
	Coefficient	t-statistic	Coefficient	t-statistic
Constant	1.15	2.47**	−.66	1.53
Background				
Female	−.002	0.00	.17	1.42
African-American	.50	2.26**	.23	1.20
African-American × female	.03	.12		
Parental Choices/Opportunities				
Average number of siblings[a]	.005	.01	−.04	1.10
Any religion	.16	.49	.23	.90
Father a high-school graduate	.20	.85	−.24	1.40
Father some college	.15	.41		
Father a college student	.14	.31		
Mother a high-school graduate	.22	1.23	−.23	1.57
Mother some college	.19	.40		
Mother a college graduate	4.45	.00		
Number of years family head disabled[a]	−.08	3.31**		
Number of years lived in SMSA[a]	−.03	1.81*	.05	2.90**
Number of household location moves[a]	−.16	4.27**	.10	2.29**
Number of years mother worked[a]	−.01	.52	−.05	2.38**
Number of years posttax family income < poverty line[a]	−.04	1.36		
Average posttax family income ÷ poverty line[a]	.15	1.49	−.06	.95
Average number of years family head unemployed[a]			.03	.88
Family ever received AFDC[a]			.34	2.08**
Number of years lived with one parent[a]			.001	.04
Family Circumstances				
Firstborn child	.36	1.51	−.34	2.04**
Neighborhood Attributes				
Average percentage of youths who are high-school dropouts[a]	−.01	1.51		

TABLE 7.8 (*continued*)

Variable	High-School Graduation (N = 765)		Economically Inactive at Age 24 (N = 765)	
	Coefficient	t-statistic	Coefficient	t-statistic
Average adult neighborhood unemployment[a]			−.03	1.50
Goodness of Fit				
Rho	−56	1.34		
Log likelihood value	−568			

* Significant at 10 percent level.
** Significant at 5 percent level.

[a] During ages 6–15.

5 percent level. However, when the neighborhood variables are excluded from the model, the value of Rho is significant at the 1 percent level.[12] Hence, we interpret the results on the presumption that the two decisions are simultaneously related—that unmeasured experiences, tastes, or motivations are statistically related to both of the decisions.

Do the estimated results in Table 7.8 differ from those in the more direct estimates presented earlier? First, while the race and gender background characteristics of the children were significant in both the education and economic inactivity estimates, only the race variable in the education component of the bivariate probit model is statistically significant. The signs on the coefficients are the same as in the prior estimates, however.

Among the parental choice/opportunities variables, the results in Table 7.8 largely verify our earlier estimates. Parental education choices are again positively related to the probability of graduating from high school and negatively related to the probability of being economically inactive at age 24, but they are either insignificant or marginally significant in the Table 7.8 results. Parental economic resources are not significantly related to either of the outcomes in any of the specifications.

There are two changes in the estimated effect of those parental choice variables indicating stress for children 6–15 years old. While the coefficient on the number of location moves was marginally significant in the economic inactivity results of Table 7.2, it is strongly significant in the bivariate probit estimates. Similarly, the coefficient on the variable indicating whether the parents of the child ever received welfare benefits is substantially larger in the simultaneous estimates than in the single-equation estimates of Table 7.2, and becomes statistically significant.

Finally, while the effect of being the firstborn child in the family was statistically significant in the high-school graduation estimates of Chapter 5 (t-statistic = 2.35), it is only marginally significant in Table 7.8 (t-statistic = 1.51).

These changes carry the suggestion that certain of the parental choices/opportunities variables may have a longer-term and more adverse effect on children's attainments than is indicated by the estimates that do not account for the simultaneity between decisions made earlier and later in the child's life. Conversely, some of the family attributes may have less effect than the more straightforward estimates suggest.

CONCLUSION

In this chapter we explored the relationship between parental choices/opportunities and family and neighborhood characteristics when children are growing up and their activities in their mid-twenties. We define a person to be economically inactive if he or she is not occupied with work, schooling, or child-care activities for more than about one half-time. As in earlier chapters, we first explored simple relationships between our primary family and neighborhood characteristics and the indicator of inactivity, and then estimated a more complex simultaneous model.

The pattern of estimated results could be interpreted as strongly supportive of the role-model perspective discussed in Chapter 3. Children who grow up with parents that themselves are active—mothers who work, parents with a high-school education, parents who spend time with their children, families who avoided being on welfare, parents with more income—tend to have a higher probability of themselves being active. The coefficients of all of these variables have the expected sign, and all of them save the coefficient of the income variable are significant. The separate estimates of the effect of family welfare participation for the females in our sample suggests that the role of family welfare participation is an especially important factor in understanding their activity probabilities.

In addition to these effects, the probability of being active is also related to the race and gender background characteristics. The positive and significant coefficient of the African-American variable has a number of possible interpretations, but is consistent with the high pattern of minority youth joblessness, and the labor market discrimination hypothesis which is often used to explain this pattern. The positive and significant effect of being a female is consistent with the lower labor-force participation rate of women and the several cultural and economic hypotheses that predict this pattern. The positive (though not significant) coefficient of the neighborhood unemployment rate suggests the effect of labor demand on the level of observed economic activity among youths.

Finally, the interaction between the educational attainment of youths and the probability that they will be economically active at age 24 is noteworthy (see Table 7.7). Those youths who complete high school—or who have more years of completed schooling—have a higher probability of being active than those who have terminated their schooling before high school or shortly after.

NOTES

1. See, for example, National Commission on Children (1991).

2. It will be recalled that the child-care time variable is a predicted value, and hence subject to substantial measurement error.

3. Separate analysis by race and by gender suggest that this influence is significant only among females and among nonwhites. See below.

4. An alternative specification using three neighborhood variables suggests that living in an area with a higher prevalence of households headed by women may be negatively associated with the probability of being economically inactive (t-statistic = 1.5). This also is an unexpected result. The other two neighborhood variables—a 40 percent or more prevalence of both labor force participants in high-prestige occupations and youths who are high-school dropouts—are not statistically significantly associated with economic inactivity of young adults.

5. Chi-square tests for statistically significant differences in the models for males versus females and the two racial groups were conducted. For these equations, the test statistics were 28 for the racial groups and 24 for the gender groups. The relevant test values are 32 at the 10 percent level, 35 at the 5 percent level, and 42 at the 1 percent level. Hence, we fail to reject the null hypothesis that there are no significant differences in the models for men and women or the racial subgroups.

6. In the cross-tabulations, 16 percent of the youths whose mothers were high-school graduates, 23 percent of the youths whose mothers had some college, and 15 percent of the children of college graduates were economically inactive. However, the numbers of mothers in the sample who attended or graduated from college is small.

7. In the pre-adolescent years, the only time-related variable that is statistically significant is the years lived in an SMSA. The sign on the coefficient for this variable over ages 6–8 is positive, suggesting that children who live in an urban area when they are very young are more likely to be inactive; however, the sign on the variable for ages 9–11 is negative, and it too is statistically significant, suggesting that children who live in an urban area during these ages are somewhat less likely to be economically inactive at age 24. These quite different results are unexpected. No factors seem important when they occur while the individual is an adolescent— although there is some indication of a negative association with the number of years the child's mother worked, and (in the specification with two time periods), a negative association with years lived in an SMSA.

8. We tested to see if there was a statistically significant difference between the structure of the model fit over gender- and race-specific samples and the full model. The null hypothesis that either the gender- or race-specific models differed in their structure from the full model could not be rejected at the 10 percent level in this case either.

   We also explored interactions of the gender variables with the family-received-AFDC dummy variable and with the years-family-received-AFDC variable, and only in the case of the female interaction with the family-received-AFDC dummy variable was the coefficient of interaction term even marginally significant. (The positive coefficient of this interaction variable was significant, which is consistent with the results shown in Table 7.5.)

9. The signs on the two terms of the spline function are of the opposite signs, and both are significant. Because the magnitudes of the coefficients are similar, the spline specification indicates that welfare receipt for two years has a positive and significant effect on the probability that the youth will be inactive, but that additional years of recipiency have no additional effect on the probability. A simulation using the spline coefficients suggest a nonlinear influence of duration of welfare receipt on the probability of economic inactivity. Holding all of the other variables constant at their mean values, the estimated probability that a youth will be inactive at age 24 is .24 (unweighted); this probability becomes .06 if a child grew up in family that had no welfare experience at all. However, if the family of the child is simulated to have been on welfare for all 10 years, the probability is .12.

10. The coefficients of the remaining variables in the specification in Columns 3 and 4 remained virtually unchanged. The father's education variable changed from being significant to being marginally significant.

11. One might wish to study the influence of eliminating poverty on children who grew up experiencing a spell of family poverty when they were age 6–15. We simulated this impact of economic resources as well, and find very little impact. The average probability of inactivity for this group of vulnerable children was .251; the simulated effect on the average probability of eliminating poverty reduced this to .249.

12. The value of Rho in the model without neighborhood variables is nearly −1, which is statistically significant at the 1 percent level. The Wald test-statistic is 80, compared to a critical value of 6.63 at the 1 percent level. As expected, the statistical significance of some of the remaining variables is increased when the neighborhood variables are excluded, indicating the importance of including in the estimation a rich selection of background, parental choice/opportunity, family attribute, and neighborhood characteristics.

8

Our Findings and Some Policy Implications

INTRODUCTION: CHILDREN'S WELL-BEING AND PUBLIC POLICY

We began this book by citing evidence that children have not done well in this country over the past three decades. Much has been written about the decline in the status and performance of the nation's children as a whole, and especially of the precarious situation of many children who grow up in poor, unstable, and single-parent families. Both the overall decline in well-being and the special problems for the nation's most at risk children have serious implications for the nation's future.

The current status of the nation's children and their prospects for future success are central elements in public discussions regarding economic and social policy. It is claimed that we have neglected the economic prospects of our children: cited in evidence are low absolute and relative levels of private saving and capital investment, persistent federal government deficits, higher net tax burdens imposed on future generations compared with those living today,[1] deteriorated public infrastructure, and sagging indicators of child and youth attainments. We are allowing a large and increasing share of our children to grow up in families living below the poverty line. Indeed, official poverty rates show that today's children are poorer than other groups in society, poorer than they have been in the past, and poorer than children in many other Western developed countries. In discussions of Social Security, intergenerational conflict is asserted: while we have done well by our older citizens, we have neglected children.

Children also get caught up in policy debates over other issues. Support through welfare for unmarried women caring for children at home

237

seems incongruous with the fact that most women with children are now employed. Housing policy debates reflect the belief that past policies bear much of the responsibility for having concentrated children in neighborhoods that today are noteworthy for their high rates of joblessness, school failure, drug use, and crime. The debate over education reform—school choice, magnet schools, busing—reflects the judgment that neither schools nor neighborhoods are serving children the way we would have them.

In this concluding chapter, we attempt to pull together a variety of themes concerning the level and trend in children's well-being and the potential for public policy to intervene effectively in this area.

In the second section of this chapter we review the most salient facts regarding children's status and success, and then restate our perspective concerning the determinants of children's attainments. By viewing children's achievements as important because of the well-being that they afford their parents and themselves, and as integral to the processes of future economic and social development—that is, by viewing children as human capital—we are able to organize our discussion of the roles of government (or society), families, and children themselves in fostering success and attainment. The insights of this perspective for our research are described in the next section.

The research that we have presented in this book focuses on the effect of decisions taken by parents, and the circumstances in which families find themselves, on the attainments of children. In the fourth section we summarize our findings.

Finally, we nest our findings in those broader public discussions regarding the role of public policy in increasing the success of children, and thereby securing a more productive, more successful future for our next generation.

HOW, IN FACT, ARE CHILDREN FARING?

By any number of standards—for example, America's children in the past, or today's children in other industrialized nations—today's American children do not fare well. Numerous facts confirm this assessment. We shall recall here only a few of them selected from the longer list in Chapter 1.

The nature of the families in which children are raised is perhaps the most vivid indication of this deterioration. About 25 percent of today's children have been born to an unwed mother, and less than 75 percent of them live with two parents. For African-American children the situation is far worse—nearly 70 percent of African-American children are born to a nonmarried mother, and less than 40 percent of them live with two parents. Moreover, with increasing numbers of both single and married mothers in the labor force, the amount of parental child-care time is less than it could be, and than it was. Whereas in 1965 the average child spent about 30 hours per week interacting with a parent, by the late 1980s this figure had dropped to about 17 hours.

Conditions that children encounter in the home have clearly eroded. The rising rate of marital dissolution—an increase of more than 30 percent from 1970 to 1987—has increased the extent to which children are exposed to this form of stress. Whereas during the 1960s, 19 percent of American children experienced their parent's marital dissolution, this rate increased to 30 percent in the 1980s. The rate of child maltreatment (including abuse) now stands at more than 300 per 10,000 children, up threefold from 20 years ago. The suicide rate of teenagers from 15–19 is high, more than 11 per 100,000. Teenagers continue to drop out of high school at a 15 percent rate, with higher rates for minorities. For those who stay in high school and take the Scholastic Aptitude Test (SAT), the average combined score of slightly more than 900 is judged to be low by nearly all observers.[2]

There have also been important changes in the income available to children, and in the sources of that income. The average cash income (in real terms) of families in the lowest fifth of the income distribution is now well below that in the early 1970s. This in part reflects the decline in median earnings over this time period, but more particularly the concentration of this decline among younger men and those with limited education. It also partly reflects a decline in the real value of public income support programs. As of 1990, real AFDC benefit levels for a mother and two children on average were less than $7500, down from more than $10,000 in 1972. The effectiveness of these government programs in moving working-age, earnings-poor families out of poverty has fallen significantly; the last 20 years have been an era of retrenchment.

Not all factors contributing to child well-being have deteriorated, however. On average, today's parents are better educated than those of any previous cohort. In 1970, 61 percent of the parents of elementary-school children had completed high school; by 1987 this percentage had increased to 73.

Similarly, average family sizes have decreased over the past quarter century. The average number of births per 1000 women aged 15–44 declined from 122.7 in the mid-1950s to 67.8 in the mid-1980s and has increased only slightly since that time. As a result, the average child has fewer siblings today than in earlier decades and less competition for parental attention and resources. This decline in average number of children per family with children has been greater among African-American families than white families, although the average number remains higher among minorities than white families.

Overall, many of the more troubling of these indicators of children's status can be summarized by the nation's official poverty statistics. More than 20 percent of all children now live in poor families, and the incidence of children's poverty is above 40 percent in minority families. Nearly 12 percent of families with children younger than 18 fail to escape poverty even though someone in the family worked; about 7 percent of these families remained in poverty even though there was at least one person working at least three-fourths time.

Growing up in a family with low income conveys only a portion of the full deprivation that is experienced. Children who grow up in poor families also experience a wide range of other circumstances that thwart their opportunities. A number of them are exposed to lead and other environmental hazards, have relatively low and deteriorating health status, and are less likely to be immunized against common preventable diseases. They tend to live in neighborhoods with high rates of crime, drug dependence, and drug trafficking; to attend schools with low capacities to convey education or inspire learning; and to live in a family with no working adult. They are more likely to give birth out of wedlock and—by their own testimony—find traditional norms involving hard work, creativity, diligence, organization, stability, and loyalty to be unrewarding. To make matters worse, most of these correlates of living in a poor family are substantially higher if the children are African-American or Hispanic.

While these statistics are discouraging, they clearly do not apply to all children. The admonition to "beware the mean" also applies to statistics on the incidence of adverse circumstances. The average American child today has access to substantial economic resources as well as a number of other advantages. A large part of the problem of children's status is rooted in differences among children, rather than the status of the average child: the gaps among children today are far larger than they have been since statisticians have been keeping track. It is at the bottom of the nation's income distribution that these problems are concentrated.

CHILDREN AS HUMAN CAPITAL: OUR RESEARCH PERSPECTIVE

In our view, one of the most useful ways of understanding the level of children's success and attainment in our society is by viewing children as human capital.

In this perspective, children's success is determined by the choices made by society, by families, and by children themselves. The choices made by society (primarily the government) concern the opportunities that are available to children and the families in which they grow up. We have referred to this as the "social investment in children." The choices made by parents involve the level of resources that they make available to their children, and involve not only financial resources but also time, energy, love, and support: we called these the "parental investment in children." Finally, there are the choices that children make on their own behalf—how they spend their time and choose their friends, how they mold their own future.

This way of characterizing the problem provides a *sequential view* of the process of children's attainments. Society (government) acts first, making some direct investments in children and families, but more importantly setting the economic environment in which both parents and children operate. Given this environment, parents choose how much to work and earn (given their talents) and how much time to spend with their children, and then, given their income, they decide how much to devote to their children.[3] They also make decisions about family structure and location that serve their own interests, but that also affect their children. Finally, given their own talents, the resources that have been invested in them, and the incentives that they confront, children—at least older children—make choices about their education, their reproduction behavior and family structure, and their work effort. We observe the outcome of these choices—children's attainments.

Government

Society—or government, as its agent—sets the basic environment within which families and children make their choices. In this view, government controls a wide variety of policy instruments: taxing policies, spending policies, regulatory policies, and judicial pronouncements. The use of any of these instruments will affect families and their children in a wide variety of ways. Government decisions, we presume, reflect the collective attitudes of its citizens. They also reflect the resource constraints of the society, and the structure of relative prices.

Government policies can have both a *direct* and *indirect* effect on children's well-being and on their ultimate chances for success. Those policies that have direct effects on children comprise the social investments in children.

Parents

Like government, but even more directly, the decisions made by parents influence how children develop and the level of success that they achieve when they are young adults. Like government, parents have objectives, and these may reflect their own well-being or that of the entire family. Parents make choices that reflect their objectives, and in so doing they establish the environment in which their children are raised. Within a set of constraints, they choose how many children to have, and when; whether or not to work, and how much to earn; where and in what sort of conditions to live; how much time to spend with their children; and so on. All of these choices (and many others, as well) have influences on their children. Together they determine the level of parental investment in children.

The objectives of parents often conflict, requiring consideration of trade-offs. Although the provision of time and resources for children appears on the list of things that give parents satisfaction, they are not the only things. Having a new car may conflict with hiring a tutor to work with a child who is performing poorly in school. Working two jobs may detract from quality time spent with children, although it will generate additional income in which children will share.

In evaluating these trade-offs and making these choices, parents also confront constraints. They may wish to earn income, but they may not be able to find a job. They are constrained by their own background and characteristics: they may have little education, few abilities, poor health, or limited language proficiency. The relative prices and wages they face are also constraints, as are prevailing social mores. If marital separation and divorce meet with social disapproval, or if accepting welfare benefits is frowned on by family and friends, choosing these options will appear more costly, and choices will be effectively constrained.

Operating in a social and economic environment that is influenced by the decisions and choices made by governments, parents make choices that directly influence the success of their children.

Children

The approach that we have suggested for viewing both the choices of society (government) and parents also applies to children—at least older children. At least after some point during their adolescence years, they too can be viewed as rational decision makers. We, therefore, presume that older adolescents have carefully weighed the gains and losses associated with the options available to them, and have made the choices that we observe, constrained by circumstances or limitations that affect their available choices.

CHOICES, INVESTMENTS, AND CHILDREN'S SUCCESS: OUR RESEARCH APPROACH AND FINDINGS

The research that we have presented has been guided by this investment-choices framework. Wherever possible, we have attempted to assess the relationship between choices made by governments and parents—and various other family and neighborhood characteristics—and the attainments of a representative sample of young adults. Such public and parental choices (and characteristics) are interpreted as reflecting various levels of investment in children. We study the relationship of these investments on the attainments of children when they become young adults in a context in which these youths, themselves, make choices.

Our Data on Children and Their Families

Within this overall investment-in-children framework, our research approach has been largely determined by the survey data that we have available. Although it would have been desirable to have a nationally representative sample of children with detailed, year-by-year information on the child's peers, the characteristics of the schools attended, performance in school, the attributes of neighborhoods, and the constraints on and incentives for choosing among the options available to them—in addition to detailed information on family choices and circumstances—no such longitudinal data set exists.

The data we have assembled include 21 years of information on about 1700 children born about 1965 and who were 25–31 years old in 1992, and on their families. These data are from the University of Michigan Panel Study of Income Dynamics (PSID). All of these children were living in 1968, at which time they ranged in age from 0–6. Each of these children was "dropped in on" in each of the subsequent 21 years (until 1988), and in each year the characteristics of their families and other living arrangements were observed and recorded.

For each child, then, we are able to know a number of basic unchanging characteristics, such as race, gender, and year of birth. We are also able to obtain detailed information on the kind of family in which the child lives during each year of childhood—the income of the family, its religion, the number of parents present and their education levels, whether these parents work, how much they work if they do work, how many other children are in the family, whether the family is on welfare or not, where the family lives (whether in a central city, and in what region of the country), and so on.

More importantly, because we have a snapshot of the child in each year, we are able to include information about a number of important changes and events that occurred during the child's lifetime. These include events such as the separation of the child's parents; the unemployment of the head of the child's family; if the family went on welfare, or changed location, or if the family head became disabled. Finally, we know some of the things that have happened to the child, such as losing a grade in school.

We enriched these basic PSID data by adding information on the number of hours of care time that parents spend with their children; detailed characteristics of the neighborhoods in which the families lived (obtained by matching on an annual basis, information available in our data with detailed tract information available in the 1970 and 1980 Censuses), and the year-by-year value of welfare-type benefits that are available in the state in which the child lives.

Aspects of Success in Young Adulthood

The outcomes or attainments of the children that we have chosen to study are among the most important in terms of forecasting ultimate success. The first outcome that we analyzed is education. Did the youth finish high school, or did he or she drop out? If he or she graduated from high school, were additional years of schooling or training chosen? How many years of schooling were completed?

We also explored the choices that the girls in our sample made regarding whether or not to have a child out of wedlock while they were teenagers, and if they became an unmarried teenage mother, whether or not they then chose to go on welfare.

A third choice that we study related to the activities of these young adults when they are in their mid-twenties. Some of them are not in school, or working, or required to engage in child care—we call them "economically inactive."

While these are basic outcomes, there are a variety of other aspects of success that would have been worthwhile to study—aspects of behavior related to drugs, crime, or sexual activities; mental or physical health problems; achievements in extracurricular or sports activities; reproductive or marital choices; and ultimate economic success such as earnings or income. For some of these attainments and outcomes, data are simply unavailable; for others, the length of time for which we have information constrains the research that is feasible.

Our Research Findings Summarized

Our research has attempted to establish the relationship of several aspects of children's attainments to a rich set of family choices/circumstances and neighborhood characteristics. The sheer number of linkages between choices/circumstances and outcomes makes any summary of our findings less than complete.

In Table 8.1, we summarize the most important findings from earlier chapters. Along the top of the table, we list the five outcome measures that we have investigated. The rows of the table are the choice/circumstance variables that we judge to be the most important from both a social-scientific and a policy perspective. In each cell of the table, we provide information on the following aspects of the relationships we have studied[4]:

- The direction of effect, as reflected in the sign on the estimated coefficient

- Whether or not the estimated effect was statistically significant

- A judgmental assessment of whether the estimated effect is quantitatively large or small, conditional on the effect being statistically significant

- A quantitative indication of the change in the level of attainment in response to a change in the specified family choice/circumstance or neighborhood characteristic

**TABLE 8.1 Summary of Empirical Findings
on the Determinants of Children's Attainments**

Parental Choices/Opportunities	Graduated From High School (Table 5.1)	Years of Schooling (Table 5.2)
Parental Education	Positive, statistically significant, quantitatively large Were all parents high-school graduates, probability child would drop out falls by nearly one-half	Positive, statistically significant, quantitatively large Were all parents high-school graduates, mean years of schooling of nation's children increases by 4.3 percent
Family Living in Poverty	Negative, not statistically significant, not quantitatively large Were poverty for all of nation's children eliminated, the probability a child would drop out falls by 3 percent Among those who grew up in a family that experienced poverty, the probability a child would drop out falls by 6 percent if poverty were eliminated	Negative, statistically significant, not quantitatively large Were poverty for all of nation's children eliminated (vs. a mean number of years in poverty equal to 1), mean years of schooling of nation's children would increase by .3 percent Were poverty eliminated for those children who experienced poverty, they would have a 1 percent increase in years of schooling
Number of Years on Welfare, When Poor[a]	Negative, not statistically significant, not quantitatively large If all children living in poverty received AFDC (vs. no children in poverty received AFDC) the probability a child would drop out increases by 4 percent	Positive, statistically significant, not quantitatively large Were all poor children on welfare (vs. no poor children on welfare), mean years of schooling of nation's children would increase by .3 percent

Teenage Out-of-Wedlock Birth (Table 6.2)	Received Welfare after Teenage Out-of-Wedlock Birth (Table 6.2)	Economic Inactivity (Table 7.2)
Mother a high-school graduate = 1; negative, statistically significant, quantitatively large Were all mothers high-school graduates, probability that daughter has teenage nonmarital birth falls by one-half	Negative, not statistically significant	Negative, statistically significant, quantitatively large Were all parents high-school graduates, probability of inactivity among nations' youths falls by 26 percent
Family predicted income/needs; statistically significant, quantitatively small Were poverty for all of nation's children experiencing poverty eliminated (vs. a mean number of years in poverty equal to 2.3), probability of teenage nonmarital birth would fall 3 percent Were poverty eliminated for those children who experienced it as a child, the probability of a teenage nonmarital birth among this group would fall by 4 percent	Family predicted income/needs; negative, statistically significant, quantitatively small Were family income/needs for all poor children raised to poverty line, probability of welfare recipiency would fall 4 percent Were poverty eliminated for those children who experienced poverty, the probability that they would receive welfare falls by 5 percent	Family predicted income/needs; positive, not statistically significant, quantitatively small
Parents ever received welfare = 1; negative, not statistically significant	Parents ever received welfare = 1; positive, statistically insignificant	Positive, statistically significant, quantitatively large Were no parents to receive welfare (vs. a mean number of years of recipiency of .6), probability of inactivity among nation's youths would fall by 8 percent

247

TABLE 8.1 *(continued)*

Parental Choices/Opportunities	Graduated From High School (Table 5.1)	Years of Schooling (Table 5.2)
Number of Years Mother Worked[a]	Positive, statistically significant, quantitatively large Were mother working all 10 years (vs. no years), probability child would drop out falls by 43 percent	Positive, statistically insignificant Were all mothers working 10 years (vs. no years), mean years of schooling of nation's children would increase by 1 percent
Number of Years Living in Single-Parent Family[a]	Negative, marginally significant, not quantitatively large Were all 10 years in intact family (vs. mean of 8.5 years), probability child would drop out falls by 8 percent	Negative, statistically significant, quantitatively large Were all of nation's children to spend 10 years in intact family (vs. mean of 8.5 years), schooling of nation's children increases by 1 percent
Number of Family Structure Changes (parental separations, remarriages)[a]	No measurable effect	Number of parental separations not statistically significant; number of remarriages negative, statistically significant, quantitatively small
Number of Years Living with Disabled Parent[a]	Negative, statistically significant, quantitatively large Were all parents disabled zero years (vs. 10 years), probability child would drop out falls by 53 percent	Negative, statistically significant, quantitatively large Were all parents disabled zero years (vs. 10 years), means years of schooling of nation's children increases by 3 percent

Teenage Out-of-Wedlock Birth (Table 6.2)	Received Welfare after Teenage Out-of-Wedlock Birth (Table 6.2)	Economic Inactivity (Table 7.2)
		Negative, statistically significant, quantitatively large Were all mothers working 10 years (vs. no years) probability of inactivity among nation's youths would fall by 45 percent
		Negative, not statistically significant, quantitatively large
Number of parental separations; positive, statistically significant, quantitatively large; number of remarriages negative, statistically significant Were the number of parental separations of all children experiencing separation to decrease by one, probability of teenage nonmarital birth falls 27 percent		Number of parental separations negative, not statistically significant; number of remarriages positive, not statistically significant
		Negative, not statistically significant

249

TABLE 8.1 (*continued*)

Parental Choices/Opportunities	Graduated From High School (Table 5.1)	Years of Schooling (Table 5.2)
Number of Household Location Moves [a]	Negative, statistically significant, quantitatively large Were the number of location moves of all children zero (vs. 4 moves), probability child would drop out falls by one-half	Negative, statistically significant, quantitatively large Were the number of location moves of all children zero (vs. 4 moves), mean years of schooling of nation's children increases by 3 percent
Number of Years Living in Neighborhood with "Bad" Characteristics [a,b]	Negative, statistically significant, quantitatively large Were a child to grow up in a "good" neighborhood (vs. "bad"), probability that child would drop out falls by more than one-half If those who grew up in a "bad" neighborhood were to grow up in a "good" neighborhood, probability of dropping out falls by 52 percent	Negative, marginally significant, quantitatively large Were all children to grow up in a "good" neighborhood (vs. "bad"), mean years of schooling of nation's children increases by 6 percent If those who grew up in a "bad" neighborhood instead grew up in a "good" neighborhood, their mean years of education increases by 6 percent If those poor children who grew up in a "bad" neighborhood were to grow up in a "good" neighborhood, their mean years of education increases by 7 percent

[a] Measured over ages 6–15.
[b] See text for definition of variables.

We also include in the table a discussion of the quantitative effect of a change in family or neighborhood circumstances on two subgroups of our sample: those who spent at least one year living in poverty and those who grew up in a bad neighborhood. These effects are based on a special set of simulations run on these children at risk.

In the following paragraphs, we summarize what we find in the table

Teenage Out-of-Wedlock Birth (Table 6.2)	Received Welfare after Teenage Out-of-Wedlock Birth (Table 6.2)	Economic Inactivity (Table 7.2)
Positive, marginally significant, quantitatively large Were the number of location moves of all girls zero (vs. 4 moves) probability of teenage nonmarital birth falls by 31 percent	Positive, marginally significant, quantitatively large Were the number of location moves zero (vs. 4 moves), probability of welfare recipiency decreases by 11 percent	Positive, not statistically significant Were the number of location moves zero (vs. 4 moves), probability of inactivity among nation's youths falls by 22 percent
Positive, not statistically significant If those who grew up in "bad" neighborhood were to grow up in a "good" neighborhood, their probability of having a teenage nonmarital birth falls by 18 percent		Positive, not statistically significant

regarding the effects of the various family and neighborhood characteristics on children's attainments.

Parental Education

The most robust—and the strongest—finding concerns the effects of the *education of the parents* on the children that we have studied. For all of the outcomes, more years of parental schooling are associated with greater success and attainments. In all cases save that of welfare recipiency after a teenage nonmarital birth, this effect is statistically significant and quantitatively large. This result is consistent with much of the literature discussed in Chapter 3 and, like that literature, the tie between determinant and outcome is strongest for variables that are similar in character. Thus, additional schooling for parents tends to have its largest effect on the educational choices and success levels of the children.

Moreover, the effect of additional parental education appears to be more important at the bottom end of the distribution of parental educational levels than at the top. If we undertake the mental experiment of bringing all parents (or mothers) without a high-school diploma to matriculation, holding all of the other variables included in the estimates constant, the national high-school dropout rate would be cut in half, the number of years of schooling of the nation's children would increase by about 4 percent, the rate of teenage nonmarital births would be halved, and the incidence of inactivity of youths in their mid-twenties would be reduced by one-quarter. These changes are large in size, and securing them would substantially alter some of the adverse trends in children's success that we have described.[5]

The impact of parental education on two of the groups of children who are at greatest risk in the population—those who grew up in a family that spent one or more years living in poverty and those who grew up in a bad neighborhood—are also worthy of mention. The estimates that serve as the basis for this summary are reported in Table 8.2.

The impact of more years of parental schooling on these subgroups of children is larger than that for the entire group of children. For the entire sample, the probability of graduating from high school increases by 6 percentage points, but for those who grew up in a family that experienced poverty for at least one year, the simulated gain is 10 percentage points. For those who grew up in a bad neighborhood, the simulated gain is 18 percentage points (from 60.8 percent to 78.8 percent).[6]

Economic Circumstances

The *economic circumstances* of the families in which children grow up also matter. In the table, family economic circumstances are reflected in the variables measuring: (1) the number of years that the families of the children are in poverty when they were aged 6–15, (2) the number of years that the family received welfare during this period, and (3) the number of years that the child's mother worked.

Eliminating Poverty for the Families of Children. Consider, first, the extent to which the child's family was poor. While poverty status, by itself, tends to decrease the probability that the child will complete high school, the relationship is not statistically significant. However, the extent of schooling beyond high school is significantly affected by the economic circumstances of the family. Indeed, if those families of the children we studied that experienced poverty could have avoided being poor, the national level of educational attainment of children would have increased by about .3 percent. While this change may not seem quantitatively large, over the entire decade of the 1980s the median number of years of schooling of young adults aged 25–29 was 12.4 and did not change at all. Hence, our simulations suggest that the elimination of poverty, by itself, would achieve an increase in national educational attainment larger that which was, in fact, achieved over the past decade.[7]

The elimination of poverty while growing up would also reduce both the probability that a girl would give birth out of wedlock as a teenager, and the probability that the girl would be a recipient of welfare after giving birth. Our estimates suggest that both the rate of teenage nonmarital birth and the rate of conditional welfare receipt would fall by about 3 percent because of this effect alone. Finally, while economic resources—as reflected in the experience of poverty while growing up— appear to reduce the probability of economic inactivity when children are in their twenties, the effect is not statistically significant.

Turning to the groups of at-risk children, elimination of poverty is expected to increase the probability of graduating from high school among children who experienced at least one year living in poverty by 6 percent. In terms of years of education, the expected increase for these children is simulated to increase by .13 years, which is about three times the change estimated for all children.

Among the girls in our sample who grew up experiencing poverty, the elimination of poverty is simulated to decrease the probability of having a nonmarital birth by .7 percentage points, compared to .2 percentage points for the entire group of children. For another at-risk group, children who grew up in a bad neighborhood, elimination of poverty is expected to increase the probability of graduation by more than 1 percentage point, and to increase the number of years of education by .07 years.

For girls who grew up in a bad neighborhood, the base probability of having an out-of-wedlock birth as a teenager is four times that of the overall sample of girls we studied (.324 versus .08). Our simulation

TABLE 8.2 Predicted Values of Attainment Variables and Percentage Change from Population Base Value: Selected Subgroups of Our Sample

Parental Choices/Opportunities	Graduated from High School (Table 5.1)		Years of Schooling (Table 5.2)	
	Probability of High-School Graduation	Percentage Change from Base*	Mean Years of Schooling	Percentage Change from Base
Panel A: Those Who Spent One or More Years in Poverty, Ages 6–15				
Base	.774		12.27	
Mother/Father High-School Graduates	.877	+45.5	12.91	+5.2
Family Zero Years in Poverty †	.788	+6.2	12.40	+1.0
No Years in Single-Parent Family †	.799	−11.2	12.43	+1.3
Grew Up in "Bad" Neighborhood †	.675	−43.6	11.84	−3.5
Grew Up in "Good" Neighborhood †	.839	+28.5	12.63	+2.9
Panel B: Those Who Grew Up in a Bad Neighborhood				
Base	.607		11.90	
Mother/Father High-School Graduates	.788	+45.9	12.71	+6.8
Family Zero Years in Poverty †	.620	+3.2	11.97	+0.6
No Years in Single-Parent Family †	.627	+5.0	12.00	+0.9
Grew Up in "Good" Neighborhood †	.844	+60.3	12.59	+5.8

*This column is calculated as a proportional change from the probability of not completing high school, which is the reciprocal of the reported base probability for high-school graduation.
†During ages 6–15.

Teenage Out-of-Wedlock Birth (Table 6.2)		Received Welfare after Teenage Out-of-Wedlock Birth (Table 6.2)		Economic Inactivity (Table 7.2)	
Probability of Teenage Out-of-Wedlock Birth	Percentage Change from Base	Probability of Receipt of Welfare Benefits, after Teenage Out-of-Wedlock Birth	Percentage Change from Base	Probability of Economic Inactivity	Percentage Change from Base
Panel A: Those Who Spent One or More Years in Poverty, Ages 6–15					
.188		.800		.251	
.098	−47.9			.158	−37.0
.180	−3.9	.760	−4.9	.249	−1.0
				.286	+13.9
.211	+12.2			.212	−15.8
.167	−10.9			.280	+11.5
Panel B: Those Who Grew Up in a Bad Neighborhood					
.324				.244	
.182	−43.8			.158	−35.4
.312	−3.5			.242	−.7
				.291	+19.4
.258	−20.2			.340	+39.3

estimates suggest that the elimination of poverty would decrease the probability of having a nonmarital birth by more than 1 percentage point compared to .2 percentage points for the overall population.

Years the Mother Worked. Another aspect of the economic resources of the family of the child is reflected in the extent to which the mother worked during the child's ages 6–15. The expected effect of a change in this factor is ambiguous. A higher number of years of the mother's work would tend to reduce the level of nurturing and monitoring activities, which would be expected to lead to a reduction in children's attainments. On the other hand, the additional income that the mother would earn may mean economic resources available to the child and provide a role model of hard work.

The effect of the mothers' work on children's attainments is large. If the mothers of these children are simulated to be working for all 10 years during which the child was aged 6–15 (as compared to not working at all), the high-school dropout rate of this cohort of children is predicted to fall by 43 percent, the average number of years of schooling to increase by 1 percent, and the percent of children who would be inactive at age 24 to decrease by 45 percent. All of these effects are substantial and in excess of what one would expect from simply the increase in family income from the mother's work.[8] The very large impact in reducing the economic inactivity of the children is particularly noteworthy.

Receipt of Welfare by the Child's Family. Like the effect of the mother's work, the receipt of welfare by the child's family carries with it both success-inhibiting stigma and dependence effects and increases in available family income. In the case of schooling, if the families of children who are poor were to be denied welfare benefits (holding all of the other variables constant), the average number of years of schooling of the children in this cohort would be decreased (by about .03 years). Similarly, were participation in welfare by the child's family during the growing-up years to be eliminated, our simulations suggest that the probability that the child would be inactive at age 24 would be reduced by about 8 percent.[9]

Family Structure

The potential effects of *family structure* on children's attainments is one of the most controversial and policy-relevant issues in this area. Does divorce and separation, or having a child out of wedlock, have serious long-term consequences for the child? In our research, we have employed two variables that measure this relationship—the number of years that children live with a single parent while they are aged 6–15, and the number of parental disruptions (separations and remarriages) experienced over this period.

As Table 8.1 indicates, growing up in a single-parent family appears to have adverse, statistically significant, and large effects on children's attainments. Our simulation results indicate that if all children could live in an intact family throughout the entire growing-up period,[10] the probability of dropping out of school would decrease by 2 percent, and the number of years of schooling completed would increase by 1 percent.

Experiencing the changes involved with family restructuring (parental separations and remarriages) also has an adverse effect on children. Having controlled for the number of years that a child has lived in a single-parent arrangement, the stress involved with the change in family structure does not appear to significantly affect the probability that the child will graduate from high school, but remarriages have a negative effect on the number of years of schooling completed.

Our estimates of the effects of these stressful, family-change factors on the nonmarital birth-welfare recipiency outcomes reveal some large impacts.[11] For example, we estimate that reducing by one the number of parental separations experienced by children who have gone through a family breakup would reduce the probability that the daughter would have a teenage nonmarital birth by about one-fifth.

The impact of remarriages is more mixed and generally small. The simulated effect of the number of parental (re)marriages on the probability of teenage nonmarital births and economic inactivity is negative, suggesting that this parental decision has a positive effect on the choices of the young adult. Perhaps the parental choice of a married lifestyle rather than continuing as a single parent, or the introduction of a working adult into the family, introduces a positive role model into the family, thereby influencing the goals and the choices of the children. On the other hand, the influence of remarriages on the years of schooling appears to be negative, perhaps reflecting the limited access by the child to the family's (stepparent's) economic resources.

Stressful Family Events and Circumstances

The previous results on the effects of parental separation and remarriage suggest that *stressful family events and living arrangements* do take a toll on the performance and attainments of children. Table 8.1 presents results on two additional family choices/circumstances that may affect children's success: the number of years that the head of the child's family was disabled and the number of location moves experienced by the child. In both cases, large, adverse, and statistically significant impacts are recorded.

Living in a Family with a Disabled Head. The effects of growing up in a family in which the head is disabled are particularly noteworthy. In our simulations, we calculated the effect on the various outcomes of living for 0 and for 10 years in a family with a disabled head.[12] Holding all other variables constant, moving all of the children from living 10 years in such a living arrangement to 0 years is estimated to cut the high-school dropout rate by an amount equal to somewhat more than one-half of the reported rate. Such a simulated change would also increase the average number of years of schooling attained by over 3 percent.

The Number of Location Moves. The disruptive effects of location moves (or those unmeasured parental characteristics that may be associated with the number of location moves) is also substantial. We estimate that if all children were to experience zero location moves during the age 6–15 period (relative to four), the dropout rate would decrease by one-half, and the mean years of schooling would increase by 3 percent. In both cases, the effects are statistically significant.[13] The disruptive impact of location moves on the probability that the youth will be economically inactive at age 24 is also substantial; we estimate that if all children experienced zero moves compared to four, the probability of economic inactivity would decrease by more than 20 percent. The frequency of location moves also has an adverse effect on the probability of having a teenage nonmarital birth and subsequent welfare recipiency for the girls in our sample. Decreasing the number of moves for all girls in the sample from four to zero suggests a reduction of more than 30 percent in the probability of a teenage nonmarital birth, and an 11 percent reduction in the probability of subsequent welfare recipiency.

While common experience suggests the disruptive effects of geographic moves on children—often involving school changes, the loss of friends, and the establishment of new friendship networks—these results are among the first to report the quantitative effects of such disruptions. The magnitude of the effects is noteworthy.

Neighborhood Characteristics

The final simulation effect reported in Table 8.1 concerns the relationship of the *characteristics of the neighborhoods* in which children grow up and their educational attainments.

In our studies of the determinants of educational success, we categorized neighborhoods into extreme categories that we labeled "good" and "bad."[14] While neighborhood quality so measured is a statistically significant determinant of the probability of graduating from high school, the coefficient of this variable is marginally significant in the years of schooling estimation.

On the basis of these estimated results, we performed the mental experiment of, first, assuming that children spent all of their growing-up years in a bad neighborhood, and then assuming that all of those years were spent in a good neighborhood. Moving from the all-in-a-bad-neighborhood case to the all-in-a-good-neighborhood case had a substantial effect on the predicted schooling outcomes of the children. The probability that the child would drop out of high school prior to graduation was cut by more than one-half when such a change was made; similarly, the number of years of completed schooling of the child was increased by 6 percent.

Coefficients on the neighborhood variables in estimates of choices with regard to teenage out-of-wedlock birth and welfare participation are not significant but of the expected sign. In the case of teenage nonmarital births, the estimated effect of growing up in a bad neighborhood is large and suggests a decrease in the probability of a teenage birth by about 20 percent! Among those adolescents who grew up experiencing poverty, moving to a good neighborhood also appears to have a large effect: in this case, the probability of a teenage nonmarital birth is reduced by 21 percent. The measure of neighborhood in our estimate of the determinants of economic inactivity is the unemployment rate of adults in the area. The coefficient of this variable has an unexpected sign in the equation for economic inactivity, but it is not significant.

FROM RESEARCH TO POLICY

The research that we have presented is motivated by the belief that children in the United States are not doing well. Erosion in the circumstances in which many of them are growing up has been documented, and the conclusions are discouraging. At the same time, several aspects of children's success and attainments appear to be in decline. Our research was also guided by a concern with policy; our hope was to be able to identify public measures capable of increasing both the well-being and the attainments of children.

Can our findings, in fact, leaven discussion and thinking about policy toward children? Are there insights from our research that can guide the actions of citizens concerned with policy? This question, itself, is a controversial one. It presumes that public policy can affect community, parental, or children's choices, and hence influence children's success.

Because our research has focused primarily on the effects of parental choices regarding children and the circumstances of the families in which children grow up, any policy lessons that we might draw would have to involve either measures that could alter parental choices and circumstances, or interventions that might correct or offset the effects of these choices and circumstances. The implication of parents and families in policy discussions designed to reverse the deteriorating status of the nation's children—and to increase their attainments—is controversial. Although it is generally agreed that the contributions of parents to children's nurturing, support, and motivation are lower today than in prior times, and of reduced quality, the question of why families today seem to be less effective than in the past is clouded.

For some, it is a matter of *values*. In this view, the "moral climate" [15] of the nation has eroded, and today's parents reflect the erosion of the values that comprise this climate. Parents, it is claimed, place more emphasis on self-gratification, self-realization, and career advancement than in former days—and less on responsibilities to spouses and children, moral obligation, self-sacrifice, and living according to rules. The result is decreased family stability, increased nonmarital parenthood (especially among young minority women), reductions in the amount of time that parents spend with children, and erosion in the support of community and neighborhood institutions.

Some versions of this values perspective place the blame for the deteriorating status of children on the shoulders of government policy. Expanding welfare program generosity and accessibility in the 1960s and 1970s, some assert, encouraged reductions in self-sufficiency and independence. In addition to the expansion of welfare programs, we have experienced expanded legal rights and decriminalization, and these have encouraged lawbreaking. We have less restrictive divorce laws, changed custody rules, and a failure to enforce child-support payments, and these have encouraged family breakups and nonmarital parenthood.[16] From this perspective, the changes in family behavior that follow from these public social policies have imposed serious and adverse consequences on children: they increasingly grow up in mother-only households, in poverty, in dysfunctional neighborhoods, and dependent on welfare.

An implication of this position is that government should return to the rules of the past, and that further expansion of government programs to improve the environment of children will only make things worse. Perhaps an exception is the use of moral suasion to change values and the moral climate, and thereby to improve the lot of children.[17]

To other observers, the declining status of the nation's children and the growth of social problems in general is largely attributable to *economic changes*. Mean annual earnings of full-time, full-year workers have been stagnant since the early 1970s. As a result, young families have not experienced the economic gains that were taken as "natural" by their parents, and their hopes for home ownership, vacations, and college educations for their children were more uncertain than expected. Wives increased their work time in part to enable families to attain the economic gains on which even modest dreams are built. While the average worker experienced no gains over this period, the typical worker with only a high-school diploma witnessed a decline in full-time earnings of about 16 percent over this period; those who failed to graduate from high school saw their real earnings decline by one-third, even though they worked full time.

In the face of such changes, it is suggested, family circumstances and behaviors have also changed. With more two-worker families has come less time for childrearing and nurturing. Economic pressures encouraged delayed marriages, and probably encouraged cohabitation outside of marriage—and with it increased nonmarital childbearing. To some, these economic pressures—most seriously reflected in job losses and a lack of work opportunities in inner cities—have led to a decline in the pool of marriageable males, and greater acceptance of childbearing out of wedlock. For those who find themselves with children, without a spouse and without education, welfare is often a more attractive option than working.

Those who take this position arrive at a quite different conclusion regarding the role of government. Public measures, it is emphasized, are necessary to provide jobs at family-supporting wages to those able to work, even if they do not have a high-school diploma. Moreover, financial access to medical care must be provided to increase the attractiveness of work relative to welfare. These observers also suggest that a variety of other interventions—expanded pre- and postnatal care, public provision of children's vaccinations, full funding of Head Start, government-guaranteed child-support enforcement, and expansion of the Earned Income Tax Credit—are also necessary for marked improvements in the circumstances in which children grow up, and in their ultimate attainments.

The implications of our research for policy are basic, fundamental, and general. They suggest areas where public intervention might be effective; they suggest children who are at particular risk and hence might benefit from intervention. However, the effectiveness of many of the more specific policy proposals under discussion is not evaluated.

Given the detailed summary of the findings of our research above, here we present a set of general propositions that are both consistent with these results and relevant for policy.

1. Children who face a large number of adverse parental choices and circumstances—for example, low parental education, poverty, and many location moves—have markedly poorer outcomes than those experiencing fewer disadvantages. While the effects of these factors may not be multiplicative, they are at least additive. This suggests concentrating interventions on those children who have experienced or are experiencing large numbers of these risks.

2. Policy should foster and support increased levels of education for all young people. They are tomorrow's parents, and, perhaps among all of the factors that we have studied, parental education is the most powerful. Ensuring that all young people complete high school would appear to be an important goal in terms of their own success, their children's success, and the success of the younger residents in their neighborhoods.

3. Irrespective of marital status, policymakers should seek effective ways of increasing the income available to families. This statement, of course, finesses the question of whether the best income-generating strategy for families with the lowest income levels should come via macroeconomic policy, job-training efforts, reform of labor markets, employment subsidies, or increased income transfers. Although little specific guidance on this question is available in our research findings, there are some suggestions that the effect of increased family economic resources secured from earnings have a more positive effect on children's attainments than increases secured through welfare.

   Further, while our research findings do not directly address the merits of specific proposals for improving the economic prospects of families, they do offer implicit support for attempts to raise the skill levels, the earnings, and the incomes of parents who are able to work.

4. Increasing the incidence of intact and supportive families would also have payout in terms of children's educational and economic success.[18] Again, suggesting that public policy adopt this as a goal leaves

aside large and perplexing questions regarding how—and if—this objective can be attained.

5. There is no evidence in our research that children who grow up with mothers who work have lower levels of success and attainments than those whose mothers stay at home. Indeed, the opposite effect would seem to predominate. In the interests of children and their attainments, policy should not discourage, but perhaps encourage, women's work outside the home.

6. Prosperous and well-functioning communities and neighborhoods appear to have important positive effects on children's attainments. Our findings suggest that growing up in those neighborhoods with the greatest concentrations of social problems and the worst economic deficits has a particularly deleterious effect on children's outcomes. There appears to be a productive role for targeted policies designed to improve living conditions in the nation's weakest and poorest neighborhoods. And there appears to be a positive role for policies that discourage teenagers in these neighborhoods from dropping out of high school.

7. Finally, our research suggests that children from families that have experienced multiple stresses (e.g., location moves, parental separations, remarriages, and parents with disabilities or health problems), or which confront serious economic or educational deficits, deserve special attention. Programs providing support and counseling for such children, either in schools or out, could have important effects in offsetting the adverse consequences of these parental decisions or circumstances.

At one level, these policy implications seem too general to be of specific use. At another level, however, our research results do set a direction for public action, and do provide a basis and a rationale for a variety of public interventions. Stated most concretely, and perhaps too baldly, the message to policymakers is:

Seek to strengthen American families and enable them to exercise their desires to be economically self-sufficient. Help them to live in neighborhoods that will support their economic goals and instincts for stability. Where serious deficits in resources and stability—or excesses of family-based stress—plague particular children, provide intensive support and counseling designed to offset these problems. And, above all, seek to increase the educational attainment of the next set of the nation's parents, concentrating efforts on minimizing the number of those without even a high-school diploma.

NOTES

1. See, for example, Kotlikoff (1992) and Kotlikoff and Gokhale (1993).

2. As noted above, the proportion of those in high school taking the exam has increased somewhat, which may partly explain the lower SAT scores.

3. Society also may intervene if certain decisions of parents toward their children, such as abandonment, nutritional deficiency, or lack of (or limited) primary-school attendance occur.

4. Some of the cells of the table are empty due to the specific empirical models estimated in the chapters. As described in the chapters, the specification of these models depended on: (1) judgments regarding the relevance of particular choices/circumstances to specific outcomes; (2) the interaction of variables depicting different aspects of the same choice/circumstance, and in some cases; (3) constraints imposed by the nature of the econometric models that were estimated.

5. To the extent that the coefficients of parental schooling capture the characteristics of parents that are not measured in our data—for example, motivation, intelligence, or values—these simulations may overstate the likely impact of increased education among parents. Because these unmeasured characteristics may not be influenced by increased schooling, the simulated effects on attainments from changing only schooling may be biased.

6. As noted in Tables 8.1 and 8.2, these simulations are based on the estimates reported in Chapters 5, 6, and 7.

7. It should be emphasized that the simulation on which this is based measures only the direct effect of eliminating poverty on the years of completed schooling. The indirect effects that would accompany poverty reduction, such as improvements in neighborhood school quality, are not reflected in this estimate. However, our simulated effect may overstate the effects of eliminating poverty if the poverty variable is capturing the effects of other factors unmeasured in our data (see note 5).

8. Note the far smaller simulated changes in response to the elimination of poverty discussed above.

9. This large impact may be explained by the indirect effect of eliminating welfare participation on the labor-force participation of single mothers.

10. For our national sample, the overall probability that a randomly chosen child-year would find the child in a single-parent family is .15. The simulation involves reducing this probability to zero. We mention again that this does not take into account those unobserved factors—such as personality—that may both affect the child's performance and explain why some parents are single. To the extent that observing a single-parent family captures the effect of these unmeasured factors as well as the impact of living with but one parent, the simulation may overstate the effects of the change in family structure (see note 5).

11. These analyses, it will be recalled, did not control for the number of years that the girl lived in a single-parent family. As a result, the family-change variables may be measuring this duration effect as well as the independent effect of the change.

12. Relatively few children—about 10 percent—spend any years living in a family headed by a disabled person. Hence, the simulation that we report only indicates the sizable impact that such a living arrangement has on a child with this experience. The earlier warnings regarding the potential effects of unmeasured variables hold in this case as well (see note 5).

13. Again, because few children experience either zero or four location moves during childhood, these simulated results are only suggestive of the importance of this factor in determining educational attainments.

14. A "bad" neighborhood is one with more than 40 percent of youths who are high-school dropouts, more than 40 percent of families are headed by a single female, and less than 10 percent of the employed persons hold professional or managerial jobs. A "good" neighborhood is one with less than 10 percent of youths who are high-school dropouts, less than 10 percent of families are headed by a single female, and more than 40 percent of the employed persons hold professional or managerial jobs.

15. James Q. Wilson (1993) has defined "moral climate" to be "the set of habits that govern the daily relationships of people in a particular institution." [p. 112]

16. An interesting discussion about the extent of changing values and their role in explaining the problems of today's children is found in a Symposium published in the special Winter, 1993 issue of *The Aspen Institute Quarterly*. See especially the articles by David Gergen, William Galston, and James Q. Wilson.

17. James Q. Wilson speaks of the possibility for government to "use laws to enforce a culture." Referring to the 1960s and civil rights, he states:

   We didn't want merely to offer carrots and sticks to Mississippi sheriffs and to segregationist schools, we wanted to tell them that what they were doing was wrong. We wanted to do that not only to change their behavior but to deliver a lesson to everyone else. "You young people growing up in this society—we believe this is a wrong, and stop thinking these racist and invidious thoughts, and begin to treat people with some human decency." If we spoke that way on that problem, we can speak that way on [the decline of family values]. [p. 116]

18. Galston, in the *Aspen Institute Quarterly*, goes further and states that "the best anti-poverty program for children is a stable, intact family." [p. 68]

Appendix A
Our Data on Children
and Young Adults

We here describe the data on children and young adults that we have assembled, and on which our analyses rest.

These data are observations of children from U.S. families that were included in the stratified sample of households included in the Michigan Panel Study of Income Dynamics (PSID). There are about 1700 children in this data set, and they have been tracked from their early childhood through young adulthood. For each child, these data include information on family status, income and source of income, parental education, neighborhood characteristics, changes in family status, and background characteristics such as race, religion, and geographic location. They also include information on a variety of children's attainments.

The first section of this appendix includes a discussion of the data set, its construction, and the supplementary information we have added to it. In the second section, the more important variables describing childhood circumstances and living arrangements are identified and defined. The third section presents the variables measuring children's attainments and outcomes. The means and distributions of these variables are provided. In the last section, the question of attrition that plagues all longitudinal data sets is addressed.

LONGITUDINAL DATA ON 1705 CHILDREN
AND THEIR FAMILIES
FROM THE PANEL STUDY OF INCOME DYNAMICS

Basic Data

Our basic data set consists of 21 years of information on 1705 children from the Michigan Panel Study of Income Dynamics (PSID). The PSID data provide longitudinal information on 6000 families beginning in 1968. As of 1991, 21 years of data were available—from 1968 through 1988. We selected children who were aged 0–6 in the beginning year of the survey, and followed them for the full 21 years. By the final year, the children have become young adults, ranging in age from 21 to 26 years. Only those individuals who remained in the survey for each year through 1988 are included.[1]

In order to analyze the influence of various family and neighborhood characteristics during the childhood period on success and attainments of these children when they have become young adults, we transformed those data elements that do not describe the permanent characteristics of either the child or his or her parents into an age-indexed data set. That is, rather than have the information defined by the year of its occurrence (say, 1968 or 1974), we converted the data so that this time-varying information is assigned to the child by the child's age (say, age 6 or 7).[2] We transform the data in this way in order to be able to compare the process of attainment across individuals with different birth years. Doing so allows us to analyze whether the *timing* of particular events—whether an event or circumstance occurs when the children are young or adolescents—has a differential influence on their attainments when they become young adults.

Many of the variables describing parental or social investments in children—such as family income—are stated in monetary units. To compare income and other monetary values over time, all dollar values from the PSID were converted to 1976 prices using the Consumer Price Index for all items.

In a few cases, observations could not be used and are excluded from the analysis. For the full sample, these include those persons with two or more contiguous years of missing data. Those observations with but one year of missing data were retained and the missing data were filled in by averaging the data for the two years contiguous to the missing year.[3]

Added Child-Care Time, State Welfare Generosity, and Neighborhood Data

Because a number of important aspects of family and social investments in children are not included in the information contained in the PSID, we merged three additional types of information onto our basic PSID data.

First, to estimate the amount of time that parents spent with their children, we used data from the University of Michigan's Time Use Data Set. In this study, interviewers collected detailed information on individual time allocation, asking respondents to complete a time diary. In the diary, respondents stated the time spent in a number of activities during a "typical" day, including time spent with children. For each parent in the Time Use Data Set who had at least one child under the age of 19, we summed together the time spent in activities that we classified as "time allocated primarily to children."[4] We transformed this daily information into an annual estimate, and then regressed this estimate of annual child-care time on a set of background, family status, and labor market activity variables that are common to the Time Use and PSID data sets. This estimation was done separately for mothers and fathers.[5] The coefficients from these regressions were then used with information on every parent in every family in every year of our PSID sample to obtain an estimate of mother's and father's child-care time.[6]

Second, we merged onto our basic PSID data an annual, state-specific series of welfare generosity variables. For each state, we have annual data from 1968 through 1988 on the state maximum benefits for the Aid to Families with Dependent Children (AFDC) program, the maximum Food Stamp benefit, and the average Medicaid expenditures for AFDC families. In incorporating this information into our data set, we match maximum benefits for a family of four, in 1976 dollars (deflated by the personal consumption expenditure deflator, base 1982) for the years when the child is aged 6 to 21. This is the maximum amount paid by the state as of July of that year to a family of four with no other income. For Food Stamps, the benefit is the amount of the allotment (or the allotment minus the purchase requirement) for a family of four with no other income, again measured as of July of that year.[7] Finally, average Medicaid expenditures for a family of four for each state are calculated as the product of three and the state-specific fiscal year per child Medicaid expenditures for dependent children under 21 who are in categorically needy families, plus the state-specific average per person annual Medicaid payments for adults in categorically needy families.[8] These are deflated into 1976 dollars using the Consumer Price Index for medical care, base 1982.[9]

The final information that we have merged onto our PSID data are neighborhood data constructed by matching small-area information from the 1970 and 1980 Censuses to the location of the children in our sample. The links have been (painstakingly and painfully) accomplished by the Michigan Survey Research Center (SRC). Using 1970 and 1980 Census data, the SRC analysts created a link between the neighborhood in which each family in the PSID lives and small-area information collected in the national Census.[10] Based on this link, we are able to include information on the racial composition, mean family income, proportion of persons living in poverty, proportion of young adults who are high-school dropouts, adult and male unemployment rates, proportion of families that are female headed, vacant housing units, and an underclass count (see Ricketts and Sawhill, 1988) for each family in our sample, based on the neighborhood in which they reside for each of the years from 1968 to 1985.

For the years 1968 to 1970, the 1970 Census data are used in this matching; for the years 1980 to 1985, the 1980 Census data are used. For years 1971 to 1979, a weighted combination of the 1970 and 1980 Census data are used. The weights linearly reflect the number of years from 1970 and 1980.[11] All dollar values for these neighborhood variables are converted to 1976 dollars using the all-item CPI index.[12]

THE EXPLANATORY VARIABLES

In Table A-1, we present the mean, standard deviation, and minimum and maximum values of the variables that serve as the explanatory variables in our analyses presented in Chapters 4–7. Panel A contains the values for the unweighted sample of 1705 individuals; panel B provides weighted measures.[13]

How do the characteristics of our population, over the ages of 6–15, compare to those of the overall U.S. population? We highlight a few of the variables that are of particular interest.[14]

Race

According to data in the *Statistical Abstract of the United States,* as of 1988, 12.2 percent of the population aged 6–15 were African-

TABLE A.1 Explanatory Variables Based on 1705 Observations

Variable	Mean	Standard Deviation	Minimum	Maximum
		Panel 1: Unweighted Statistics		
Background				
Education of Parents				
Father a high-school graduate*	0.23	0.42	0	1.00
Father some college*	0.10	0.30	0	1.00
Father a college graduate*	0.09	0.29	0	1.00
Mother a high-school graduate*	0.39	0.49	0	1.00
Mother some college*	0.08	0.27	0	1.00
Mother a college graduate*	0.04	0.21	0	1.00
Father a high-school graduate or more*	0.42	0.49	0	1.00
Mother a high-school graduate or more*	0.52	0.50	0	1.00
Religion				
Any religion*	0.92	0.27	0	1.00
Catholic*	0.20	0.40	0	1.00
Jewish*	0.02	0.12	0	1.00
Protestant*	0.71	0.45	0	1.00
Other Background Variables				
Number of years family head disabled, ages 6–15*	1.56	2.59	0	9.00
Number of years lived in South, ages 6–15*	4.57	4.91	0	10.00
Ever lived in South, ages 6–15*	0.47	0.50	0	1.00
Average annual hours with parents, ages 6–15	941.51	301.71	92.90	1851.60
Number of years lived with one parent, ages 6–15*	2.79	3.96	0	10.00
Number of years lived in SMSA, ages 6–15*	7.21	4.24	0	10.00
Number of years mother worked, ages 6–15*	5.74	3.65	0	10.00
Average number of siblings, ages 6–15	2.52	1.61	0	8.50
Firstborn child*	0.23	0.42	0	1.00
Female*	0.51	0.50	0	1.00
Nonwhite*	0.48	0.50	0	1.00
African-American*	0.46	0.50	0	1.00

Variable	Mean	Standard Deviation	Minimum	Maximum
Head foreign-born*	0.02	0.14	0	1.00
Head's parents poor*	0.53	0.50	0	1.00
Mother's age at first birth	22.13	5.31	0	62.00
Mother had out-of-wedlock birth*	0.17	0.38	0	1.00
Stress Variables				
Number of parental separations, ages 6–15	0.24	0.47	0	3.00
Number of parental (re)marriages, ages 6–15	0.14	0.38	0	3.00
Number of household location moves, ages 6–15	1.60	1.77	0	9.0
Number of other changes in family, ages 6–15	0.20	0.44	0	4.00
One parent in 1968*·†	0.14	0.35	0	1.00
No parents in 1968*·‡	0.10	0.29	0	1.00
Average number of years head unemployed, ages 6–15	1.29	2.63	0	10.00
Income and Other Resources				
Average occupational status of head, ages 6–15§	3.25	1.43	1.00	5.00
Average pretax family income ÷ poverty line, ages 6–15	2.28	1.78	0	24.69
Average posttax family income ÷ poverty line, ages 6–15	2.34	1.73	0	24.69
Number of years family received AFDC, ages 6–15	1.33	2.66	0	10.00
Family ever received AFDC, ages 6–15	0.29	0.45	0	1.00
Number of years family posttax income < poverty line, ages 6–15	2.24	3.16	0	10.00
Maximum AFDC benefits in state, ages 6–15	427.91	170.70	121.80	704.50
Maximum AFDC benefits in state in 3 years after birth	370.03	155.34	118.25	666.00
Maximum welfare benefits in state, ages 6–15	614.74	144.09	355.60	938.00
Maximum welfare benefits in state in 3 years after birth	550.47	117.53	349.00	838.00

TABLE A.1 (*continued*)

Variable	Mean	Standard Deviation	Minimum	Maximum
Panel 2: Weighted Statistics				
Background				
Education of Parents				
Father a high-school graduate*	0.28	0.45	0	1.00
Father some college*	0.16	0.36	0	1.00
Father a college graduate*	0.16	0.37	0	1.00
Mother a high-school graduate*	0.47	0.50	0	1.00
Mother some college*	0.11	0.31	0	1.00
Mother a college graduate*	0.08	0.27	0	1.00
Father a high-school graduate or more*	0.61	0.49	0	1.00
Mother a high-school graduate or more*	0.66	0.47	0	1.00
Religion				
Any religion*	0.91	0.29	0	1.00
Catholic*	0.29	0.45	0	1.00
Jewish*	0.03	0.18	0	1.00
Protestant*	0.59	0.49	0	1.00
Other Background Variables				
Number of years family head disabled, ages 6–15*	1.03	2.12	0	9.00
Number of years lived in South, ages 6–15*	2.78	4.38	0	10.00
Ever lived in South, ages 6–15*	0.30	0.46	0	1.00
Average annual hours with parents, ages 6–15	899.09	288.19	92.90	1851.60
Number of years lived with one parent, ages 6–15	1.65	3.13	0	10.00
Number of years lived in SMSA, ages 6–15	6.78	4.38	0	10.00
Number of years mother worked, ages 6–15	5.75	3.55	0	10.00
Average number of siblings, ages 6–15	2.07	1.41	0	8.50
Firstborn child*	0.28	0.45	0	1.00
Female*	0.50	0.50	0	1.00
Nonwhite*	0.17	0.37	0	1.00
African-American*	0.14	0.35	0	1.00
Head foreign-born*	0.03	0.16	0	1.00
Head's parents poor*	0.43	0.50	0	1.00
Mother's age at first birth	22.28	5.32	0	62.00

Variable	Mean	Standard Deviation	Minimum	Maximum
Mother had out-of-wedlock birth*	0.10	0.30	0	1.00
Stress Variables				
Number of parental separations, ages 6–15	0.23	0.47	0	3.00
Number of parental (re)marriages, ages 6–15	0.14	0.38	0	3.00
Number of household location moves, ages 6–15	1.49	1.78	0	9.0
Number of other changes in family, ages 6–15	0.15	0.37	0	4.00
One parent in 1968*·†	0.09	0.28	0	1.00
No parents in 1968*·‡	0.01	0.10	0	1.00
Average number of years head unemployed, ages 6–15	0.65	1.77	0	10.00
Income and Other Resources				
Average occupational status of head, ages 6–15§	2.82	1.46	1.00	5.00
Average pretax family income ÷ poverty line, ages 6–15	3.02	2.03	0	24.69
Average posttax family income ÷ poverty line, ages 6–15	3.05	2.01	0	24.69
Number of years family received AFDC, ages 6–15	0.61	1.77	0	10.00
Family ever received AFDC, ages 6–15	0.15	0.36	0	1.00
Number of years posttax family income < poverty line, ages 6–15	1.06	2.25	0	10.00
Maximum AFDC benefits in state, ages 6–15	457.08	163.47	121.80	704.50
Maximum AFDC benefits in state in 3 years after birth	394.77	150.58	118.25	666.00
Maximum welfare benefits in state, ages 6–15	639.30	140.39	355.60	938.90
Maximum welfare benefits in state in 3 years after birth	569.19	114.40	349.00	838.00

*Dummy variable that equals 1 if person has the described characteristic.

†Hence, no education variable is available for one parent.

‡Hence, no education variable is available for either parent.

§Occupation is a simple index that takes on five values, from 1 for a high-prestige occupation to 4 for an unskilled occupation, and 5 for unemployed.

American; 84 percent were white, and 3.3 percent were other. In our sample, 46 percent are African-American—a clear overrepresentation. However, using weights, the sample is 14 percent African-American and 3 percent other, suggesting a very slight overrepresentation of non-whites, and a very slight underrepresentation of whites.[15]

Religion

Ninety-one percent of the U.S. population claimed a religious preference in 1988; the percentage in our sample is also 91. The breakdown by religions in our weighted sample is nearly identical to that of the country as a whole: 59 percent report being Protestant compared to 56 percent nationally; 29 percent report being Catholic versus 28 percent for the nation; and 3 percent report being Jewish, compared to 2 percent for the nation.

Parent's Education

According to national statistics in 1970, a date close to the beginning date of our data and the year in which we measure parent's education, 55 percent of males and 57 percent of females 25+ were high-school graduates (*Statistical Abstract of the United States,* 1975, p. 145). Our weighted sample suggests a more highly educated population, with 66 percent of the women and 60 percent of the men having completed high school. This reflects the lower mean age of the fathers and mothers in our sample—in their mid-twenties in 1970—relative to that of all adults nationally. We note that as of 1978, the median school years completed for all adults was 12.9 but only 12.4 (11.0) for those 45–55 (55+), (*Ibid,* p. 145).

Family Structure

In 1970, 11.9 percent of all children aged 18 or less in the United States lived with one parent. By 1980, this percentage was 19.7. An average centered around 1976, when the children were 8–13, is 16.6 percent. The comparable statistic for our sample of children is unavailable, given that they were aged 0–6 in 1968. However, we can tabulate the mean percentage of years that the children in our sample lived with one parent while they were aged 6–15; it is 16.5 percent. This value is close to the 16.6 percent national statistic centered on the time when these children were in the similar age bracket.

Geographic Moves

In our weighted sample of children, the mean number of moves over ages 6–15 was 1.6 (1.5 in the unweighted sample). This is equivalent to an annual rate of moves of .16 (.15). For the U.S. population as a whole, about 18 percent of the population moved at least once per year from 1969 to the mid-1980s.[16] This is equivalent to an annual rate of moves of .18, which is slightly greater than for the young children in our sample. Using data on geographic mobility from the P-20 series from the Current Population Survey, we can more closely measure the number of moves of children aged 6–15 over the 1968 to 1983 period. These ranged from about 9 to 14 percent, somewhat lower than the rate in our sample.[17]

Residence

In our sample, the mean number of years that a child lived in an SMSA is 7.2 (unweighted) and 6.8 (weighted). This translates into about 72 percent (unweighted) or 68 percent (weighted) of the children living in an SMSA in any given year, a value that is very close to the 68 percent of the U.S. noninstitutional population that lived in an SMSA in 1978.

Years the Mother Worked

During their ages 6–15, the children in our sample experienced an average of 5.7 years (weighted and unweighted) in which their mothers worked. Stated alternatively, in any particular year a mean of 57 percent of our children had a mother who worked. According to Current Population Survey data, 51.4 percent of mothers of children aged 6–17 worked as of 1970; by 1980 this percentage was 64.1. Taking a weighted average of these national data and centering them on 1976 provides an estimate of 59 percent of mothers of children aged 6–17 in the work force. Given that the mean age of children in the national statistic is somewhat older than the mean age of the children in our sample, we consider the two numbers comparable.

Welfare Recipiency

Over the years 1970 to 1980, the proportion of children less than 18 years old who lived in families that received AFDC benefits ranged from 8.7 percent to 11.4 percent, and equaled 11.8 percent in 1976. For the children in our sample, the mean annual AFDC recipiency rate is 13.3 percent unweighted, and 6.6 percent weighted. Probably because of the underreporting of AFDC benefit receipt in surveys, our 6.6 percent weighted figure lies below the national figure, which is based on recipient counts from administrative records.[18]

THE NEIGHBORHOOD VARIABLES

Given the special character of the neighborhood data that we have merged onto our sample of children, we have chosen to present their summary statistics separately, in Table A.2. As described in the first section of this appendix, the neighborhood variables are based on the 1970 and 1980 U.S. Censuses. The match is done on the basis of the smallest area with a population over 30 persons that can be tied to the location of the residence of the child or his/her family.

The variables whose summary statistics we report here are those that we have merged onto our children's data set, even though not all of them are used in our analyses. We report the mean values of these variables for selected years from 1968 through 1985. They include measures of the neighborhood's racial composition, unemployment, income and poverty, underclass, prevalence of workers in high-status occupations, prevalence of female-headed households, and prevalence of youths who have failed to complete high school.

The racial composition of the neighborhoods in which the children in our sample lived reflects the increasing proportion of the nation's population that is nonwhite (African-American and nonwhite Hispanic). From 1968 through 1985,[19] the children in our data set went from living in neighborhoods that were about 88 percent white to neighborhoods that were about 84 percent white. (Recall that the racial composition of the sample itself is unchanging.)

The measures of economic status of the neighborhood—mean income and the proportion of families living in poverty—show little change over the period, although the proportion of households in these communities who report household income below the poverty line decreased from about 14 percent to 12 percent over the period.

Two measures of neighborhood unemployment are shown: the adult rate and the male rate. Both show a pattern of increasing unemployment in the neighborhoods in which our sample of children reside. By 1985, the average male unemployment rate in these areas is 6.7 percent, up

TABLE A.2 Neighborhood Variables, Selected Years, 1968–1985, $N = 1705$

Variable	1968	1970	1975	1980	1985
Panel 1: Unweighted Means					
Percentage white	65.7	66.6	64.7	62.9	63.7
Percentage households living in poverty	21.0	20.2	18.8	18.4	17.6
Family income	$13,869	$14,102	$14,138	$14,231	$14,249
Adult unemployment rate	5.4	5.3	6.6	8.7	8.4
Male unemployment rate	4.9	4.8	6.4	8.8	8.5
Percentage of workers in professional and technical occupations	11.6	11.8	12.3	12.9	13.1
Percentage of workers in executive and managerial occupations	6.3	6.5	7.0	7.9	8.2
Underclass count*	0.9	0.8	0.6	0.8	0.8
Percentage underclass count of 4†	4.8	4.2	0.5	2.9	2.9
Percentage of families female headed	17.0	16.6	18.7	21.7	21.3
Percentage of young adults who are dropouts	19.1	18.8	16.1	14.8	14.8
Panel 2: Weighted Means					
Percentage white	87.8	88.5	86.3	85.0	84.3
Percentage households living in poverty	13.8	13.1	12.7	12.6	12.3
Family income	$16,068	$16,337	$16,217	$16,185	$16,191
Adult unemployment rate	4.5	4.4	5.3	7.1	6.8
Male unemployment rate	4.0	3.9	5.1	7.1	6.7
Percentage of workers in professional and technical occupations	14.0	14.2	14.4	14.7	14.7
Percentage of workers in executive and managerial occupations	8.0	8.2	8.6	9.7	9.9
Underclass count*	0.4	0.4	0.3	0.4	0.4
Percentage underclass count of 4†	1.1	0.7	0.2	0.5	0.5
Percentage of families female headed	11.4	11.1	12.6	14.5	14.7
Percentage of young adults who are dropouts	14.6	14.3	13.2	12.4	12.7

*Whether the neighborhood is more than one deviation above the average of tracts on each of four indicators: percentage of female-headed families, percentage of young adults 16–19 who are high-school dropouts, proportion of males 16+ employed less than 26 weeks, and proportion of households receiving public assistance.
†Proportion of neighborhood with an underclass count of 4.

from about 4.0 percent in 1968. The adult unemployment rate follows a similar pattern.

The percentage of employed persons engaged in high-prestige occupations has increased somewhat over the 1968 to 1985 period, reflecting a general increase in the prevalence of these occupations in the nation. By 1985, the average child in our sample lived in a neighborhood in which more than 25 percent of the workers were in high-prestige occupations, up from 22 percent in 1968.

The final set of neighborhood variables are measures of "underclass" status, as defined by Ricketts and Sawhill (1988). Their definition is based on the prevalence of dysfunctional behaviors exhibited in a neighborhood. These behaviors are those that both differ substantially from accepted norms and that inhibit mobility and, when transmitted to children, are likely to have a negative influence on future attainments. An underclass neighborhood, then, is one in which a sizeable proportion of the inhabitants engage in a number of such behaviors.[20]

Table A.2 provides, for each of the years, the mean of this count for the neighborhoods in which the children in our sample live and the proportion with a count of four. Using weighted data, the average underclass count has stayed much the same over time. While about 1 percent of children lived in underclass neighborhoods in 1968, it had fallen to about .5 percent in 1985, suggesting some improvement in the average neighborhood in which children (and young adults) reside. (The unweighted means suggest a similar pattern, although the rate itself is far higher, as expected.)

The table also contains separate entries for two of the four components of the count—the percentage of female-headed households and the percentage of youths aged 16–19 who are neither in school nor are high-school graduates. The table shows the average (mean) percentage of the population of children and youths in neighborhoods with these characteristics. These indicators of neighborhood show different patterns: the proportion of female-headed families has increased in these neighborhoods while the proportion of young adults who are dropouts has declined, suggesting an improvement in the neighborhoods over the time period that we observe these children. These changes, it should be noted, parallel changes nationally in the prevalence of female-headed families and high-school dropouts over this period.

Table A.3 presents these neighborhood variables in the form in which they enter our analysis: i.e., averages over ages 6–15 of the observations in our sample. Three additional variables are included: county me-

TABLE A.3 Neighborhood Variables, Ages 6–15, Based on 1705 Observations

Variable	Mean	Standard Deviation	Minimum	Maximum
	Panel 1: Unweighted Statistics			
Neighborhood Variables				
County median income in 1974	$9,370.81	$2,081.12	$0	$16,708.00
Average county unemployment rate, ages 6–15	6.32	1.64	1.70	11.50
Bad neighborhood in 1976*	0.95	1.30	0	5.00
Average percentage of female heads, ages 6–15	18.84	13.00	0.90	75.80
Average percentage of families below poverty line, ages 6–15	18.78	12.99	1.00	69.30
Average median family income, ages 6–15	$14,150.44	$5,236.15	$4,534.30	$63,473.80
Average percentage of youths who are high-school dropouts, ages 6–15	16.10	9.47	0	87.40
Average underclass count, ages 6–15†	0.66	0.95	0	4.00
Average percentage of underclass neighborhood, ages 6–15‡	0.014	0.08	0	1.00
Average adult neighborhood unemployment, ages 6–15	6.73	4.06	0	25.60
Average male neighborhood unemployment, ages 6–15	6.54	4.58	0	27.70
Average percentage white, ages 6–15	64.52	35.69	0	100.00
Average percentage of workers with professional or technical occupations, ages 6–15	12.27	6.29	0.50	54.80
Average percentage workers with executive or managerial occupations, ages 6–15	6.96	4.20	0	29.50
Average percentage of workers in high-prestige occupations, ages 6–15	19.23	9.71	2.80	63.20
Average extreme percentage of female heads, ages 6–15§	1.90	5.35	0	41.45
Average extreme percentage of adult dropouts, ages 6–15§	1.12	3.78	0	61.81

279

Variable	Mean	Standard Deviation	Minimum	Maximum
Average extreme percentage of high-prestige occupations, ages 6–15§	4.06	6.95	0	43.44

Panel 2: Weighted Statistics

Neighborhood Variables
County median income in 1974	$9,767.80	$2,218.79	$0	$16,708.00
Average county unemployment rate, ages 6–15	6.37	1.78	1.70	11.50
Bad neighborhood in 1976*	0.65	4.75	0	5.0
Average percentage of female heads, ages 6–15	12.55	8.27	0.90	75.80
Average percentage of families below poverty line, ages 6–15	12.64	9.96	1.00	69.30
Average median family income, ages 6–15	$16,266.11	$5,926.30	$4,534.00	$63,474.00
Average percentage of youths who are high-school dropouts, ages 6–15	13.02	9.39	0	87.40
Average underclass count, ages 6–15†	0.30	0.64	0	4.00
Average percentage of underclass neighborhood, ages 6–15‡	0.002	0.03	0	1.00
Average adult neighborhood unemployment, ages 6–15	5.45	3.14	0	25.60
Average male neighborhood unemployment, ages 6–15	5.22	3.46	0	27.70
Average percentage white, ages 6–15	86.34	23.10	0	100.00
Average percentage of workers with professional or technical occupations, ages 6–15	14.32	6.90	0.50	54.80
Average percentage of workers with executive or managerial occupations, ages 6–15	8.64	4.59	0	29.50
Average percentage of workers in high-prestige occupations, ages 6–15	22.95	10.50	2.80	63.20

Variable	Mean	Standard Deviation	Minimum	Maximum
Average extreme percentage of female heads, ages 6–15 §	0.40	9.31	0	41.45
Average extreme percentage of adult dropouts, ages 6–15 §	0.84	16.44	0	61.81
Average extreme percentage of high-prestige occupations, ages 6–15 §	6.31	37.00	0	43.44

*The sum of positive responses to (1) burglaries and robberies, (2) muggings, rapes, pushers, junkies, or too few police, (3) crowded area with too many people, too much noise, and bad traffic, (4) a poor neighborhood for kids, or (5) unkempt yards, grounds, houses poorly kept up, or infrequent or sloppy garbage pickups being a problem in the neighborhood.
†Whether the neighborhood is more than one standard deviation above the average of tracts on each of four indicators: percentage of female-headed families, percentage of young adults 16–19 who are high-school dropouts, proportion of males 16+ employed less than 26 weeks, and proportion of households receiving public assistance.
‡Proportion of neighborhoods with an underclass count of 4 (see note †).
§Proportion greater than, or equal to, 40 percent.

dian income in 1974, bad neighborhood in 1976, and county unemployment rates, the last is averaged over the ages 6–15 of our sample. All of these are directly available in the PSID, but are for substantially larger geographic areas than the census-based tract data. Three variables that attempt to measure the extent to which children in our sample live in neighborhoods with very high (or "extreme") values of particular characteristics of interest are also included. These variables measure the percentage of children in our sample whose families live in a neighborhood that is one standard deviation or more above the mean of the distribution of all neighborhoods in terms of each of three characteristics—the percentage of households headed by a female, the dropout rate of youths 16–19 years old, and the percentage of workers in high-prestige occupations. These extreme characteristics are presented to give a more complete picture of the living conditions of the neighborhoods in which the children in our data resided.

African-Americans generally live in poorer neighborhoods relative to those of other races. There are particular large differences in the average proportion of families headed by a female, the proportion of families below the poverty line, and the average underclass count.

THE ATTAINMENT (OUTCOME) VARIABLES

In the estimation results presented in Chapters 4–7, we attempt to understand the relationships between a rich set of our family and neighborhood variables—many reflecting parental and social decisions affecting children—and a variety of indicators of the success or attainments of children. The outcomes that we study in detail are variables that answer the following questions:

- Did the child *graduate from high school?*
- Did the child *attend college,* if he or she graduated from high school?
- How many total *years of schooling* did the child complete?
- At age 24, was the child—now a young adult—*economically active or inactive?*
- For females, did the child give *birth out of wedlock as a teenager?*
- If the daughter did have a nonmarital teenage birth, did she subsequently *receive welfare?*

The precise definition of most of these variables is clear. However, in two cases additional clarification is necessary. *Economic inactivity* is measured for each child at age 24; youths are inactive if they fall into none of the following categories: (1) a mother of an infant, or of two or more children one of whom is less than 5 years old; (2) working 1000 or more hours per year; (3) a full-time student; (4) a part-time student and working at least 500 hours per year; or (5) a mother of one child 1–5 years old and a part-time student. The *receipt of welfare* subsequent to a teenage nonmarital birth is defined as receiving AFDC benefits within 3 years of giving birth out of wedlock.

Table A.4 presents relevant summary statistics for these outcome variables. Of the 1705 children in our sample, 80 percent completed high school.[21] Of the high-school graduates, 33 percent continued on to postsecondary schooling, some after a period out of school. On average, 12.4 years of school were completed; some of the children had completed at least 1 year of schooling beyond college, while at the other extreme, at least one child had only 2 years of schooling. Of our sample, 17 percent were not economically active at age 24. Among the females, 8 percent had a teenage birth out of wedlock (14 percent in our unweighted sample), and of these 73 percent received AFDC benefits within three years of the birth.

TABLE A.4 Outcome Variables Based on 1705 Observations

Variables	Mean	Standard Deviation	Minimum	Maximum
Panel 1: Unweighted Statistics				
Graduated from high school*	0.76	0.43	0.0	1.00
Years of schooling	12.21	1.78	2.0	17.00
Attend college*	0.31	0.46	0.0	1.00
Economic inactivity*·†	0.24	0.43	0.0	1.00
Teenage out-of-wedlock birth*				
(females only)	0.14	0.35	0.0	1.00
Received welfare*·‡ (females only)	0.18	0.39	0.0	1.00
Panel 2: Weighted Statistics				
Graduated from high school*	0.88	.32	0.0	1.00
Years of schooling	12.90	1.71	2.0	17.00
Attend college*	0.43	0.50	0.0	1.00
Economic inactivity*·†	0.17	0.37	0.0	1.00
Teenage out-of-wedlock birth*				
(females only)	0.08	0.28	0.0	1.00
Received welfare*·‡ (females only)	0.11	0.32	0.0	1.00

*Dummy variable that equals 1 if person has the described characteristic.
†Work < 1000 hours; not a full-time student, or a part-time student and working at least 500 hours; not a mother of an infant or two or more children, one of whom is < 5: nor of one child 1–5 plus a part-time student. Defined only for those 24 years old or above.
‡Within 3 years of giving birth.

ATTRITION FROM, AND ACCURACY OF, OUR SAMPLE

In order for our study to provide insight into the factors that influence the success of all children when they are young adults, we require a sample that is representative of all children in this country. The basic PSID data that we use is a stratified random sample of the U.S. population, in which the low-income population and minority population is oversampled in order to obtain statistically reliable information for such children. Sample weights are then constructed at the inception of the sample to allow researchers to recreate the structure of the entire U.S. population; such weights reflect the stratified character of the survey.

A problem exists, however, if there is a high nonresponse rate for any segment of the population, or if there is a high attrition rate (drop-out rate) among particular segments of the population. Nonresponse or attrition patterns could imply that the sample is not representative of the entire population. If there are systematic patterns of nonresponse or attrition, the sample becomes a selected sample that can no longer describe the entire U.S. population. Analyses based on such samples could yield estimated relationships that fail to describe patterns within the overall population.

To adjust for the differential patterns of attrition, SRC analysts have periodically reweighted the remaining observations in the PSID so as to enable the weighted sample again to reflect the national population. If this reweighting is done appropriately, there should not be a significant problem in terms of the representativeness of the sample relative to the entire U.S. population.

In this section, we discuss the potential problem of attrition from the PSID data and its implications for the representativeness of our sample. We conclude that the periodic reweighting efforts of the SRC analysts have adequately adjusted for the changing composition of the population due to nonresponse and attrition.

As of 1968, the first year of the PSID survey, there were 3120 children aged 0–6 in the sample; by 1988, this number had fallen to 1750. Hence, 1370 children who started in the sample in 1968 are no longer included in 1988 (Wave 21 of the PSID). The Michigan Survey Research Center does not follow families once they are omitted from the survey for a single year. The Center tries for 6 months to contact those not reached on the first attempted contact in a year. A child (dependent) can reenter the survey after missing a year, if the family continued to be interviewed.

We have used the "attrition tape" that provides information on the age, gender, and race of the persons no longer in the sample; the reason for the nonresponse; the year of initial nonresponse; and the status of the child's family as of 1968. Twenty-eight of our potential sample of 3120, or less than 1.0 percent, have died over this period. The children no longer in the sample are rather evenly divided across gender and ages 0–6 in 1968. Nearly 40 percent (39.2) of those who are no longer in the survey, as compared with 51.5 percent in the remaining sample, are white, suggesting a greater probability for nonwhites than whites to drop out from the sample.

About 10 percent of our original sample of children aged 0–6 in 1968

TABLE A.5 Attrition from Our Sample of Children, 1969–1988

Year of Attrition	Number
1969	317
1970	74
1971	45
1972	64
1973	60
1974	38
1975	49
1976	70
1977	52
1978	35
1979	58
1980	67
1981	63
1982	51
1983	68
1984	52
1985	62
1986	66
1987	48
1988	31

dropped out of the survey after the first year (see Table A.5). The number of those dropping out in 1969, 317, represents 23 percent of the total number of those lost over the 21 years, and accounts for the largest annual attrition recorded in the sample. This is a somewhat lower attrition rate than for the entire PSID sample, where 12 percent dropped out after the first year. The mean year of attrition for all those who dropped out is 1976. For most other years after 1969, somewhere between 35–70 persons dropped out; the exceptions are the 74 persons in 1970, and the 31 persons in 1988.

The major reported reasons for the substantial dropout rate in 1969 were: (1) eligible family members refused to participate (117), and (2) all family members were lost or could not be located (95). Thirty-seven of the children (now 1–7) had moved out of the main family—perhaps into foster homes or the homes of grandparents—and were not eligible for interviewing as a new unit because of their age.

For what reasons were those who dropped out from our sample after 1969 lost to the sample? Eight persons were not interviewed because they were in jail or prison, all of whom were lost in the 1980s. Fifty-three were not interviewed because they were in the armed forces: most of these were also lost in the 1980s, more than 30 from 1981 to 1983. Forty-eight were not followed when they attended an educational institution. These were lost during the years 1981 to 1986. Nineteen were not followed due to an "office error" at SRC headquarters. A total of 215, or nearly 16 percent of the total number of attriters, were lost when they moved from the main family, and were not eligible to be interviewed because they were too young (under 18 years of age). Nearly 500 (491) were lost when all eligible family members refused to participate in the sample. After 1969, 254 were lost when the interviewers were unable to locate any member of the family unit within the time allocated for the search. Small numbers dropped out for a variety of other reasons, such as that the family moved too far away for interviewer contact, the eligible respondent could not participate because of a disability or death, the individual was in another type of institution, or "other office error."

Has the pattern of attrition caused systematic biases? Becketti, Gould, Lillard, and Welch (1988) have recently conducted a study on the representativeness of the remaining sample of the PSID. They compared the distributions of age, sex, schooling, income, and related variables for the Current Population Survey and the PSID. They have also compared estimates from earnings equations for male heads of households, female heads of households, and wives using Wave 1 (1968) and Wave 14 (1981) data from the PSID to similar estimates derived from the broader-based cross-sectional sample of the Current Population Survey (CPS). They conclude on the basis of such comparisons that there is no substantial bias in the PSID for cross-sectional studies of the sort they are testing—earnings equations. They state: "While there are statistically significant differences in the empirical distributions of observable characteristics, most of these differences are of no practical significance or can be explained by known differences in coding of answers across the two surveys. . . . The most important conclusion from our efforts is that there appear to be no major biases in the areas we have considered."

Although this study provides some assurance that attrition bias is not significant, there can be no guarantee of this conclusion for our sample.

The quality of the PSID data has been assessed from other perspectives as well. One of these is a simple comparison of the original 1968 survey to the 1968 Current Population Survey. The purpose of this was

TABLE A.6 Coefficients and Standard Errors from Time-Use Data Regressions

Variables	Men	Women
Constant	256.4	1051.9**
	(276.1)	(492.1)
Number of children	3.5	39.9
	(13.3)	(33.1)
Age	−0.1	−7.3
	(4.4)	(6.7)
Spouse age	−3.3	−7.9
	(4.5)	(7.5)
Education		
8–11	−4.8	296.7*
	(65.8)	(174.7)
High-school graduate	−11.9	23.8
	(61.4)	(145.8)
Some college	−51.4	80.3
	(84.9)	(175.2)
College graduate	−36.0	19.8
	(87.6)	(190.9)
Spouse Education		
8–11	65.9	−110.0
	(74.1)	(152.0)
High-school graduate	27.0	−134.4
	(49.3)	(114.2)
Some college	34.5	39.0
	(68.9)	(152.4)
College graduate	4.1	−50.8
	(90.5)	(145.3)
Hours (market) work	−0.5	−18.1**
	(3.1)	(8.3)
Hours work squared	−0.03	0.2
	(0.04)	(0.2)
Spouse hours work	−0.8	−3.7
	(1.0)	(3.0)
Owned house = 1	−66.7	−75.5
	(76.8)	(103.2)
Family income	0.0026	−0.0112*
	(0.0016)	(0.0063)
Spouse present = 1	216.7	647.8*
	(193.5)	(341.6)
Adjusted R^2	.102	.200

*Significant at 10 percent level.
**Significant at 5 percent level.

to assess whether there were biases created by the sample design itself. Both Duncan and Hill (1989) and Becketti, Gould, Lillard, and Welch (1983) compared the demographic characteristics of the two samples. The results suggest that the samples are comparable on all dimensions with two exceptions: racial composition and income distribution. For the former, PSID has a lower proportion of white households than does the CPS, although the actual percentage difference is less than 3 percent. For the latter, PSID has fewer families with incomes of less than $10,000 than does the CPS; however, this is likely to reflect greater accuracy of PSID relative to the CPS. Duncan and Hill (1989) also measure the accuracy of the PSID in capturing income from public transfer programs, including AFDC, other welfare, SSI and emergency assistance. For the entire set of welfare programs, the PSID was found to account for 89 percent of official aggregates. The AFDC income reported accounted for about 92 percent of the national aggregate, and SSI reports accounted for about 84 percent of the national aggregate. Similar studies of the CPS find that it regularly underestimates the level of transfer incomes. A study by Minarik (1975) found that PSID (CPS) accounted for 87.3 (83.7), 94.7 (87.7), and 95.7 (88.8) percent, respectively, of aggregate income including transfer incomes in 1967, 1971, and 1972.

On the basis of these cross-sectional studies, it appears that the PSID sample that we employ does not have a problem of representativeness based on either the original nonresponse rate or on the attrition pattern over time. Nor does it appear to have a problem in terms of its representativeness according to later cross-sectional comparisons. The attrition analysis suggested only limited cause for concern (the differential racial attrition rate). This combination of evidence on nonresponse/attrition patterns and on the periodic reweighting efforts provides some reassurance that there are no major selectivity issues associated with our analyses of the data. A full study of attrition from the PSID is under way at this time (1994) and should provide a more detailed answer to this concern when completed.

NOTES

1. In 1968, there were 3120 children aged 0–6 in the PSID. During the subsequent 21 years, 1370 children were lost from the sample due to a variety of reasons for sample attrition over such a long period. In the fourth section of this appendix we discuss the implications of this attrition for our

research. We note that some children in our sample were missing from the sample for a year or two. If their families were continuously interviewed, however, they could reenter the survey. A few did reenter, and for this reason there may be 1 or 2 years of missing data on these children. There are 46 children who had data missing for 2 or more years, or had missing information on the years of education completed; these observations are excluded from our data base.

2. Thus, for two children, one aged 2 and the other aged 6 in 1968, comparable information for each from ages 6–18 is obtained using data from 1972 to 1984 for the first child, and data from 1968 to 1980 for the second child.

3. For the first and last year of the data, this averaging of the contiguous years is not possible. In these cases, the contiguous year's value is assigned and is adjusted if appropriate using other information in the PSID.

4. These activities included child-care time, time teaching children to learn, time spent helping with homework, time spent reading to the child, time spent playing with the child, and time spent listening to the child.

5. The two regressions are reported in Table A.6. The equation for men is considerably weaker than that for women: none of the variables in the men's equation are statistically significant at the 5 percent level; the R^2 is .102, compared to .20 for women. Although predictions from this equation are very imprecise, they are the best estimates that we have of the amount of time fathers spend with their children.

6. If a family unit includes only one parent in a particular year, the family child-care time estimate is based on the imputed value for that parent alone. The presence or absence of a spouse is one of the independent variables in the child-care time regressions. It has the expected positive sign and is large and significant in the child-care time equation of mothers. It is positive but not significant in the time estimate for fathers.

7. Beginning in 1987, it is for the calendar year rather than as of July.

8. For years prior to 1975, these Medicaid estimates are based on more crude approximations.

9. These data were provided to us by Robert Moffitt, and we thank him. The underlying sources for the data are: U.S. House of Representatives, Committee on Ways and Means, *Background Material and Data on Programs within the Jurisdiction of the Committee on Ways and Means* (known as *The Green Book*) for various years; Kasten and Todd (1983), unpublished data from the U.S. Department of Health and Human Services (for Medicaid, the data are from unpublished tables from the U.S. Department of Health and Human Resources [State Medicaid Tables for 1975–1988], and the *Economic Report of the President*).

10. In most cases, this link is based on a match of the location of our observations to the relevant Census tract or block-numbering area (67.8 percent for 1970 and 71.5 percent for 1980). (A block-numbering area is analogous to a tract but is typically located in a small city that is blocked rather than

tracted.) These are the smallest areas (neighborhood measures) available, and hence the most preferred match. The next most common match (25 and 14 percent for 1970 and 1980, respectively) is on the basis of Minor Civil Division/Census County Division. (A minor civil division is a legal subdivision of a county, typically a township or a city, and is used as a substitute in areas where tract, enumeration district, and block numbering area are not available.) The third most common match in both 1970 and 1980 is for zip codes (5 and 11.7 percent, respectively). Zip codes, or U.S. Postal Service Zoning Improvement Plan areas, are another substitute when tract, enumeration district, and block-numbering area are not available. The fourth—and least common—match, accounting for about 2 percent of the matches for both years, is enumeration district. These are the "basic work areas for a single Census enumerator" and are used as an approximation for a neighborhood in rural areas. Less than 1 percent of individuals in our sample did not have a neighborhood match.

11. The specific weights are .1 1980 and .9 1970 for 1971, .2 1980 and .8 1970 for 1972, etc.

12. The adjustments are .681898 for 1970 and 1.44815 for 1980 data.

13. The weights (denominators) used are those for the 1988 sample. Note that the neighborhood variables are discussed separately below.

14. For most of the discussion, we use national data for a year or set of years while these children were growing up. For permanent characteristics of the sample, we use national data tied to the date of our weighted data—1988. For variables measuring the experience of the children when they were growing up, the discussion is centered on variables measured as of 1978 when these children were aged 10–16. In other cases, the data used are tied to the point at which we measure the variable: for example, parent's education is measured in the first year of the survey (1968).

15. The design of the PSID includes an oversampling of the low-income population and minorities. The oversampled part of the sample is known as Office of Economic Opportunity (OEO) sample.

16. For example, the annual percentages were 19 in 1969, 17.7 in 1976, and 17 in 1982.

17. From 1975 to 1980, the annual rate of moves for children aged 5–9 years (10–14 years) was 11.7 (8.8). From 1981 to 1984, the annual move rate for children aged 10–14 was about .13 to .14.

18. These data are taken from *The Green Book* (1990).

19. The estimates for years other than 1970 and 1980 should be interpreted cautiously; they are based on weighted averages of the values in the 1970 and 1980 Censuses.

20. In particular, an underclass neighborhood as defined by Ricketts and Sawhill (1988) is one that is more than one standard deviation above the national tract mean on each of four behavioral indicators: the percentage

of female-headed families, the percentage of young adults 16–19 who are high-school dropouts, the proportion of males 16 and over who were employed fewer than 26 weeks, and the proportion of households receiving public assistance.

21. This discussion reports weighted statistics.

Appendix B
The Econometric Structure
of the Bivariate Probit Models
# of Chapters 5, 6, and 7

In this appendix we lay out the bivariate models that we use in Chapters 5, 6, and 7. Each of these models is of two discrete but related choices, I_1 and I_2. The three bivariate models specified in this study all use the following general form of a simultaneous equations system:

(1) $I_1^* = Z_1 \gamma_1 + \epsilon_1$
(2) $I_2^* = Z_2 \gamma_2 + \epsilon_2$

where I_1^* and I_2^* are the two choices or dependent variables "explained" within the bivariate model. In Chapter 5, I_1^* is the high-school graduation choice, and I_2^* is the postsecondary schooling choice; in Chapter 6, I_1^* is the choice of giving birth out of wedlock as a teenager, and I_2^* is the choice of receiving AFDC benefits subsequent to giving birth out of wedlock as a teenager; in Chapter 7, I_1^* is the high-school graduation decision, and I_2^* is the decision of whether or not to be economically active.* The Z vector contains exogenous variables that are expected to influence the choices made (I_1 and I_2), and γ_1 and γ_2 are the coefficients on the explanatory variables. ϵ_1 and ϵ_2 are the error terms.

In the bivariate probit model, the error terms are assumed to be corre-

---

*The version of this model as it applies to the out-of-wedlock birth and welfare choices is discussed in more detail in An, Haveman, and Wolfe (1993).

lated with each other, and this is tested as part of the empirical estimation of the model. A negative correlation implies that there are unobserved factors that increase the likelihood of one outcome while simultaneously decreasing the likelihood of the other; a positive correlation suggests that the unobserved factors work in the same way to either increase or decrease the likelihood of both outcomes.

The choices or dependent variables observe the following selection rules:

(3) $I_1 = \begin{cases} 1 \text{ if } I_1^* > 0 \\ \\ 0 \text{ otherwise} \end{cases}$ [Graduating from high school (Chapters 5 and 7)] [Giving birth out of wedlock as a teenager (Chapter 6)]

(4) $I_2 = \begin{cases} 1 \text{ if } I_2^* > 0 \text{ and } I_1^* = 1 \\ \\ \\ \\ 0 \text{ if } I_2^* \le 0 \text{ and } I_1^* = 1 \end{cases}$ [Graduating from high school and having postsecondary schooling (Chapter 5)] [Giving birth out of wedlock as a teenager and receiving AFDC (Chapter 6)]

or

(5) $I_2 = \begin{cases} 1 \text{ if } I_2^* > 0 \\ \\ 0 \text{ otherwise} \end{cases}$ [Being economically inactive at age 24 (Chapter 7)]

By normalization, $V(\epsilon_1) = V(\epsilon_2) = 1$. Then, the covariance matrix between (1) and (2) is given by

$$\sum = \begin{matrix} [1 \ \rho] \\ [\rho \ 1] \end{matrix}$$

where ρ measures the extent of the simultaneous interrelationship between the two decisions.*

Depending on the question, we partition the original sample into either three or four mutually exclusive subsamples. Chapters 5 and 6 employ a three-way partition; Chapter 7 employs a four-way partition.

---

*The ρ indicates whether or not the relationships being estimated are simultaneous or independent. The value of ρ must lie between 0 and 1. Values close to 0 suggest no simultaneity or independence. A Wald test is traditionally used to test whether the ρ is significantly different from 0. The test uses the square of the t-statistic on the ρ, which has a chi-square distribution with 1 degree of freedom.

The Three-Way Partition Formulation (Chapters 5 and 6)

Under selection rules (3) and (4), the probability P_j that the individual will fall into the jth subsample is given by:

(6) $P_1 = \Pr(I_1 = 0) = \mathrm{PR}(I_1^* \leq 0)$
$= \mathrm{PR}(\epsilon_1 \leq -Z_1\gamma_1) = 1 - F(Z_1\gamma_1)$

(7) $P_2 = \Pr(I_2 = 0) = \Pr(I_1^* > 0, I_2^* \leq 0)$
$= \mathrm{PR}(\epsilon_1 < -Z_1\gamma_1, \epsilon_2 \leq -Z_2\gamma_2)$
$= G(Z_1\gamma_1, -Z_2\gamma_2; \rho)$

(8) $P_3 = \mathrm{PR}(I_2 = 1) = \Pr(I_1^* > 0, I_2^* > 0)$
$= \mathrm{PR}(\epsilon_1 > -Z_1\gamma_1, \epsilon_2 > -Z_2\gamma_2)$
$= G(Z_1\gamma_1, Z_2\gamma_2; \rho)$

where $F(\cdot)$ and $G(\cdot)$ denote the standardized univariate and bivariate normal distribution functions, respectively.

Chapter 5:

S_1:   Those who do not graduate from high school;
S_2:   Those who graduate from high school but do not choose postsecondary schooling; and
S_3:   Those who graduate from high school and choose postsecondary schooling.

Chapter 6:

S_1:   Those who do not give birth out of wedlock as a teenager;
S_2:   Those who give birth out of wedlock as a teenager, but do not receive AFDC benefits; and
S_3:   Those who give birth out of wedlock as a teenager and receive AFDC benefits.

For each of the analyses with three subgroups, the likelihood function for the entire sample has the following form:

(9) $$L = \prod_{S_1} [1 - F(Z_1\gamma_1)] \cdot \prod_{S_2} G(Z_1\gamma_1, -Z_2\gamma_2 ; \rho)$$
$$\cdot \prod_{S_3} G(Z_1\gamma_1, Z_2\gamma_2 ; \rho)$$

The Four-Way Partition Formulation (Chapter 7)

Under selection rules (3) and (5), the probability P_j that an individual will fall into the jth subsample is given by:

(10) $P_1 = \text{Pr}\,(I_1 = 1,\, I_2 = 0) = \text{Pr}\,(I_1^* > 0,\, I_2^* \leq 0)$
      $= \text{Pr}\,(\epsilon_1 > -Z_1\gamma_1,\, \epsilon_2 \geq -Z_2\gamma_2) = G(Z_1\gamma_1,\, -Z_2\gamma_2;\, \rho)$

(11) $P_2 = \text{Pr}\,(I_1 = 1,\, I_2 = 1) = \text{Pr}\,(I_1^* > 0,\, I_2^* > 0)$
      $= \text{Pr}\,(\epsilon_1 > -Z_1\gamma_1,\, \epsilon_2 > -Z_2\gamma_2) = G(Z_1\gamma_1,\, Z_2\gamma_2;\, \rho)$

(12) $P_3 = \text{Pr}\,(I_1 = 0,\, I_2 = 0) = \text{Pr}\,(I_1^* \leq 0,\, I_2^* \leq 0)$
      $= \text{Pr}\,(\epsilon_1 \leq -Z_1\gamma_1,\, \epsilon_2 \leq -Z_2\gamma_2) = G(-Z_1\gamma_1,\, -Z_2\gamma_2;\, \rho)$

(13) $P_4 = \text{Pr}\,(I_1 = 0,\, I_2 = 1) = \text{Pr}\,(I_1^* \leq 0,\, I_2^* > 0)$
      $= \text{Pr}\,(\epsilon_1 \leq -Z_1\gamma_1,\, \epsilon_2 > -Z_2\gamma_2) = G(-Z_1\gamma_1,\, Z_2\gamma_2;\, \rho)$

For Chapter 7, we partition the original sample into four mutually exclusive subsamples.

S_1:   Those who graduate from high school and are not economically inactive at age 24;

S_2:   Those who graduate from high school, but who are economically inactive at age 24;

S_3:   Those who do not graduate from high school and are not economically inactive at age 24; and

S_4:   Those who do not graduate from high school and are economically inactive at age 24.

For the analysis with four subgroups, the likelihood function for the entire sample has the following form:

(14) $$L = \prod_{S_1} [G(Z_1\gamma_1,\, -Z_2\gamma_2;\, \rho)] \cdot \prod_{S_2} [G(Z_1\gamma_1,\, Z_2\gamma_2;\, \rho)] \cdot \prod_{S_3} [G(-Z_1\gamma_1,\, -Z_2\gamma_2;\, \rho)] \cdot \prod_{S_4} [G(-Z_1\gamma_1,\, Z_2\gamma_2;\, \rho)]$$

The maximization of (9) and (14) with respect to γ_1, γ_2, and ρ yields consistent estimates $\hat{\gamma}_1$, $\hat{\gamma}_2$, *and* $\hat{\rho}$.

References

Aaron, Henry J. 1978. *Politics and the Professors: The Great Society in Perspective.* Washington, D.C.: The Brookings Institution.

Abrahamse, Allan F., Peter Morrison, and Linda Waite. 1987. "Single Teenage Mothers: Spotting Susceptible Adolescents in Advance." Paper presented at the annual meeting of the Population Association of America, Chicago.

Acs, Gregory, and Sheldon Danziger. 1993. "Educational Attainment, Industrial Structure and Male Earnings." *Journal of Human Resources, 28(3):* 618–648.

Alan Guttmacher Institute. 1992. *Facts in Brief: Teenage Sexual and Reproductive Behavior.* New York: Alan Guttmacher Institute.

Alexander, Karl L., and Bruce K. Eckland. 1975. "Contextual Effects in the High School Attainment Process." *American Sociological Review, 40:* 402–416.

Alexander, Karl L., Bruce K. Eckland, and Larry J. Griffen. 1975. "The Wisconsin Model of Socioeconomic Achievement: A Replication." *Journal of Sociology, 81:* 324–342.

Alwin, Duane, and Arland Thornton. 1984. "Family Origins and the Schooling Process: Early versus Late Influence of Parental Characteristics." *American Sociological Review, 49 (December):* 784–802.

Amato, Paul R., and Alan Booth. 1991. "Consequences of Parental Divorce and Marital Unhappiness for Adult Well-Being." *Social Forces, 69(3):* 895–914.

Amato, Paul R., and Bruce Keith. 1991. "Parental Divorce and Adult Well-being: A Meta-analysis." *Journal of Marriage and the Family, 53:* 43–58.

An, Chong Bum, Robert Haveman, and Barbara Wolfe. 1992. "The 'Window Problem' in Studies of Children's Attainments: A Methodological Exploration." Institute for Research on Poverty, Discussion Paper no. 977–92, University of Wisconsin-Madison.

An, Chong Bum, Robert Haveman, and Barbara Wolfe. 1993. "Teen Out-of-Wedlock Births and Welfare Receipt: The Role of Childhood Events and Economic Circumstances." *Review of Economics and Statistics, 75(2):* 195–208.

Annie E. Casey Foundation. 1992. *Kids Count Data Book.* Washington, D.C.: Center for the Study of Social Policy.

Antel, John. 1988. "Mother's Welfare Dependency Effects on Daughter's Early Fertility and Fertility Out-of-Wedlock." Unpublished paper, University of Houston.

Antel, John. 1992. "The Inter-generational Transfer of Welfare Dependency: Some Statistical Evidence." *Review of Economics and Statistics, 74(3):* 467–473.

Ashenfelter, Orley, and Alan Krueger. 1993. "Estimates of the Economic Return to Schooling from a New Sample of Twins." Industrial Relations Section, Working Paper No. 34, Princeton University.

Astone, Nan Marie, and Sara McLanahan. 1991. "Family Structure and High School Completion: The Role of Parental Practices." *American Sociological Review, 56:* 309–320.

Averch, Harvey A., et al. 1972. *How Effective Is Schooling? A Critical Review and Synthesis of Research Findings.* Santa Monica, Calif.: RAND Corporation.

Bane, Mary Jo, and David Ellwood. 1983. "Dynamics of Dependence and the Routes to Self-Sufficiency." Final report to the U.S. Department of Health and Human Services. Cambridge, Mass.: Harvard University, Kennedy School of Government.

Becker, Gary S. 1960. "An Economic Approach to the Analysis of Fertility." In *Demographic and Economic Change in Developed Countries,* Universities-National Bureau of Economic Research, Special Conference Series, no. 11. Princeton: Princeton University Press.

Becker, Gary S. 1981. *A Treatise on the Family.* Cambridge, Mass.: Harvard University Press.

Becker, Gary S., and H. Gregg Lewis. 1973. "On the Interaction between the Quantity and Quality of Children." *Journal of Political Economy, March/ April, Pt. II:* S279–S288.

Becker, Gary S., and Nigel Tomes. 1986. "Human Capital and the Rise and Fall of Families." *Journal of Labor Economics, 84(4):* S143–S162.

Becketti, Sean, William Gould, Lee Lillard, and Finis Welch. 1983. "Attrition from the PSID." Santa Monica, Calif.: Unicorn Research Corp.

Becketti, Sean, William Gould, Lee Lillard, and Finis Welch. 1988. "The Panel Study of Income Dynamics after Fourteen Years: An Evaluation." *Journal of Labor Economics, 6(4):* 472–492.

Behrman, Jere. 1984. "Sibling Deviation Estimates, Measurement Error and Biases in Estimated Returns to Schooling." Mimeo, Department of Economics, University of Pennsylvania.

Behrman, Jere, Zdeneck Hrubec, Paul Taubman, and Terrance Wales. 1980. *Socioeconomic Success: A Study of the Effects of Genetic Endowments, Family Environment and Schooling.* Amsterdam: North-Holland.

Behrman, Jere, and Paul Taubman. 1990. "The Intergenerational Correlation between Children's Adult Earnings and Their Parents' Income: Results from the Michigan Panel Survey of Income Dynamics." *Review of Income and Wealth, 36:* 115–127.

Behrman, Jere, Paul Taubman, and Terrance Wales. 1977. "Controlling for and Measuring the Effects of Genetics and Family Environment in Equations for Schooling and Labor Market Success." In Paul Taubman (ed.), *Kinometrics: Determinants of Socioeconomic Success within and between Families.* Amsterdam: North-Holland.

Belsky, Jay, Lawrence Steinberg, and Patricia Draper. 1991. "Childhood Experience, Interpersonal Development, and Reproductive Strategy: An Evolutionary Theory of Socialization." *Child Development, 63(4): 647–670.*

Bianchi, Suzanne. 1990. "America's Children: Mixed Prospects." *Population Bulletin, 45(1): 1–42.*

Bishop, John. 1989. "The Productivity Consequences of What Is Learned in High School." School of Industrial and Labor Relations, Working Paper no. 88–18, Cornell University.

Blankenhorn, D., S. Bayme, and J. B. Elstain (eds.) 1990. *Rebuilding the Nest: A New Commitment to the American Family.* Milwaukee, WI.: Family Service America.

Blau, Peter, and Otis D. Duncan. 1967. *The American Occupational Structure.* New York: Wiley.

Bound, John, Zvi Griliches, and Bronwyn Hall. 1986. "Wages, Schooling and IQ of Brothers and Sisters: Do the Family Factors Differ?" *International Economic Review, 27:* 77–105.

Bowles, Samuel. 1972. "Schooling and Inequality from Generation to Generation." *Journal of Political Economy, 80 (Part II, May/June):* S219–S251.

Bowles, Samuel, and Herbert Gintis. 1972–1973. "I. Q. in the U. S. Class Structure." *Social Policy, 3:* 65–96.

Bowles, Samuel, and Herbert Gintis. 1976. *Schooling in Capitalist America: Educational Reform and Contradictions of Economic Life.* New York: Basic Books.

Bowles, Samuel, and Henry Levin. 1968. "The Determinants of Scholastic Achievement: An Appraisal of Some Recent Evidence." *Journal of Human Resources, 3:* 3–24.

Bowles, Samuel, and Valerie Nelson. 1974. "The 'Inheritance of IQ' and the Intergenerational Reproduction of Economic Inequality." *Review of Economics and Statistics, 56 (February):* 39–51.

Brittain, John. 1977. *The Inheritance of Economic Status.* Washington, D.C.: The Brookings Institution.

Bronfenbrenner, Uri. 1979. *The Ecology of Human Development.* Cambridge, Mass.: Harvard University Press.

Bronfenbrenner, Uri. 1989. "Ecological Systems Theory." *Annals of Child Development, 6:* 187–249.

Bronfenbrenner, Uri, and Ann C. Crouter. 1983. "The Evolution of Environmental Models in Developmental Research." In Paul H. Musser (ed.), *Handbook of Child Psychology: Vol. I History, Theory, and Methods.* New York: Wiley.

Brooks-Gunn, Jeanne, Greg Duncan, Pam Kato, and Naomi Sealand. 1991. "Do Neighborhoods Influence Child and Adolescent Behavior?" Ann

Arbor, Mich.: Mimeo, University of Michigan, Institute for Survey Research.

Bryk, Anthony S., and M. E. Driscoll. 1988. *The High School as Community: Contextual Influences, and Consequences for Students and Teachers*. Madison, Wis.: National Center on Effective Secondary Schools.

Bumpass, Larry, and Sara McLanahan. 1989. "Unmarried Motherhood: Recent Trends, Composition, and Black-White Differences." *Demography, 26(2):* 279–286.

Bumpass, Larry, and James Sweet. 1989. "Children's Experience in Single-Parent Families: Implications of Cohabitation and Marital Transitions." *Family Planning Perspectives, 21(6):* 256–260.

Cain, Glen G. 1974. "Review of *Socioeconomic Background and Achievement*, by Duncan, Featherman, and Duncan." *American Journal of Sociology, 79:* 1497–1509.

Cain, Glen G., and Harold Watts. 1970. "Problems in Making Inferences from the Coleman Report." *American Sociological Review, 35:* 228–242.

Card, David, and Alan Krueger. 1992. "Does School Quality Matter? Returns to Education and the Characteristics of Public School in the United States." *Journal of Political Economy, 100(1):* 1–40.

Carnegie Council on Adolescent Development. 1989. *Turning Points: Preparing American Youth for the 21st Century*. New York: Carnegie Corporation.

Carver, Charles S., and Michael F. Scheier. 1981. *Attention and Self-regulation: A Control-theory Approach to Human Behavior*. New York: Springer-Verlag.

Case, Anne, and Lawrence Katz. 1991. "The Company You Keep: The Effects of Family and Neighborhood on Disadvantaged Youths." National Bureau of the Economic Research, Working Paper no. 3075, Cambridge, Mass.

Center for Population Options. 1990. "Teenage Pregnancy and Too-Early Childbearing: Public Costs, Personal Consequences." Washington, D.C.

Chamberlain, Gary, and Zvi Griliches. 1975. "Unobservables with a Variance-Components Structure: Ability, Schooling and the Economic Success of Brothers." *International Economic Review, 16(2):* 422–449.

Chamberlain, Gary, and Zvi Griliches. 1977. "More on Brothers." In Paul Taubman (ed.), *Kinometrics: Determinants of Socioeconomic Success within and between Families*. Amsterdam: North-Holland.

Chase-Lansdale, P. Lindsay, and E. M. Hetherington. 1991. "The Impact of Divorce on Life-Span Development: Short and Long Term Effects." In Paul Baltes, David Featherman, and Richard Lerner (eds.), *Life-Span Development and Behavior*. Hillsdale, N.J.: Lawrence Erlbaum Associates.

Cherlin, Andrew (ed.). 1988. *The Changing American Family and Public Policy*. Washington, D.C.: Urban Institute Press.

Children's Defense Fund. 1990. *S.O.S. America! A Children's Defense Budget*. Washington, D.C.: Children's Defense Fund.

Coleman, James S., et al. 1966. *Equality of Economic Opportunity*. Washington, D.C.: Government Printing Office.

Collette, Nancy Donohue. 1979. "Support Systems after Divorce: Incidence and Impact." *Journal of Marriage and the Family,* 41: 837–845.

Committee for Economic Development. 1991. *The Unfinished Agenda: A New*

Vision for Child Development and Education. New York: Committee for Economic Development.

Corcoran, Mary. 1980. "Sex Differences in Measurement Error in Status Attainment Models." *Sociological Methods and Research, 9:* 199–217.

Corcoran, Mary, and Linda Datcher. 1981. "Intergenerational Status Transmission and the Process of Individual Attainment." In Martha Hill, Daniel H. Hill, and James M. Morgan (eds.), *Five Thousand American Families— Patterns of Economic Progress,* Vol. 9. Ann Arbor, Mich.: University of Michigan, Institute for Social Research.

Corcoran, Mary, Roger Gordon, Deborah Laren, and Gary Solon. 1992. "The Association between Men's Economic Status and Their Family and Community Origins." *Journal of Human Resources, 27(4):* 575–601.

Council of Economic Advisors. Various years. *Economic Report of the President.* Washington, D.C.: U.S. Government Printing Office.

Crain, Robert, and Rita Mahard. 1978. "School Racial Composition and Black College Attendance and Achievement Test Performance." *Sociology of Education, 51:* 81–101.

Crane, Jonathan. 1991. "The Epidemic Theory of Ghettos and Neighborhood Effects on Dropping out and Teenage Childbearing." *American Journal of Sociology, 96(5):* 1226–1259.

Danziger, Sheldon. 1990. "Antipoverty Policies and Child Poverty." *Social Work Research and Abstracts, 26(4):* 17–24.

Danziger, Sheldon, and Robert Wood. 1992. "Black Male Joblessness, 1979 to 1989." Ann Arbor, Mich.: Mimeo, University of Michigan.

Datcher, Linda. 1982. "Effects of Community and Family Background on Achievement." *Review of Economics & Statistics, 64:* 32–41.

Datcher-Loury, Linda. 1986. "Effects of Mother's Home Time on Children's Schooling." Ann Arbor, Mich.: Mimeo, University of Michigan.

Dryfoos, Joyce. 1989. *Youth at Risk: One in Four in Jeopardy.* New York: Carnegie Corporation.

Duncan, Greg and Daniel Hill. 1975. "Attitudes, Behavior, and Economic Outcomes: A Structural Equations Approach." In Greg Duncan and James Morgan (eds.), *Five Thousand American Families—Patterns of Economic Progress,* Vol. 3. Ann Arbor, Mich.: University of Michigan, Institute for Social Research.

Duncan, Greg, and Daniel Hill. 1989. "Assessing the Quality of Household Panel Data: The Case of the Panel Study of Income Dynamics." *Journal of Business and Economic Statistics, 7(4):* 441–452.

Duncan, Greg, Martha Hill, and Saul Hoffman. 1988. "Welfare Dependence within and across Generations." *Science, 231:* 467–471.

Duncan, Greg, and Saul Hoffman. 1989. "The Use and Effects of Welfare: A Survey of Recent Evidence." *Social Service Review, 62(2):* 238–257.

Duncan, Greg, and Saul Hoffman. 1990a. "Teenage Welfare Receipt and Subsequent Dependence among Black Adolescent Mothers." *Family Planning Perspectives, 22(1):* 16–20.

Duncan, Greg, and Saul Hoffman. 1990b. "Welfare Benefits, Economic Opportunities, and the Incidence of Out-of-Wedlock Births among Black Teenage Girls." *Demography, 27(4):* 519–557.

Duncan, Greg, and Deborah Laren. 1990. "Neighborhood and Family Correlates of Low Birthweight: Preliminary Results on Births to Black Women from the PSID-Geocode File." Ann Arbor, Mich.: Mimeo, University of Michigan, Survey Research Center.

Duncan, Greg, Deborah Laren, and Wei-Jun Yeung. 1991. "How Dependent Are America's Children on Welfare—Recent Findings from the PSID." Ann Arbor, Mich.: Mimeo, University of Michigan, Survey Research Center.

Duncan, Greg, and Willard Rodgers. 1991. "Has Children's Poverty Become More Persistent?" *American Sociological Review, 56:* 538–550.

Duncan, Otis D., David L. Featherman, and Beverly Duncan. 1972. *Socioeconomic Background and Achievement.* New York: Seminar Press.

Duncan, Otis D., and Ralph W. Hodge. 1963. "Education and Occupational Mobility." *American Journal of Sociology, 68:* 629–644.

Elder, Glen H., Jr. 1974. *Children of the Great Depression.* Chicago: University of Chicago Press.

Elder, Glen H., Jr. 1985. "Families, Kin, and the Life Course: A Sociological Perspective." In Glen H. Elder, Jr. (ed.), *Life Course Dynamics: From 1968 to the 1980s.* Ithaca, N.Y.: Cornell University Press.

Ellwood, David. 1986. "Targeting 'Would Be' Long Term Recipients of AFDC." Report prepared for the U.S. Department of Health and Human Services. Princeton, N.J.: Mathematica Policy Research, Inc.

Engle, Robert. 1984. "Wald, Likelihood Ratio, and LaGrange Multiplier Tests in Econometrics." In Zvi Griliches and Michael Intrilligator (eds.), *Handbook of Econometrics.* Amsterdam: North-Holland.

Entwisle, Doris, and Karl Alexander. 1992. "Summer Setback: Race, Poverty, School Composition, and Mathematics Achievement in the First Two Years of School." *American Sociological Review, 57 (February):* 72–84.

Evans, William, Wallace Oates and Robert Schwab. 1992. "Measuring Peer Group Effects: A Study of Teenage Behavior" *Journal of Political Economy, 100(5):* 966–991.

Featherman, David. 1979. "Opportunities Are Expanding." *Society, 16:* 4–11.

Featherman, David. 1981. "Stratification and Social Mobility: Two Decades of Cumulative Social Science." In James F. Short, Jr. (ed.), *The State of Sociology: Problems and Prospects.* San Francisco: Sage Publications.

Featherman, David, and Robert M. Hauser. 1978. *Opportunity and Change.* New York: Academic Press.

Ferguson, Ronald. 1991. "Paying for Public Education: New Evidence on How and Why Money Matters." *Harvard Journal on Legislation, 28(2):* 465–498.

Fuchs, Victor. 1990. "Are Americans Underinvesting in Their Children?" In David Blankenhorn, Steven Bayme, and Jean B. Elshtain (eds.), *Rebuilding the Nest: A New Commitment to the American Family.* Milwaukee, Wis.: Family Service America.

Fuchs, Victor and Diane Reklis. 1992 "America's Children: Economic Perspectives and Policy Options." *Science, 255:* 41–46.

Furstenberg, Frank. 1987. "Race Differences in Teenage Sexuality, Pregnancy, and Adolescent Childbearing." *The Milbank Quarterly, 65(2):* 381–403.

Furstenberg, Frank, Jeanne Brooks-Gunn, and S. Philip Morgan. 1987. *Adolescent Mothers in Later Life.* New York: Cambridge University Press.

Furstenberg, Frank, Christine W. Nord, James L. Peterson, and Nicholas Zill. 1983. "The Life Course of Children of Divorce: Marital Disruption and Parental Conflict." *American Sociological Review, 48:* 656–668.

Galston, William. 1993. "Causes of Declining Well-Being among U.S. Children." *The Aspen Institute Quarterly, 5(1):* 52–77.

Ganzeboom, Harry, Donald Treiman, and Wout Ultee. 1991. "Comparative Intergenerational Stratification Research: Three Generations and Beyond." In W. Richard Scott and Judith Blake (eds.), *Annual Review of Sociology, 17:* 277–302.

Geronimous, Arline, and Sanders Korenman. 1992. "The Socioeconomic Consequences of Teen Childbearing Reconsidered." *Quarterly Journal of Economics, 107 (November):* 1187–1214.

Glenn, Norval D., and Kathryn B. Kramer. 1985. "The Psychological Well-Being of Adult Children of Divorce." *Journal of Marriage and the Family, 47:* 905–912.

Gottschalk, Peter. 1992a. "Is Intergenerational Correlation in Welfare Participation across Generations Spurious?" Boston: Mimeo, Department of Economics, Boston College.

Gottschalk, Peter. 1992b. "The Intergenerational Transmission of Welfare Participation: Facts and Possible Causes." *Journal of Policy Analysis and Management, 11:* 254–272.

Graham, John, Andrea Beller, and Pedro Hernandez. 1992. "The Relationship Between Child Support Payments and Offspring Educational Attainment." Paper presented at the Econometric Society Meetings, New Orleans, La.

Griliches, Zvi. 1979. "Sibling Models and Data in Economics: Beginnings of a Survey." *Journal of Political Economy, 87:* 537–564.

Hamburg, David. 1991. "A Decent Start! Promoting Healthy Child Development in the First Three Years of Life." *Annual Report, 1990. Carnegie Corporation.* New York: Carnegie Corp.

Hanushek, Eric. 1986. "The Economics of Schooling: Production and Efficiency in Public Schools." *Journal of Economic Literature, 24:* 1141–1177.

Hanushek, Eric. 1992. "The Trade-off between Child Quantity and Quality." *Journal of Political Economy, 100(1):* 84–117.

Hanushek, Eric, and John Kain. 1972. "On the Value of Equality of Economic Opportunity as a Guide to Public Policy." In Frederick Mosteller and Daniel P. Moynihan (eds.), *On Equality of Educational Opportunity.* New York: Random House.

Harvard Educational Review. 1973. *Perspectives on Opportunity.* Cambridge, Mass.: Harvard Educational Review Reprint Series no. 8.

Hauser, Robert. 1973. "Socioeconomic Background and Differential Returns to Education." In Lewis Solomon and Paul Taubman (eds.), *Does College Matter?* New York: Academic Press.

Hauser, Robert. 1984. "Some Cross-Population Comparisons of Sibling Resemblance in Educational Attainment and Occupational Status." *Social Science Research, 13 (June):* 159–187.

Hauser, Robert. 1991. "Measuring Adolescent Educational Transitions among

African Americans, Hispanics, and Whites.'' Institute for Research on Poverty, Discussion Paper no. 951–91, Madison, Wis. University of Wisconsin-Madison.

Hauser, Robert and Thomas N. Daymont. 1977. ''Schooling, Ability and Earnings: Cross-sectional Findings 8 to 14 Years after High School Graduation.'' *Sociology of Education, 50:* 182–206.

Hauser, Robert, and William Sewell. 1986. ''Family Effects in Simple Models of Education, Occupation Status, and Earnings: Findings from the Wisconsin and Kalamazoo Studies.'' *Journal of Labor Economics, 4, Pt. 2:* S83–S115.

Haveman, Robert. 1987. *Poverty Policy and Poverty Research.* Madison, Wis.: University of Wisconsin Press.

Haveman, Robert. 1989. *Starting Even: An Equal Opportunity Program to Combat the Nation's New Poverty.* New York: Simon and Schuster.

Haveman, Robert, and Lawrence Buron. 1993. ''Escaping Poverty through Work: The Problem of Low Earnings Capacity in the United States, 1973–1988.'' *Review of Income and Wealth,* forthcoming.

Haveman, Robert, and Barbara Wolfe. 1984. ''Schooling and Economic Well-Being: The Role of Non-Market Effects.'' *Journal of Human Resources, 19(3):* 377–407.

Haveman, Robert, and Barbara Wolfe. 1990. ''The Economic Well-Being of the Disabled—1962–1984.'' *Journal of Human Resources, 25(1):* 32–54.

Haveman, Robert, Barbara Wolfe, and James Spaulding. 1991. ''Childhood Events and Circumstances Influencing High School Completion.'' *Demography, 28:* 133–157.

Hayes, Cheryl D. (ed.). 1987. *Risking the Future: Adolescent Sexuality, Pregnancy, and Childbearing.* Vol. 1. Washington, D.C.: National Academy of Sciences Press.

Hayes, Cheryl D., John Palmer and M. J. Zoslow, eds. 1990. *Who Cares for America's Children? Child Care Policy for the 1990s* Washington, D.C.: National Academy of Sciences Press.

Hetherington, E. Mavis. 1972. ''Effects of Father Absence on Personality Development in Adolescent Daughters.'' *Developmental Psychology, 7:* 313–326.

Hetherington, E. Mavis. 1979. ''The Development of Children in Mother-headed Families.'' In Howard A. Hoffman and David Reiss (eds.), *The American Family: Dying or Developing?* New York: Plenum.

Hetherington, E. Mavis, and Kathleen A. Camara. 1984. In Ross D. Parke (ed.), *Review of Child Development Research: Vol. 7. The Family.* Chicago: University of Chicago Press.

Hetherington, E. Mavis, Kathleen A. Camara, and David Featherman. 1983. ''Achievement and Intellectual Functioning of Children in One-parent Households.'' In Janet T. Spence (ed.), *Achievement and Achievement Motives.* San Francisco: Freeman Press.

Hill, M. Anne and June O'Neill. 1993. ''Family Endowments and the Achievement of Young Children with Special Reference to the Underclass.'' Mimeo. Baruch College. New York City.

Hill, Martha, et al. 1985a. "The Impact of Parental Marital Disruption on the Socioeconomic Attainments of Children as Adults." Survey Research Center, Institute for Social Research, University of Michigan.

Hill, Martha, et al. 1985b. *Motivation and Economic Mobility*. Survey Research Center, Institute for Social Research, University of Michigan.

Hill, Martha, and Gregory Duncan. 1987. "Parental Family Income and the Socioeconomic Attainment of Children." *Social Science Research, 16(1):* 39–73.

Hill, Martha, and Michael Ponza. 1984. "Does Welfare Dependence Beget Dependency?" Survey Research Center, Institute for Social Research, University of Michigan.

Hill, Martha S., Sue Augustyniak, and Michael Ponza. 1985. "The Impact of Parental Marital Disruption on the Socio-Economic Attainments of Children as Adults." Survey Research Center, Institute for Social Research, University of Michigan.

Hofferth, Sandra L., and Cheryl Hayes (eds.). *Risking the Future: Adolescent Sexuality, Pregnancy, and Childbearing*. Vol. 2. Washington, D.C.: National Academy of Sciences Press.

Hofferth, Sandra L., and Kristin A. Moore. 1979. "Early Childbearing and Later Economic Well-Being." *American Sociological Review, 44(5):* 784–815.

Hoffman, Saul, Michael Foster, and Frank Furstenberg. 1993. "Reevaluating the Costs of Teenage Childbearing." *Demography, 30 (February):* 1–13.

Hogan, Dennis P. 1985. "Structural and Normative Factors in Single Parenthood among Black Adolescents." Mimeo, Department of Sociology, University of Chicago.

Hogan, Dennis, and Evelyn Kitagawa. 1985. "The Impact of Social Status, Family Structure, and Neighborhood on the Fertility of Black Adolescents." *American Journal of Sociology, 90(4):* 825–855.

Hout, Michael. 1988. "More Universalism, Less Structural Mobility: The American Occupational Structure in the 1980s." *American Journal of Sociology, 93:* 1358–1400.

Huang, Fung Mei. 1993. *The Impact of Childhood Events on Educational and Early Labor Market Achievement*. Ph.D. Dissertation, University of Wisconsin-Madison.

Jencks, Christopher, Susan Bartlett, Mary Corcoran, James Crouse, David Eaglesfield, Gregory Jackson, Kent McClelland, Peter Meuser, Michael Olneck, Joseph Schwartz, Sherry Ward, and Jill Williams. 1979. *Who Gets Ahead? The Determinants of Economic Success in America*. New York: Basic Books.

Jencks, Christopher, and Marsha Brown. 1975. "The Effect of High Schools on Their Students." *Harvard Educational Review, 45:* 273–324.

Jencks, Christopher, James Crouse, and Peter Mueser. 1983. "The Wisconsin Model of Status Attainment: A National Replication with Improved Measures of Ability and Aspiration." *Sociology of Education, 56:* 3–19.

Jencks, Christopher, and Susan Mayer. 1990. "The Social Consequences of Growing Up in a Poor Neighborhood." In Larry Lynn, Jr., and Michael

McGeary (eds.). *Inner-city Poverty in the United States.* Washington, D.C.: National Academy Press.

Jencks, Christopher, Michael Smith, Henry Acland, Mary-Jo Bane, David Cohen, Herbert Gintis, Barbara Heyns, and Stephan Michelson. 1972. *Inequality: A Reassessment of the Effect of Family and Schooling in America.* New York: Basic Books.

Kamarck, E. C., and William Galston (eds.), *Putting Children First: A Progressive Family Policy for the 1990s.* Washington, D.C.: Progressive Policy Institute.

Kasten, Richard, and John Todd. 1983. "Transfer Recipients and the Poor During the 1970s." In Richard Zeckhauser and Derek Leebaert (eds.), *What Role for Government?* Durham, N.C.: Duke University Press.

Keith, Varna M., and Barbara Finlay. 1988. "The Impact of Parental Divorce on Children's Educational Attainment, Marital Timing, and Likelihood of Divorce." *Journal of Marriage and the Family, 50:* 797–809.

Kelly, Joan B., and Judith Wallerstein. 1979. "Children of Divorce." *National Elementary Principal, 59:* 51–58.

Kiker, B. F., and C. M. Condon. 1981. "The Influence of Socioeconomic Background on the Earnings of Young Men." *Journal of Human Resources, 16:* 94–105.

Kimenyi, Mwangi S. 1991. "Rational Choice, Culture of Poverty, and the Intergenerational Transmission of Welfare Dependency." *Southern Economic Journal, 57(4):* 947–960.

Kotlikoff, Laurence J. 1992. *Generational Accounting: Knowing Who Pays, and When, For What We Spend.* New York: The Free Press.

Kotlikoff, Laurence J., and Jagadeesh Gokhale. 1993. "The Equity of Social Services Provided to Children and Senior Citizens." The Ruth Pollak Working Papers Series on Economics, Working Paper no. 20, Department of Economics, Boston University.

Krein, Sheila F. 1986. "Growing up in a Single-Parent Family: The Effect on Education and Earnings of Young Men." *Family Relations, 35(1):* 161–168.

Krein, Sheila F., and Andrea Beller. 1988. "Educational Attainment of Children from Single-Parent Families: Differences by Exposure, Gender, and Race." *Demography, 25:* 221–234.

Leibowitz, Arleen. 1986. "An Economic Model of Teenage Pregnancy Decision-Making." *Demography, 23:* 67–77.

Lerner, Richard M. 1984. *On the Nature of Human Plasticity.* New York: Cambridge University Press.

Levitan, Sar, Garth Mangum, and Marion Pines. 1989. *A Proper Inheritance: Investing in the Self-Sufficiency of Poor Families.* Washington, D.C.: George Washington University.

Levy, Frank. 1980. "The Intergenerational Transfer of Poverty." The Urban Institute, Working Paper no. 1241–102 (January), Washington, D.C.

Levy, Frank, and Richard Michel. 1991. *The Economic Future of American Families.* Washington, D.C.: Urban Institute Press.

Levy, Frank, and Richard Murnane. 1991. "Jobs, Demography, and the Mismatch Hypothesis." Mimeo, University of Maryland, School of Public Affairs.

Levy, Frank, and Richard Murnane. 1992. "U.S. Earnings Levels and Earnings Inequality: A Review of Recent Trends and Proposed Explanations." *Journal of Economic Literature, 30(3):* 1333–1381.

Long, Larry. 1988. *Migration and Residential Mobility in the United States.* New York: Russell Sage Foundation.

Luker, Kristin. 1991. "Dubious Conceptions: The Controversy over Teen Pregnancy." *The American Prospect, 5 (Spring):* 73–83.

Lundberg, Shelly, and Robert Plotnick. 1990a. "Testing the Opportunity Cost Theory of Premarital Childbearing." Paper presented at the meeting of the Association of Public Policy Analysis and Management.

Lundberg, Shelly, and Robert Plotnick. 1990b. "Effects of State Welfare, Abortion and Family Planning Policies on Premarital Childbearing among White Adolescents." *Family Planning Perspectives, 22(6):* 246–251.

Macaulay, Jacqueline. 1977. "Stereotyping Child Welfare." *Society, 13:* 47–51.

Manski, Charles, Gary Sandefur, Sara McLanahan, and Daniel Powers. 1992. "Alternative Estimates of the Effect of Family Structure during Adolescence on High School Graduation." *Journal of the American Statistical Association, 87:* 25–37.

Mare, Robert D. 1980. "Social Background and School Continuation Decisions." *Journal of the American Statistical Association, 75:* 295–305.

Mare, Robert, and William M. Mason. 1980. "Children's Reports of Parental Socioeconomic Status: A Multiple Group Measurement Model." *Sociological Methods and Research, 9:* 178–198.

Marino, Cena D., and Richard J. McCowan. 1976. "The Effects of Parent Absence on Children." *Child Study Journal, 6:* 165–183.

Mattox, Jr., William R. 1991. "The Parent Trap: So Many Bills, So Little Time." *Policy Review, 55 (Winter):* 6–13.

Mayer, Susan E. 1990. "How Much Does a High School's Racial and Economic Mix Affect Graduation Rates and Teenage Fertility Rates?" In Christopher Jencks and Paul Peterson (eds.), *The Urban Underclass.* Washington, D.C.: The Brookings Institution.

Mayer, Susan E. 1991. "The Effect of Schools' Racial and Socioeconomic Mix on High School Students' Chances of Dropping Out." Mimeo, University of Chicago.

McCubbin, Hamilton I., Constance Joy, A. Elizabeth Cauble, Joan Comeau, Joan Patterson, and Richard Needle. 1980. "Family Stress, Coping, and Social Support: A Decade Review." *Journal of Marriage and the Family, 42:* 855–871.

McLanahan, Sara. 1985. "Family Structure and the Reproduction of Poverty." *American Journal of Sociology, 90:* 873–901.

McLanahan, Sara. 1988. "Family Structure and Dependency: Early Transitions to Female Household Headship." *Demography, 25(1):* 1–16.

McLanahan, Sara. 1989. "The Two Faces of Divorce: Women's and Children's Interests." Institute for Research on Poverty, Discussion Paper no. 903–89, University of Wisconsin-Madison.

McLanahan, Sara, and Larry Bumpass. 1988. "Intergenerational Consequences of Family Disruption." *American Journal of Sociology, 94:* 130–152.

Mead, Lawrence. 1988. "The Hidden Jobs Debate." *The Public Interest, 91 (Spring):* 40–58.

Michael, Robert, and Nancy Tuma. 1985. "Entry into Marriage and Parenthood by Young Men and Women: The Influence of Family Background." *Demography, 22:* 515–544.

Miller, Dale T., and William Turnbull. 1986. "Expectancies and Interpersonal Processes." *Annual Review of Psychology, 37:* 233–256.

Minarik, Joseph. 1975. "New Evidence on Poverty Count." In *Proceedings of the Social Statistics Section, American Statistical Association,* 18th edition: 554–559.

Moffitt, Terrie, Arshalom Caspi, Jay Belsky, and Phil Silva. 1992. "Childhood Experience and the Onset of Menarche: A Test of a Sociobiological Model." *Child Development, 63(1):* 47–58.

Moore, Kristin A., and Steven B. Caldwell. 1977. "The Effect of Government Policies on Out-of-Wedlock Sex and Pregnancy." *Family Planning Perspectives, 9:* 164–169.

Mott, Frank, and William Marsiglio. 1985. "Early Childbearing and Completion of High School." *Family Planning Perspectives, 17:* 234–237.

Mueller, Carol, and Hallowell Pope. 1977. "Marital Instability: A Study of the Transmission between Generations." *Journal of Marriage and the Family, 39:* 83–92.

Nathanson, Constance A. 1991. *Dangerous Passage: The Social Control of Women's Adolescence.* Philadelphia: Temple University Press.

National Center for Health Statistics. 1991. *Health, United States, 1990.* Hyattsville, Md.: Public Health Service.

National Commission on America's Urban Families. 1993. *Families First.* Washington, D.C.: U.S. Government Printing Office.

National Commission on Children. 1991. *Beyond Rhetoric: A New American Agenda for Children and Their Families.* Washington, D.C.: U.S. Government Printing Office.

National Commission to Prevent Infant Mortality. 1990. *Troubling Trends: The Health of America's Next Generation* Washington, D.C.: National Commission to Prevent Infant Mortality.

Newman, Philip R., and Barbara M. Newman. 1978. "Identity Formation and the College Experience." *Adolescence, 13:* 312–326.

Novak, Michael, et al. 1987. *The New Consensus on Family and Welfare.* Washington, D.C.: American Enterprise Institute for Public Policy Research.

Olneck, Michael. 1976. "The Effects of Education on Occupational Status and Earnings." Madison, Wis. Institute for Research on Poverty, Discussion Paper no. 358–76, University of Wisconsin-Madison.

Olneck, Michael. 1977. "On the Use of Sibling Data to Estimate the Effect of Family Background, Cognitive Skills and Schooling: Results from the Kalamazoo Brothers Study.'' In Paul Taubman (ed.), *Kinometrics: Determinants of Socioeconomic Success within and between Families.* Amsterdam: North-Holland.

O'Neill, June. 1990. ''The Role of Human Capital in Earnings Differences between Black and White Men.'' *Journal of Economic Perspectives, 4(2):* 25–45.

O'Neill, June, Laurie Bassi, and Douglas Wolf. 1987. ''The Duration of Welfare Spells.'' *Review of Economics and Statistics, 69(2):* 241–248.

Palmer, John, Timothy Smeeding, and Barbara Torrey (eds.) 1988. *The Vulnerable.* Washington, D.C.: Urban Institute Press.

Pearlin, Leonard I., and Joyce S. Johnson. 1977. ''Martial Status, Life-Strains and Depression.'' *American Sociological Review, 42:* 704–715.

Pearlin, Leonard I., and Carmi Schooler. 1978. ''The Structure of Coping.'' *Journal of Health and Social Behavior, 19:* 2–21.

Plant, Mark W. 1984. ''An Empirical Analysis of Welfare Dependence.'' *American Economic Review, 74(4):* 673–684.

Plotnick, Robert. 1983. ''Turnover in the AFDC Population: An Event History Analysis.'' *Journal of Human Resources, 18(1):* 65–81.

Plotnick, Robert. 1990. ''Welfare and Out-of-Wedlock Childbearing: Evidence from the 1980s.'' *Journal of Marriage and the Family, 53(3):* 735–746.

Preston, Samuel. 1984. ''Children and the Elderly in the U.S.'' *Demography, 21:* 435–457.

Rainwater, Lee. 1987. ''Class, Culture, Poverty and Welfare.'' Boston, Mass.: Center for Human Resources, Heller Graduate School, Brandeis University.

Rein, Martin, and Lee Rainwater. 1978. ''Patterns of Welfare Use.'' *Social Service Review, December:* 511–534.

Ribar, David. 1991. ''A Multinomial Logit Analysis of Teenage Fertility and High School Completion.'' Mimeo, Department of Economics, Pennsylvania State University.

Ricketts, Erol, and Isabel Sawhill. 1988. ''Defining and Measuring the Underclass.'' *Journal of Policy Analysis and Management, 7(2):* 316–325.

Rutter, Michael. 1980. *Changing Youth in a Changing Society: Patterns of Adolescent Development and Disorder.* Cambridge, Mass.: Harvard University Press.

Sawhill, Isabel. 1989. ''The Underclass.'' *The Public Interest, 96:* 3–15.

Schorr, L. B. 1988. *Within Our Reach: Breaking the Cycle of Disadvantage.* New York: Doubleday.

Sewell, William, and Robert Hauser. 1975. *Education, Occupation, and Earnings: Achievement in the Early Career.* New York: Academic Press.

Sewell, William, and Robert Hauser. 1977. ''On the Effects of Families and Family Structure on Achievement.'' In Paul Taubman (ed.), *Kinometrics: Determinants of Socioeconomic Success within and between Families.* Amsterdam: North-Holland.

Sewell, William, Robert Hauser, and Wendy Wolf. 1980. ''Sex, Schooling, and Occupational Status.'' *American Journal of Sociology, 86:* 551–583.

Sewell, William, and Vimal P. Shah. 1967. ''Social Class, Parental Encouragement, and Educational Aspirations." *American Journal of Sociology, 73:* 559–572.

Shaw, Lois B. 1982. "High School Completion for Young Women: Effects of Low Income and Living with a Single Parent." *Journal of Family Issues, 3:* 147–163.

Solon, Gary. 1992. "Intergenerational Income Mobility in the United States." *American Economic Review, 82:* 393–408.

Solon, Gary, Mary Corcoran, Roger Gordon, and Deborah Laren. 1991. "A Longitudinal Analysis of Sibling Correlations in Economic Status." *Journal of Human Resources, 26(3):* 509–534.

Stafford, Frank P. 1986. "Women's Work, Sibling Competition, and Children's School Performance." *American Economic Review, 77:* 972–980.

Summers, Anita, and Barbara Wolfe. 1977. "Do Schools Make a Difference?" *American Economic Review, 67:* 639–652.

Taubman, Paul (ed.). 1977. *Kinometrics: Determinants of Socioeconomic Success within and between Families.* Amsterdam: North-Holland.

Taubman, Paul, and Terence Wales. 1975. "Education as an Investment and Screening Device." In F. Thomas Juster (ed.), *Education, Income and Human Behavior.* New York: National Bureau of Economic Research.

Thornton, Arland. 1991. "Influence of the Marital History of Parents on the Marital and Cohabitational Experiences of Children." *American Journal of Sociology, 96:* 868–894.

Trussell, Jane. 1988. "Teenage Pregnancy in the United States." *Family Planning Perspectives, 20(6):* 262–272.

U.S. Bureau of the Census. 1975. *Statistical Abstract of the United States: 1975.* Washington, D.C.: U.S. Government Printing Office.

U.S. Bureau of the Census. 1979. *Statistical Abstract of the United States: 1979.* Washington, D.C.: U.S. Government Printing Office.

U.S. Bureau of the Census. 1991. *Statistical Abstract of the United States: 1991.* Washington, D.C.: U.S. Government Printing Office.

U.S. Bureau of the Census. Various years. "Geographical Mobility." Series P-20, no. 368, March 1975–1980, Table 4; no. 377, March 1980–1981, Table 4; no. 384, March 1981–1982, Table 4; no. 393, March 1982–1983, Table 4; no. 407, March 1983–1984, Table 4.

U.S. Council of Economic Advisors. 1990. *Economic Report of the President, 1990.* Washington, D.C.: U.S. Government Printing Office.

U.S. Department of Education. 1988. *Schools That Work: Educating Disadvantaged Children.* Washington, D.C.: U.S. Government Printing Office.

U.S. Department of Health and Human Services. *Quarterly Public Assistance Statistics.* April–June 1982 and April–June 1984. Washington, D.C.: U.S. Government Printing Office.

U.S. House of Representatives, Committee on Ways and Means. 1990. *1991 Green Book: Background Material and Data on Programs within the Jurisdiction of the Committee on Ways and Means.* Washington, D.C.: U.S. Government Printing Office.

U.S. House of Representatives, Committee on Ways and Means. 1991. *1992 Green Book: Background Material and Data on Programs within the Juris-*

diction of the Committee on Ways and Means. Washington, D.C.: U.S. Government Printing Office.

U.S. House of Representatives, Committee on Ways and Means. 1992. *The Green Book: Background Material and Data on Programs within the Jurisdiction of the Committee on Ways and Means.* Washington, D.C.: U.S. Government Printing Office.

U.S. House of Representatives, Select Committee on Children, Youth and Families. 1989. *U.S. Children and Their Families: Current Conditions and Recent Trends, 1989.* Washington, D.C.: U.S. Government Printing Office.

Wallerstein, Judith. 1991. "The Long-Term Effects of Divorce on Children: A Review." *Journal of American Academy of Child and Adolescent Psychiatry, 30:* 349–360.

Weiner, Bernard. 1972. *Theories of Motivation: From Mechanism to Cognition.* Chicago: Rand McNally.

Weiss, Robert S. 1979. "Growing up a Little Faster: The Experience of Growing up in a Single-Parent Household." *Journal of Social Issues, 35(4):* 97–111.

William T. Grant Foundation Commission on Work, Family and Citizenship. 1988. *The Forgotten Half: Pathways to Success for America's Youth and Young Families.* Washington, D.C.: William T. Grant Foundation.

———. 1988. *The Forgotten Half: Non-College Youth in America.* Washington, D.C.: William T. Grant Foundation.

Wilson, James Q. 1993. *Aspen Institute Quarterly, 5* (1).

Wilson, William Julius. 1981. "The Black Community in the 1980s: Questions of Race, Class, and Public Policy." *Annals of the American Academy of Political and Social Sciences, 454 (March):* 26–41.

Wilson, William Julius. 1987. *The Truly Disadvantaged: The Inner City, the Underclass, and Public Policy.* Chicago: University of Chicago Press.

Wojtkiewicz, Roger. 1991. "Parental Presence and High School Graduation: The Effects of Living with Single Parents, Stepparents, Grandparents, and Other Relatives." Mimeo, Department of Sociology, Louisiana State University.

Wolfe, Barbara. 1985. "The Influence of Health on School Outcomes: A Multivariate Approach." *Medical Care, 23:* 1127–1138.

Wolfe, Barbara. 1991a. "The Deteriorating Economic Circumstances of Children." In E. Hoffman (ed.), *Essays on the Economics of Discrimination.* Kalamazoo, Mich.: Upjohn Institute, pp. 43–66.

Wolfe, Barbara. 1991b. "Treating Children Fairly." *Society, 28(6):* 23–28.

Wolfe, Barbara. 1993. "Externalities of Education." *The International Encyclopedia of Education.* Oxford, U.K.: Pergamon Press Ltd. Forthcoming.

Zimiles, Herbert, and Valerie E. Lee. 1991. "Adolescent Family Structure and Educational Progress." *Developmental Psychology, 27(2):* 314–320.

Zimmerman, David J. 1992. "Regression toward Mediocrity in Economic Stature." *American Economic Review, 82:* 409–429.

Index

neighborhood characteristics (*continued*)
outcomes, 117, 132, 267; influencing
teenage nonmarital childbearing, 195,
199, 203

neighborhood/s, 14, 15, 43, 80, 176*n*,
263; and children's choices, 196; and
children's success, 66-70, 114, 175;
data, estimation of, 268, 269; differences, 119; effects of changes in, 13;
empirical findings on effects of years
in, **250-251,** 259; influence of, 132-
133, 161; with prevalence of female-
headed households, 114-115, **116**; quality, 167, 259, 281; racial composition
of, 269, 276; results based on multiple
regressions for, **134-135,** 136; simulated effects of growing up in different,
165, 166, 253; underclass, 278, 290*n*

neighborhoods, bad, **165, 203, 250-251,
254-255**; definition of, 265*n*; and earnings, 89*n*; effects of living in, 250,
252, 259; summary statistics for, **279,
280,** 281

neighborhoods, good, 133, **165, 250-251,**
259; definition of, 265*n*; effects of
growing up in, 66, 68, 79, 259, 263

neighborhood variables, 69-70, **134-135,**
234*n*; effect of, 136; for nonmarital
births, 202, 205, 259; related to economic inactivity, 215, 220-221, 226,
232; related to educational attainment,
154, 156, 160, 168, 171, 173; summary statistics for, 276, **277,** 278, **279-
281,** 281

Nelson, Valerie, 84*n*

non-African-Americans, 175*n*-176*n*, 179;
and economic inactivity, **225,** 225; and
nonmarital births, **182-183, 186-187,**
206, 209

nonemployment, 214; rates of young
women, 216

nonmarital births. *See* childbearing; out-
of-wedlock births

nonresponse, 283-284

nonwhites, 276, 284; inactivity rates for,
217, 217; summary statistics for, **270,
272,** 274

O

Oates, Wallace, 90*n*

objectives: government, 28; parental, 30-
31, 242

occupational attainments, 94*n*; determinants of, 59, 60; of sons, 84*n*

Occupational Changes in a Generation
(OCG), 83*n*, 84*n*, data, 60; studies, 61

occupational status, 59-60, 61; effects of
education on, 65

OCG. *See* Occupational changes in a Generation

Office of Economic Opportunity (OEO),
290*n*

Olneck, Michael, 86*n*

Omnibus Budget Reconciliation Act of
1990, 20*n*

O'Neill, June, 85*n*

one-parent families: attainments of children in, 48, 87*n*; effects of growing up
in, 53, 65, 75, 78, 91*n*, 206; effects of
living in, **140, 141, 142**; race-specific
results for schooling for, **180,** 181,
182, 184, 186; relationships, 108-111,
110, 125-126; and schooling using bivariate probit estimates, **170, 172**. *See
also* female-headed households

one-parent families, effects of years lived
in, 120, 132, 138*n*, 163, 171; on economic inactivity, **219,** 220; empirical
findings on, **248-249,** 257; on high-
school graduation, **152,** 153, 154, 155,
162; and high-school graduation/eco-
nomic inactivity using bivariate probit
estimates, **231**; on out-of-wedlock
births, 197, **198**; results based on multiple regressions for, **121, 130-131, 134-
135**; summary statistics for, **270, 272,**
274; on years of education, **157,** 159,
162

opportunities, 23, 26, 81. *See also* parental choices/opportunities

opportunity, equality of, 61

options: government, 28; of parents, 30;
of teenage girls, 194

ordinary least squares (OLS), 138*n*

outcomes: of children, 244, 262; equality of, 50n; family-based indicators of, 71; occupational, 16, 59; racial, 60. *See also* educational outcomes; negative outcomes; positive outcomes

out-of-wedlock births, mothers', **271, 273**; effects of, **198**, 199, 202, **203**, 213n

out-of-wedlock births, teenage, 95, 104, 129, **142**, 137n; baseline models of, 197; benefits from, 58; bivariate probit estimation of, 200-202, **203**, 204-207; causes of, 191-192, 193; costs and benefits of, 35; decisions regarding, 35, 44, 197, 209, 245; determinants of, 73-74, 78, 188-189, 191-196, **198-199**, 200, 209-211; and educational achievements, 214; effects of, 32-33, 34; effects of family economic resources on, 124; effects of father's education on, 123; effects of growing up in the South on, 127; effects of living with one parent on, 125-126; effects of living in SMSA on, 127, 136; effects of mother's education on, 101, **102**; effects of mother's work on, 125; effects of neighborhood on, 115, **116**, 117, **118**, 133; effects of parental education on, 252; effects of siblings on, 126; effects of stress on, 127-128, 129; empirical findings related to, **247, 249, 251**, 253, 256, 258, 259; equations, 204-206; estimates for, **255**; factors relevant for understanding decision of, 33-34; by household moves, **103**, 129; implications of, 190-191; parental separation and, **105**, 128; patterns of, 188; and poverty, **108**, 108, 253; probability of, 69, 79, 91n, 92n, 104, 106, 107-108, 138n, 139n, **255**; racial differences in, 96, **97**; rates, 282; results based on multiple regressions for, 119-120, **121-122**, 123, **131, 135**; simulated impacts on probability of change in, 207, **208**, 210, 253, 256, 257; summary statistics for, **283**; theoretical considerations regarding, 193-196; and

welfare recipiency, 111, **112,** 113, 189-192, 214, **255**; by years lived with one parent, 109, **110**

P

parental choices, 26-27, 45-46, 148, 241; constraints of, 48n, 242; for education, 174; influences of, 177n, 222; influencing children's success, 23, 30-32, 47, 161, 242-243; related to economic inactivity, 220, 221; related to teenage non-marital births, 192, 193; relationship between government and, 41, 260; variables, 120, 153, 154, 168, 169

parental choices/opportunities, 99, 120, 123-124; creating stress for children, 127-129; empirical findings related to, **246, 248, 250**; related to economic inactivity of youths, 221, 226, 228, 232, 233; related to education, 153, 154; related to nonmarital births and welfare receipt, 188, 202

parental decisions, 15, 30-32, 48n, 104, 241, 242; related to economic inactivity, 222, 229; related to education, 148, 150, 173; stress-creating, 151

parental education, 161, 167, 194-195, 239; choices, 232; and education of children, 156, 159-161, 171, 175; effects of, 9, 47, 181; empirical findings on effects of, **246-247**, 251-252; related to economic inactivity, 218, **223**, 228; related to teenage nonmarital childbearing, 195, 197, 200, 209, 210; simulated effects of, on economic inactivity of young adults, **227**, 228; summary statistics for, **270, 272**, 274; variables, 159, 167. *See also* father's education; mothers, education of

parental separations, 104, **105**, 106, **141**, 148; and economic inactivity of children, **219**; effects of, 78; empirical findings on effects of, **248-249**, 256-257; and high-school graduation, **152**, 154, 156; limited, 108; number of, 128, **140, 142**; and out-of-wedlock